The DOUBTER'S COMPANION

The DOUBTER'S COMPANION

A Dictionary of Aggressive Common Sense

JOHN RALSTON SAUL

THE FREE PRESS

New York · London · Toronto · Sydney · Tokyo · Singapore

*The Free Press
A Division of Simon & Schuster, Inc.
866 Third Avenue, New York, N.Y. 10022*

Printed in the United States of America

*printing number
10 9 8 7 6 5 4 3 2 1*

Library of Congress Cataloging-in-Publication Data

Saul, John Ralston.
    The doubters companion: a dictionary of aggressive common sense
    John Ralston Saul.
        p. cm.
    ISBN 0-02-927722-1
    1. English language—Terms and phrases—Humor.
    2. Civilization, Modern—Humor. I. Title
PR6069.A78D68 1994
428. 1'0207—dc20   94-22922
                                                                CIP

For
Adrienne

Hoc esse salsum putas?
Catullus

THE GRAIL OF BALANCE

Our civilization is unable to do what individuals cannot say. And individuals are unable to say what they cannot think. Even thought can only advance as fast as the unknown can be stated through conscious organized language, an apparently self-defeating limitation.

The power of dictionaries and encyclopaedias is thus enormous. But what kind of power? The very possibility of it invites positive or negative use. A dictionary can as easily be a liberating force as one of control.

In the humanist view, the alphabet can be a tool for examining society; the dictionary a series of questions, an enquiry into meaning, a weapon against received wisdom and therefore against the assumptions of established power. In other words, the dictionary offers an organized Socratic approach.

The rational method is quite different. The dictionary is abruptly transformed into a dispensary of truth; that is, into an instrument which limits meaning by defining language. This bible becomes a tool for controlling communications because it directs what people can think. In other words, it becomes the voice of Platonic élitism.

Humanism versus definition. Balance versus structure. Doubt versus ideology. Language as a means of communication versus language as a tool for advancing the interests of groups.

This power of mere words and sentences may be particular to the West. Other civilizations are driven more by the image or by metaphysics. These lead them to treat the relationship between the oral and the written as secondary. But in the West, almost everything we need to know about the state of our society can be extracted from the relative power of oral versus written language.

The heavier the hand of the written, the more likely it is that language will have a deadened, predictable quality about it, justified by an obscure scholasticism. The whole thing then falls easily into the service of ideology and superstition. In societies such as these—such as ours—definition becomes an attempt to close doors by answering questions.

As for oral language, it is periodically unleashed as the only force capable of freeing society from the strangling effects of the written and the ideological. Like a burst of wind it opens the shuttered windows of scholasticism, blows out the dust of received wisdom and, in the phrase of Stéphane Mallarmé, purifies the language of the tribe. In those periods, dictionaries and encyclopaedias come into their own as aggressive, questioning tools which embrace doubt and consideration.

The dichotomy between the humanist and the rational is simple. How are citizens to enter into public debate if the concepts which define our society and decide the manner in which we are governed are open neither to understanding nor to questioning? If this is impossible or even difficult, then society comes to a standstill. If this immobility is prolonged, the results are catastrophic.

The way out for the citizenry is always the same. Their language—our language—must be reclaimed from the structures of conventional wisdom and expertise. Populations know from experience that that change can only come through what will seem at first to be outrageous statements, provocation and a stubborn refusal to accept the smooth, calm, controlling formulae of conventional wisdom.

The ideologies of this century have prospered through the exploitation of what amounts to modern superstitions, each of which is justified by closely argued definitions divorced from reality. Even the most horrifying of superstitious acts—

the Holocaust—was the product of decades of written, intellectual justification, which the rest of society failed to destroy as an expressible option by passively allowing the arguments to stand.

Our current ideologies revolve around economic determinism. They use expert argument to turn almost any form of injustice into an inevitability. This infection of the citizenry with passivity is, in fact, what we used to call superstition. Whatever is defined as true we feel obliged to accept as inevitable. Knowledge, which we believed would free us, has somehow become the instrument of our imprisonment. How can a dictionary do other than attack such mystification?

Erasmus was perhaps the first to try to kill the modern scholastic system by questioning the power of written truths. With *Adagio* (1508—a collection of three thousand proverbs from classical writers) and *In Praise of Folly* (1509—a satire on scholasticism), he attacked with both enumeration and comedy. His apparent aim was to rediscover the simplicity of early Christianity. But beyond that he was searching for the humanist equilibrium.

The religious wars—with their roar of deftly argued hatred and violence—seemed to overwhelm his message. But Erasmus had sent out a long-term signal. He had declared himself in favour of the oral approach to language, communication and understanding. Thus Europe's leading intellectual rejected the ideologies, both old and new.

The next major step nevertheless contradicted Erasmus. It continued in the unfortunate direction of the new rational and national powers unleashed more or less during the wars of religion. Cardinal Richelieu hired Claude Favre de Vangelas to organize the first dictionary of the *Académie Française* (1694—*Dictionnaire de la langue française*). Favre saw "elevated usage as the proper legislator of language."[1] He wanted to establish a "new High Mode" to replace Latin. The aim was to create a dictionary of absolute authority and so to fix French in place, like an exotic butterfly pinned in a display case, at a high level of politically correct rhetoric.

He was apparently unaware of Chancelier François Olivier's maxim "The higher the monkey climbs, the more he shows his ass."[2] Indeed, each time French has attained its natural greatness over the last three centuries, it has done so by rejecting "elevated usage" in favour of clear, flexible language inspired by a burst of oral genius.

In any case, the great humanist purification was about to begin. Ephrin Chambers's two-volume *Cyclopaedia or an Universal Dictionary of Arts and Sciences* appeared in 1728. The claims he made for his work were modest—to provide "an explication of the terms and an account of the things signified therein." Explanation and account. He did not pretend to define truth.

Samuel Johnson began with the intent of imitating Favre de Vangelas. By nature he believed that "all change is of itself evil." But by 1755, when his own dictionary was published, he had realized that language was either alive and uncontrollable or controlled and therefore dead.

> ...Academies have been instituted to guard
> the avenues of...language, to retain fugitives,
> and to repulse intruders; but their vigilance
> and activity have hitherto been vain; sounds
> are too volatile and subtle for legal restraints;
> to enchain syllables, and to lash the wind,
> are equally the undertakings of pride, unwilling
> to measure its desires by its strengths.[3]

Then came the great innovation. Denis Diderot's *Encyclopédie* appeared in seventeen volumes between 1751 and 1766.[4] For the first time, an alphabetical analysis of civilization looked, not backwards but forward through innovative social ideas.[5] It was a tool for change and its publication was therefore dogged by arrests and censorship. Voltaire's *Dictionnaire Philosophique*, which appeared in varying forms over the same period, was even more consciously designed as a weapon of portable and flexible linguistic guerilla warfare.[6] By the early twentieth century, the multi-volumed Larousse encyclopaedia was describing Diderot's as an instrument of war.

But why war? And against what? Against a language which did not serve its civilization. A language which did not communicate. What the attack led by Voltaire and Diderot demonstrated was that the large and elegant beast of eighteenth-century society was an over-dressed and overly made-up sick animal.

The last steps in this opening up of communications and thought came with the *Encyclopaedia Britannica* (1718-71) and Noah Webster's two-volume dictionary in 1828.[7] Then the settling-in stage began. This was quickly succeeded by a mania for massive tomes filled with dry and sectarian definitions turned towards the past. These were in the image of a successful, self-satisfied civilization.

Flaubert poked fun at it with his little *Dictionnaire des Idées Reçues* (1880),[8] as did Ambrose Bierce in *The Devil's Dictionary* (1911).[9] But they were prodding an unmovable and increasingly unconscious animal, slumbering in comfortable self-confidence. In the twentieth century, the tools of debate and change of the eighteenth century have become scholastic monuments to truth. Since dictionaries now define not only meaning, but decide whether words really exist, people argue over which should be included. And they turn to their Oxford or their Webster's not to challenge themselves but to be reassured.

Today our civilization is not slumbering in unconscious self-confidence. Rather it resembles the wounded and confused animal of the eighteenth century. We are again the prisoners of scholastic rhetoric, which has blocked useful public communications by dividing our language up into thousands of closed specialist dialects. The result is the disappearance of almost any public language which could have a real impact on structures and actions. Instead we have an illusion of unlimited oral communications which are, in practical terms, a vast and murmuring silence.

Our élites interpret this situation as a confirmation of their indispensability. The citizenry, on the other hand, seem to have taken their distances from the existing structure and its languages. They react to the waves of expert truth which continue to wash over them with a sort of mute indifference.

An uninvolved outsider might interpret this as the first stages of a purification rite. Indifference is often the manner behind which humans consider change.

Given our history, it should be possible to decipher our intent. We are trying to think our way out of a linguistic prison. This means we need to create new language and new interpretations, which can only be accomplished by re-establishing the equilibrium between the oral and the written.

This is a situation in which dictionaries should again be filled with doubt, questioning and considerations. They can then be used as practical weapons of change.

Note: Words which are highlighted within the text of a definition are themselves to be found as entries.

The
DOUBTER'S
COMPANION

A

A *A* versus *the*. Indefinite versus definite. A suggestion that there is room for doubt, questioning, consideration. That an inclusive approach may be more interesting than the exclusive. That dogma or ideology are about control not truth.

In formal logic, however, *A* is identified as a universal affirmative. *A* asserts. The Sophists asserted rhetoric. Aristotle asserted with genius. Using Aristotle's logic, Thomas Aquinas asserted on behalf of organized Christianity. On his heels, herds of scholastics—masters of mediaeval academic obscurity—set out to capture language for their own purposes.

Then the annoying thinkers of the seventeenth and eighteenth centuries tickled and amused, cut and thrust, and above all found ways to break through the obscurity in order to communicate. They wrote encyclopaedias and dictionaries which undermined the idea of the definite—that is, of the "definition." But their suggestion of an indefinite and thus open language, full of possibilities, was quickly undercut by the formal logic of Kant and Hegel. With them came the assertions of the various ideologues of left and right, each with their own perfect logic. Finally, in the twentieth century, the mediaeval scholastics returned in modern dress. They invested their old philosophical domains and created new ones under the heading of social science. Empires of affirmation were created, each with a language so closed as to constitute a dialect, each bearing its own hermetic truths.

Interestingly enough, the Romans, when voting, used the letter *A* to signify dissent. *A* for *antiquo*, I oppose. I object. *A* to refuse an assertion. This negative sits quite happily with *alpha*, as the beginning of the Greek alphabet. The act of opening. The logicians and the scholastics seem to have mistaken *A* for *omega*, the last letter, closure, the end. See: THE.

A BIG MAC   The communion wafer of consumption. Not really food but the promise of food. Whatever it tastes like, whatever it is made of, once it touches lips A Big Mac is transubstantiated into the mythological hamburger.

It is, with Perrier, one of the sacred objects of the leading philosophical school of the late-twentieth century—public relations. Cynics often unjustly suggest that this school favours superficial appearances over content. Had this been the case, PR would have failed. Most people, after all, can easily recognize the difference between appearances and reality.

A Big Mac, for example, is not big. It doesn't taste of much. It isn't good for you. And it seems sweet. Why does it seem sweet if, as the company says, it isn't laced with sugar?

What the philosophy of PR proposes is theoretical content (such as sex appeal, fun, individualism, sophistication, the rejection of sophistication) in the place of actual content (banal carbonated water and a mediocre hamburger). This is modern metaphysics.

Because public relations are built on illusion, they tend to eliminate choice. This is an important characteristic of contemporary capitalism. A Big Mac, like so many creations of PR, is a symbol of passive conformity. As Mac McDonald put it: "If you gave people a choice, there would be chaos."[1] See: MCDONALD, RONALD and CANNIBALISM.

À LA RECHERCHE DU TEMPS PERDU   A work of genius written in bed. It opens with the narrator tucked between his sheets. It is rarely read for any length of time on a mattress.

It is also rarely read, but is often talked about and has had a major impact on many people who haven't read it, if only because of the strain of waiting for Marcel Proust to be mentioned in conversation, which can happen as many as three times in a year. The educated person may then be required to make a comment on what they have only read about.

That literature could mean, as the French novelist Julian Gracq once complained, books more talked about than read indicates the extent to which language today may be used more to obscure and control than to communicate. See: ORAL LANGUAGE.

AARON   The brother of Moses. He was instructed, along with the heads of the other eleven houses of Israel, to hand over his rod. These were placed in the tabernacle. The next day Aaron's had budded, flowered and produced almonds, which won him the position of first head priest and the perpetual privilege of priesthood for the House of Levi.

This is neither the first nor the only example of control over the miraculous—that is, the unexplained or the secret—giving power. After all, the single word "yes" from the Delphic Oracle, when asked whether Socrates was the wisest living man, convinced the philosopher of his own ignorance and set him off on the quest for truth through questioning which in turn led to his execution.

But with Aaron the concept of power through secrecy was officially integrated into the Western system. Today's experts simply conform to this tradition. See: GANG OF FIVE.

ABASEMENT   In a society of courtiers or corporatists, the question is not whether to abase or to be abased, but whether a favourable balance can be struck between the two.

Simple folk may have some difficulty mastering the skills involved, but the sophisticated understand innately how the pleasure of abasing others can be heightened by being abased themselves.

The illusion among the most skilled is that they can achieve ultimate pleasure through a type of ambition or drive, which they call competence. This causes them to rise higher and so to win ever-greater power. But what is the value of this status in a highly structured society devoid of any particular purpose except the right, for a limited time, to give more orders than are received? Courtiers used to scurry around palace corridors with much the same illusion of importance.

When the time comes to retire from the functions of power, many collapse into a psychic crisis. They feel as if they have been ejected into a void. This is because society has not been rewarding them for their competence or their knowledge, but for their occupation of positions of power. Their very success has required a disembodied abasement of the individual. And when they leave power, the agreeable sense of purpose which it conveyed simply withers away.

Of course, power must be wielded or there is no civilization. But in a society so devoted to power and run by hierarchies of expertise, the élites are unconsciously addicted to an abstract form of sadomasochism. This may explain why success so often translates into triumphalism and constant complaints about the incompetence of others. The underlying assumption of most civilizations, including our own, is the exact opposite. Success is supposed to produce a flowering of modesty and concern for others. See: CORPORATISM.

ABELARD, PETER A twelfth-century pioneer of rational theological inquiry who laid the early foundations of SCHOLASTICISM and fell in love with a seventeen-year-old student. After a tempestuous love affair followed by a secret marriage, he suffered a neutralizing encounter with a knife wielded by her male relations.

Abelard accepted the monastic life without good grace. However, in his increasingly bad-tempered dialectical teachings, he did not deal with the connection between his inquiry and his fate. See: LOYOLA and PENIS.

ABSOLUTE Nothing is absolute, with the debatable exceptions of this statement and death, which may explain why political and economic theories are presented so seriously.

Absolutism is a deadly serious business. If even a hair's breadth of space is left around the edges of a theory, doubt may be able to squeeze through. The citizen may then begin to smile and wonder whether the intellectual justifications of power are really nonsense. Few within the expert élites see themselves as ideologues and yet they quite happily act as carriers of truth in whatever their field.

Whether it reveals the dictatorship of the proletariat or the virtues of privatization, truth is ideology. Not their truths, our élites say. They are simply delivering the inevitable conclusions of facts rationally organized. Absolutism is the weakness of others. Our élites have the good fortune simply to be right. See: **DOUBT, IDEOLOGY** and **SERIOUS**.

ACADEMIC CONSULTANTS The only place organized specifically for truth to be sought and understanding to be taught is the **UNIVERSITY**. In the late twentieth century some professors have reinterpreted the long-standing premise that since truth is a supreme value, it is therefore without price. If it's so supreme, it must have a market value.

Academics are the chief custodians of Western civilization's memory and as such of its ethical framework. Academic independence was fought for over a thousand years, with the gradual spread of **TENURE** over the last century and a half constituting the final step in the protection of intellectual freedom.

What does it mean, then, if a sizable portion of today's academics—in particular the social scientists—sell their expertise to corporations and governments? What they have to sell, after all—their aura of independent expertise—has a real use and therefore a quantifiable value.

When lawyers and lobbyists take up this kind of public activity it is monitored and licensed by government. Sometimes it is called influence peddling, sometimes lobbying. The social scientists escape these controls precisely because universities are thought of as independent. The question their commercial activity raises is whether a professor has the moral right to cash in on the independence of academia and on the value which society has assigned to the freedom of inquiry.

Since the rise of the European universities early in the second millennium, there has been a gradual change in the stature of professors. At first they were priests or freelance men of knowledge whose income came directly from the students. Professors who didn't teach what the students expected to learn were fired or chased through the streets. This had its disadvantages but kept the professors on their toes. Some, like the philosopher Giambattista Vico in Naples, did suffer in spite of their brilliance. He was a bad teacher. But Vico and his ideas nevertheless survived.

As the power of learning grew, universities became places which those with power sought to control. Initially the churches assumed this task, so one of the central goals of the Enlightenment was to release the universities from religious control. The new democratic élites of the nineteenth century declared the universities to be the custodians of intellectual freedom. In reality this young political order financed the institutions just as the old one had and sought to impose its "standards."

Despite being edged with hypocrisy, the idea of academic independence was an important pillar of the new democratic nation state. Higher education gradually came to offer the basic training required by anyone who hoped to occupy a position with any power at all. In short, a university degree became a proof of membership in the ruling élite.

With the decline of the influence of religion to an ever-narrower area—often no more than the places of worship—the whole domain of public training in ETHICS and morality was left unaccounted for. Much of that role was gradually conferred upon the universities, where it was taken over by independent thinkers and teachers. A university education became the true finishing school of the responsible citizen in a democracy.

Most philosophers of the seventeenth and eighteenth centuries earned little, expected little public respect, ran constantly on the edge of the law and were rarely employed in any regular manner. They would have looked upon the invention of the twentieth-century tenured professor as one of the great victories of the Enlightenment. They would also have been surprised to learn that an increasing number of them acted as if freedom of thought combined with secure employment and widespread respect was not enough. What the modern professors really wanted was more money. And they were willing to sacrifice all the rest in order to get it.

In fairness, the initiative had been taken by the corrupters not the corruptees. It began seriously after the Second World War with politicians seeking out ever-more academic advisers. They weren't paid much and they were exercising their own right to have political opinions. But as social and economic programming grew, with its inherent tendency to reduce the unlimited power of the large corporations, so those corporations began to mount a counter-attack.

Their answer to the practical and ethical arguments being made in favour of a stable and fair society was to develop absolute truths related to the market-place. Very early on they identified the need to cultivate their own independent experts capable of delivering truth. They began funding "independent" foundations dedicated to learning. Independence and learning were intended here to mean the development of ideas that would bolster the position of the corporation. On the leading edge of this movement were the **THINK TANKS** which went on to produce bevies of authoritative studies and annual reports intended to legitimize higher oil prices, deregulation, lower taxes, the debt crisis or whatever was the current agenda of their private-sector funders.

The final stage began in the 1970s when the social scientists began to notice a well-paid growth industry known as management consultancy. More and more, these academics began to think of themselves as consultants. And this was by no means limited to economists and professors of business administration.

The corporations and their foundations were far too sophisticated to concentrate on such a narrow and direct approach. Their mandate was to redefine half a millennium of Western evolution by re-examining how citizens see themselves and their society. In order for economic revisionism to make sense, there had to be a new view of philosophy, history, sociology and culture.

For a few years reform-minded governments competed against corporations in the race to purchase the aura of academic freedom. But most of the reform governments were gone by the early eighties and the spreading economic crisis limited the investment that public budgets could make. By then, the universities, the press and even the public seemed to have accepted without protest the new role of the professors.

The ideal of academic freedom and independence has now been severely damaged. To undo the corrupt system in place may be as complex as the eighteenth- and nineteenth-century battle to separate church and learning. There are some relatively simple problem areas. Should business administration be part of university education? Should a professor have the right to the ethical seal of approval of a university if he or she sells that aura in a separate business?

Universities are now desperate for money and only too eager to prostitute themselves. Presidents and their boards accuse the departments, who do not bring in their share, of fleeing reality. But do they have the right to destroy an essential creation of modern civilization? Rectors might well answer that the public purse is starving them. And yet the worst of all possible approaches would be to go on pretending that academic consultants are the descendants of Peter Abelard at the Sorbonne, in the twelfth century, or Giambattista Vico in Naples, in the early eighteenth. See: **TENURE** and **UNIVERSITY**.

ACADÉMIE FRANÇAISE Housed in the most beautiful palace in Paris, the Academy, whose role it is to control language, has a particularly elegant cupola and internal staircase. The Perpetual Secretary occupies a wonderful apartment in the west wing, overlooking the Seine and the Louvre. The Academy also owns a large chateau and park in the Forêt de Senlis where Academicians go to relax.

The task of the Academicians is to identify correct meaning and use, then put it in an official dictionary. This may force them to favour the truth and beauty of language over the pedestrian needs of communication. The female members of the Academy, for example, must be addressed as if they were male, because *Académicien* is a masculine word.

The Academicians are self-perpetuating—that is, when one dies, they elect another—which may explain why they are called the Immortals. The chairs in the official meeting room upstairs are historic but uncomfortable. On being elected, members receive a sword after their own design. See: SCHOLASTICISM.

ACAPULCO There are no sharks at Acapulco. The Mexican authorities are formal on this matter. If certain foreign tourists choose not to return home after their holidays, that is entirely their affair.

Furthermore, the sharks are not attracted to the waters around Acapulco by the raw sewage the hotels recycle into the bay. Suggestions of this sort are merely proof of the anti-Mexican sentiment found among foreign intellectuals, who disguise their prejudices in self-serving principles by suggesting, for example, that Mexican journalists are regularly murdered for expressing unflattering political opinions. These individuals are not journalists. Upon investigation by the responsible judicial authorities, it is often discovered that they are money-lenders or homosexuals who have managed to get press-cards under false pretences, and have then been murdered by poverty-stricken widows, whom they have been exploiting, or by under-aged male prostitutes.

These American intellectuals and their imitators in Canada are the same people who suggest that many Mexican workers live in cardboard shacks and that corruption is an integrated factor in the governmental system. This desire to maintain the Mexicans in a state of inferiority *vis-à-vis* the United States, by denigrating their accomplishments, is simply unacceptable, particularly when it is expressed with the do-gooding hypocrisy of the American élites who are themselves indifferent to the suffering of their own aboriginal peoples. See: FACTORIES.

ACCEPTANCE SPEECH   The triumph of banality over ego. See: AWARD SHOW.

AD HOMINEM   The obverse of HERO worship. Both indicate an unwillingness to deal with content.

Public figures have complained for decades about the growing tendency to judge them by violent personal attacks, often aimed at their private lives. But as public actors have chosen to assume Heroic guises—whether majestic, saintlike, martyred, romantic or touching—so those they attempt to seduce have reacted with personalized integral vilification.

There is nothing new about such *ad hominem* attacks. They were widely used for political purposes in the late eighteenth and nineteenth centuries. If public figures paid a little more attention to history, they would know that their predecessors led a much rougher life. Today they are protected by concentrated media ownership, the obsession of the large professional élites with respectable public behaviour and, in most countries, overly strict libel laws. Given that ours is a management-oriented society, we give far too much importance to the smoothness of public discourse and fear serious open verbal conflict.

Contemporary *ad hominem* resembles that of an earlier period—the seventeenth and eighteenth centuries. This was a society of courtiers constantly in pursuit of meaningless power. Court life was measured by personal details—orgasms, medals, gloves, cleavages and titles. *Ad hominem* fed the endless appetite for gossip which filled the salons and occupied the days of those caught up in the complex structures of the state. These were powerless people living by irrelevant criticisms in the shadow of false human gods—the absolute monarchs. That such detached *ad hominem* attacks have returned with a vengeance in the late twentieth century suggests that we have also returned to the courtier-based society of the great palaces, which have been transformed into the great professions and the great organizations of the public and private sectors.

ADVERTISING A once-important word now used in ever-narrower circumstances because it is in such direct contradiction with its traditional meaning.

Samuel Johnson said to advertise was "to inform another; to give intelligence." Advertising was thus linked with the moral value given to knowledge. This no longer being the case, the professionals have taken to using "public relations" where they once used advertising. This phrase suggests a self-interested negotiation rather than communication. See: **BAD PEOPLE** and **CONSUMPTION**.

AGRICULTURE See: **IRRADIATION**.

AIR-CONDITIONING An efficient and widely used method for spreading disease.

One of the keys to the revolution in architecture and planning which struck Western cities after the Second World War was the gradual realization by engineers and architects that systems of forced air could heat and cool large numbers of people in a cost-effective manner.

This removed one of the major restrictions on the size of buildings. If windows needn't be opened, then neither density nor height had to be limited. Once heated or cooled, the air could be endlessly recycled through buildings.

This revolution was soon being applied in the air. Before the arrival of the Jumbo Jet, most commercial planes expelled air continually and took in fresh air, which then had to be brought to cabin temperature. With the Jumbo, fuel savings were chosen over air quality. Passengers, from first-class to steerage and smoking to non-smoking, began travelling across the Atlantic in a classless fug. Fifty per cent of the air was recycled. After a few hours in the plane, passengers began to feel as if they were breathing dead air. It was as if each airplane contained a single pair of lungs shared among three to four hundred bodies.

By the early 1980s, standard frequent-flyer rhetoric referred to air travel as exhausting. People began to notice that working in large office towers was far more draining than in buildings where windows could be opened. Then a dramatic incident focused attention. A group of old American veterans staying in a hotel to attend a convention began to die, as if struck by a plague. It was explained that legionnaires' disease was the result not of recycled air but of defective recycling.

There were more common experiences which weren't fatal. People began to expect that following one flight out of every two or three they would fall sick. Sometimes they merely caught a cold; increasingly it was a virulent strain of what was called the flu. But these flus could bring on vomiting, dangerous temperatures and exhaustion. They often killed the elderly or fragile. In fact, they seemed to come in international waves which changed character each season. Every few months there would be a mutation in the type of virulence. The planes made these flu strains instantly international. And the office towers then spread them around in each city. What passengers didn't know was that some airlines were cutting back further on the fresh air quota in order to save money in the hard times brought on by **DEREG-ULATION** and the **DEPRESSION**.

Modern hospitals were also being built with these air-flow

systems and it soon became common knowledge that hospitals were places in which you caught things. The hard-learned medical lessons of physical isolation clarified in the nineteenth and early twentieth centuries seemed to have been forgotten.

Much of modern medicine is based upon controlling diseases by controlling movements. Now there were new and unexpected waves of viral diseases. Small epidemics in fact. One year it would be viral pneumonia. The next there would be a line of executives struck by ill-defined symptoms which exhausted them, sometimes for several years.

Air-conditioning also became a clear example of the inflexibility of modern industry and of technocratic structures generally. Economics seemed to be painfully linear. Every hour of work lost to a company through sickness is also money lost. It is common during the winter in places with moderate climates to find that 20 to 30 per cent of office workers are home sick. There seemed to be no room for applied thought which used practical observation in order to re-evaluate earlier policies.

This absurd rigidity is reminiscent of the old European colonial armies in the tropics. Well into the twentieth century British soldiers in India wore heavy clothing to protect them from the sun. In addition, a flat metal cross wrapped in cloth was placed beneath their jacket. This cross ran down the spine and over the shoulders. It was meant to stop the rays. Regiments functioned with permanently elevated levels of soldiers in hospital suffering from heat prostration. Attempts to bring in light clothing were resisted by most of the General Staff, who argued that the army would be decimated by the sun. When the change was at last introduced, and the hospital beds emptied, the Staff was amazed.

In manufacturing circles it is widely known that the least advanced area of aeronautics engineering is air treatment. In public, the press officers busily deny there is a problem. The number of formal complaints, they insist, are "statistically insignificant."[2] But then airline industry organizations don't compile data on these sorts of complaints. In 1993

American government officials investigated the case of a
flight attendant with tuberculosis who seemed to have
infected twenty-three other crew over a short period of time.
TB is spread by airborne bacteria. Uncirculated air was
therefore a likely factor. However, the mechanism of general
DENIAL kept turning.

Corporations inquiring whether windows can be made to
open in office towers are told by architects and the construction industry that this is impossible, or only for a signif-
icant extra charge, plus long-term air-management costs. In
spite of thousands of books about management and competitiveness, many of which talk about getting the most out of
executives and other employees through leadership, training
and encouragement of individual talents, there seems to be
no calculus for integrating the costs of sick-leave into those
of air-conditioning.

In truth, the only barrier to airplanes taking in a constant
stream of fresh air, cooling it and then expelling it is the
absence of pressure from passengers, the airlines' employees
and the airlines. The case of office towers is even simpler. The
air-conditioning system is rarely mentioned by companies
when they build, buy or rent. Nothing prevents them from
demanding air-conditioning systems limited to small areas—
less than a floor—and which constantly take in and expel air.
Nothing, that is, except the inability of our system to integrate
widely recognized medical costs with those of engineering.

ALLIES See: SPECIAL RELATIONSHIPS.

AMORALITY A quality admired and rewarded in modern
organizations, where it is referred to through metaphors
such as professionalism and efficiency.

Amorality is corporatist wisdom. It is one of the terms
which highlights the confusion in society between what is
officially taught as a value and what is actually rewarded by
the structure.

Immorality is doing wrong of our own volition. Amorality is doing it because a structure or an organization expects us to do it. Amorality is thus worse than immorality because it involves denying our responsibility and therefore our existence as anything more than an animal. See: BLOOD (1) and ETHICS.

ANGLO-SAXONS A racial group composed mainly of Celts, Chinese, Germans, Italians, Ukrainians, French and other peoples who have been conquered by or immigrated to the English-speaking world. To blame for everything. See: XENO-PHOBIA (PASSIVE).

ANIMISM Religion devoid of abstraction and therefore resistant to use by sophisticated power structures.

The last few decades have seen animism make a determined comeback, particularly among disaffected members of the rational élites. What their beliefs are has never been clear. Some talk of souls and spirits. Some of popular culture. Jung's archetypes have been remarkably popular.

Underlying all of this is a large group of highly educated people reaching for an integrated view of existence. The straightforward hill-tribe beliefs of Southeast Asia probably come as close as any to expressing their idea. Everything has life. Humans are alive, but then so are trees and rocks. We are all part of a single process so we must act in concert with the whole.

The large intellectual religions have little difficulty understanding each other, whatever their rivalries. They share almost identical ideals as well as their corruption by society. These religions also share a disdain for animism.

This usually takes the form of an attack on superstition. Some of it is justified. But most animistic superstition consists not of destructive fear but of populist ways to deal with social problems. Dietary rules. Marriage restrictions. The abstract religions do the same, except that their rules on everything from eating pork to fornication are apparently received as direct instructions from God.

What bothers the intellectual religions about animism is not the idea that everything from rocks to humans contains life, but that humans are therefore no more than a constituent part of a living whole which is the earth. That this view denies special rights and powers to the human is upsetting. That it denies special rights and powers to the structures of society is unacceptable.

Large organized societies are dependent on the separation of the human race from all the rest. This denial or demotion of the non-abstract frees us to act as if we were not limited by our physical realities. Without this liberation much of our PROGRESS would not have been possible.

And yet we are limited by physical realities. So our liberation has been built upon a great deal of self-delusion, which has turned gradually into very real political, social and economic weaknesses.

The argument today between those who see themselves as the forces of progress and those who appear to be resisting is a continuation of the old drive by the abstract religions to eliminate the animist view. Yet many of the new animists— environmentalists and sociologists, among others—are the product of a strange cross-breeding. They call for the reintegration of humanity into the worldly whole, but belong themselves to the intellectual structures of their enemies.

The professional environmentalists are a good example of this contradiction. They lobby like arms contractors. Haunt international conferences. Fight for tiny amendments in government and corporate behaviour. Small changes in content rules. They have the strength of fighting with their opponents' best weapons.

But after only twenty years in existence much of the environmental movement has taken on the form of just another corporation or interest group. Their interest may be disinterest, but their methods are one with the rational élites and are therefore limited to the details of corporatist life. These new animists are attempting to justify restraint and a common-sense approach to self-respect with the use of intellectual tools designed to eliminate both.

Still, they are a sign of more than dissatisfaction. There are dozens of other signs of people trying to take their distances from the rational system. Often these attempts seem silly or naïve and are discounted by the corporatist structures. But these people are reaching in the same direction, away from the isolation of our society. What they are seeking is some sense of integration or balance.

ANOREXIA A condition aspired to by most middle-class women. See: **MONARCHS**.

ANSWERS A mechanism for avoiding questions.

This might be called obsessional avoidance or a manic syndrome. It is based on the belief that the possession of an education—particularly if it leads to professional or expert status and, above all, if it involves some responsibility or power—carries with it an obligation to provide the answer to every question posed in your area of knowledge. This has become much more than the opiate of the rational élites. It may be the West's most serious addiction.

Time is of the essence in this process. An inability to provide the answer immediately is a professional fault. The availability of unlimited facts can produce an equally unlimited number of absolute answers in most areas. Memory is not highly regarded. Right answers which turn out to be wrong are simply replaced by a new formula. The result of these sequential truths is an assertive or declarative society which admires neither reflection nor doubt and has difficulty with the idea that to most questions there are many answers, none of them absolute and few of them satisfactory except in a limited way.

Answers are the abstract face of **SOLUTIONS**.

ANTI-INTELLECTUALISM   A self-validation ritual created by and for intellectuals.

There is no reason to believe that large parts of any population wish to reject learning or those who are learned. People want the best for their society and themselves. The extent to which a populace falls back on superstition or violence can be traced to the ignorance in which their élites have managed to keep them, the ill-treatment they have suffered and the despair into which a combination of ignorance and suffering have driven them.

Given the opportunity, those who know and have less want themselves or their children to know and have more. They understand perfectly that learning is central to general well-being. The disappearance of the old working-class in Germany, France and northern Italy between 1945 and 1980 is a remarkable example of this understanding.

Yet political movements continue to capitalize on the dark side of populism. Throughout the 1980s and early 1990s a number of groups gathered public support—Jean-Marie Le Pen and his *Front National* in France, Ross Perot in the United States, the new German Right, the Reform Party and the Bloc Québécois in Canada, the Northern League, Silvio Berlusconi's *Forza Italia* and the Neo-Fascist movement in Italy. These movements share the same message, each in their local way. It combines a simplistic as opposed to straightforward approach to public affairs with an ability to tap the public's disgust over the established élites.

The conclusion drawn by the PLATOnists—who account for most of our élites—is that the population constitutes a deep and dangerous well of ignorance and irrationality; if our civilization is in crisis the fault must lie with the populace which is not rising to the inescapable challenges. And yet civilizations do not collapse because the citizenry are corrupt or lazy or anti-intellectual. These people do not have the power or influence to either lead or destroy. Civilizations collapse when those who have power fail to do their job. Ross Perot was created by Harvard, not by illiterate farmers.

Our élites are concerned by what they see as intellectual **LUD-DITISM** all around them—television, films and music prospering at the lowest common denominator; spreading functional illiteracy; a lack of public appreciation for the expertise which the élites see as guiding all aspects of human life. It appears to them as if the populace is stubbornly refusing to fill an appropriate role in a **CORPORATIST** society.

Perhaps this is because the anti-intellectualism over which the élites make such a fuss is in fact the reply of the citizenry to both the élites' own pretension of leadership and their failure to lead successfully. This profoundly pyramidal model of leadership takes the form of obscure language, controlled information and the reduction of individual participation at almost all levels to one of pure function.

The élites have masked their failures by insisting that the population is lazy, reads junk, watches television and is badly educated. The population has responded by treating the élites with a contempt reminiscent of the attitudes of the pre-modern underclasses.

If **ECONOMICS** are rendered incomprehensible except to experts and in addition are unable to deal with our economic problems, why should anyone respect economists? If the corporate managerial élites cannot explain in a non-dogmatic, reasonable manner what they are doing and why, is there any reason to believe that their decisions will serve the general good? If those who create the tools of public communication—such as fiction—write novels that do not communicate, why should the public consider these works relevant or important?

It's not that everyone must understand everything; but those who are not experts must see that they are being dealt with openly and honestly; that they are part of the process of an integrated civilization. They will understand and participate to the best of their ability. If excluded they will treat the élites with an equal contempt. See: **CIVILIZATION**.

ANTS Ants do nothing 71.5 per cent of the time. They are
trying to think of what can usefully be done next. And this in
spite of their reputation—shared with beavers and BEES—as
hard-working role models for the human race.

Most humans in positions of responsibility work more
than 28.5 per cent of the time. It could be argued that, being
brighter than ants, we need less time to think. This is a technically correct and reassuring argument. Yet a comparison of
the incidence of error among ants versus that among human
beings would not come out in our favour. We could counter
that, by risking error, human society—or at least human
knowledge—has progressed, while that of the ants remains
stable. But if we are so bright, then why are we so eager to
spend as long as possible on the non-intellectual tasks which
hard work represents, while desperately economizing on the
time spent thinking? An outside observer, an ant for example, might wonder whether we are afraid of our ability to
think and more precisely of the self-doubt which it involves.
See: HARD WORK.

APPLE Spherical object created by thirty-two chemical products, then dipped in wax, then gassed. In the long run an
apple is as likely to bring on a doctor as to keep one away.

APPLIED CIVILIZATION A gift of the physically or economi-
cally stronger to the weaker. See: CIVILIZATION.

APPLIED CORPORATISM The mediocre usually gain power
because of long service, corruption, back-room manipulations, error or luck. But from time to time they arrive at the
top precisely because they are the accurate image of the
power structure in place. And so occasionally, when a leader
not good enough for the job wins office, the citizenry should
be grateful for what amounts to a moment of truth.

George Bush was the exact reflection of a corporatist

society. In his experience and attitudes he combined the interests of several business and government sectors. The standard ideological view—both that of the Right and of the Left—was that the Bush presidency presented an opportunity for special interests to cash in. And of course they did, leaving some happy and others outraged. But the principal role of a corporatist leader is not to help his friends grow rich. They will do that anyway. Nor is it to worry about the management of any one interest group.

The job of a corporatist president is to manage the relationships between the groups. In helping the arms industry to work with the Pentagon to work with the security agencies to work with the oil industry to work with the environmental agencies and so on, he encourages nationwide stability. If successful he will have indirectly eliminated interference from that rival system—citizen-based democracy—which technically maintains legal control over the constitutional structures of the Republic.

Criticisms of the Bush presidency based on accusations of corruption or of upper-class social indifference or of deficient domestic economic strategies missed the point. Corporatist leaders do not have policy strategies any more than they have ethical standards. What they do believe in is the stable management of cooperation between interest groups. This, they are convinced, will make society work effectively.

Even if the counterweight of ethics, democracy and justice is laid aside in such an argument, history proves the corporatists wrong. Interest groups are devoid of the broad common sense required to see beyond immediate self-interest. Without it they are little more than idiot savants, unable to avoid disasters and unable to understand why. Thus the superficial stability which President Bush produced was unsatisfactory and even unpleasant and was ultimately unacceptable to the voter. The one disadvantage attached to the inevitable dismissal by the public of a corporatist president is that the removal of an individual does not alter reality. See: **CORPORATISM.**

ARMAMENTS Extremely useful for fighting wars. A dead weight in any civil economy.

Throughout history functioning societies have accepted that an appropriate quantity of arms is a necessary burden which must be paid for, even though they cannot contribute to prosperity. There are two reasons for this endemic negative weight:

1. Arms are a consumer good. They either sit on the shelf like unused lipstick or are used to destroy other arms and people. In the process a large part of them disappear. They either explode or are exploded by the other side.

   In short, the purpose and use of arms includes none of the intrinsic qualities of capital goods. They cannot, for example, be used to make other goods or to provide services. That is, they contain almost no multiplier effect. Steel used for weapons has a multiplier of one—steel into weapons. But steel into road-building equipment and trucks is another matter. The equipment produces roads which permit transport, which uses trucks, which carry goods which create trade in other areas.

2. Arms have no market value. They cannot have one because the seller is a single government, and the buyer is a single government. And the seller and the buyer are usually one and the same government.

   That the company producing the weaponry may be privately owned, or that there are several rival privately owned companies, is irrelevant. Markets (competition) are created by demand, not by production. There is no economic demand for arms. They are required only to protect the state or to destroy another state. This is not an economic function.

   In order to create real market values for arms, we would have to set expressed values—fixed or floating—for each person killed or each object destroyed. During the French/English Indian wars of the eighteenth century this was tried. Scalps were assigned a cash value. A market was launched. The result was military and social disaster for all three sides (the English, the French and the Indians). A somewhat less specific market system was attempted during the Renaissance with the mercenary armies, especially the *condottieri* in Italy. It was equally disastrous.

The problem with linking military activity to any market-place has always been that if you set values for destruction you encourage destruction, which is not the same thing as preventing or winning wars, which is, after all, the purpose of armies and of arms.

Curiously enough, since the early 1960s—and in particular since President Kennedy's special message to Congress of February 6, 1961—the Western technocratic élites have been attempting to convert weaponry into a positive economic force. This imposition of an abstract idea onto a non-conforming reality is the sort of economic determinism which resembles alchemy, the obsessive mediaeval belief that base metal could be turned into gold. There is nothing unusual about the alchemist approach. Charles Mackay described sixteen phenomena similar to our armaments folly in his mid-nineteenth century masterpiece *Extraordinary Popular Delusions and the Madness of Crowds*.[3]

Kennedy and his Secretary of Defense, Robert McNamara, treated arms as if they were automobiles and so the armaments industry began to act as if it were Detroit. These two sectors were artificially linked by imaginary truths such as **TRICKLE-DOWN ECONOMICS**. National weapons needs were to be paid for by massive exports of more or less the same weaponry. Around the world a fresh new technocracy followed suit. Productive civil economies were transformed into falsely productive military economies.

The Reagan/Bush partnership took this illusion a step further and turned the arms "business" into a make-work program. Around the world more people followed suit. Arms were soon the single most important element in international industrial trade—some $900 billion per year. Research and Development (R and D) everywhere came to be dominated by military imperatives.

The third and current phase began with the fall of the Soviet Bloc. Something called the **PEACE DIVIDEND** raised its head briefly only to evaporate. Governments began to act as if the principal reason for building weapons was to save jobs.

Early in 1994 the most important American advocate of a new policy was nominated as Secretary of Defense. William Perry, a quiet technocrat, became the new-model McNamara. The ideas advancing behind him are presented in such an inoffensive, number-crunching way that few people have noticed them. This third stage involves total integration of the civil and military economies under a concept called **DUAL USE**, which subjects defence needs to market forces.

We are distracted from this by various international disarmament successes which amount to little more than a year-end clear-out in a cosmetics store. The old lipstick is swept from the shelves into the garbage or is sold off at knock-down prices in provincial markets. This makes room for the new consumer models.

The end result of our three-step, three-decade evolution has been the inversion of the meaning of the word armaments. What for thousands of years was a non-productive necessity of warfare has been dressed up as a productive necessity of both job creation and technological innovation. Where the public ownership of arsenals had once given some guarantee that weaponry would relate to defence and attack, the privatization of production puts the requirements of national protection on the back burner. In other words, the only way to reduce expenditures while ensuring the production of the right quantity of the right weapons without international proliferation would be to reverse the current policy: establish a monopoly of state production and openly assume the costs of defence.

ARMPITS   See: REALITY.

ASPEN INSTITUTE A supermarket of conventional wisdom for middle-level executives.

Corporate life, particularly for those not on the fast track, has all the bureaucratic pitfalls of directionless boredom. To distract these confused but loyal servants from what Thoreau called their "lives of quiet desperation," they are periodically shipped off to rest camps where, over the period of a few days, they are taught important things which can change their lives, their company, the world. Failing that, the experience may help them to hold on a bit longer. See: BUSINESS CONFERENCES.

AUTOBIOGRAPHY
1. A by-product of fiction which combines the dramatic methods of the romance novel with those of the adolescent adventure story.
2. A product of Heroic mythology usually written by a false Hero.
3. A celebration of the author's moral weakness.
4. Exhibitionism by someone too old to take his clothes off in public.
5. An obscuring of the author's actions behind his emotions and subjective state.
6. A plea by the author to be accepted as he is; that is, an excuse for his actions; that is, an attack on ETHICS. See: BIOGRAPHY.

AWARD SHOW Mechanism by which the members of a given profession attempt to give themselves the attributes of the pre-modern ruling classes—the military, aristocracy and priesthood—by assigning various orders, decorations and medals to each other.

These shows are a superficial expression of CORPORATISM. As with the pre-modern classes, their awards relate principally to relationships within the profession. Each time the words "I want to thank" are used by someone being decorated, they indicate a relationship based on power. The awards have little to do with that corporation's relationship to the outside world—what you might call the public—or for that matter with quality. See: **BALLROOM**.

B

BABEL, TOWER OF Multilingualism remains the source of movement and growth in a civilization.

The ability to fill the house of reality, intellect and imagination with different furniture is a great pleasure and a great strength. The strengths of comparison and of contradiction. The ability to draw on the originality or strengths of one to enrich another.

But for this to happen, writers and intellectuals must play their role, carrying words, images, emotions and ideas back and forth between languages. Unilingualism is one result of the acceptance by writers of professionalism. As they embrace the related idea that creativity is a sufficient justification for writing, so many become lost in the worship of a single tongue. The only status worse than this involves seeing themselves as the professional voice of a culture or a nation.

The laziest intellectuals have been produced by the four or five dominant cultures of the West. They claim that it is hard to write well if you speak more than one language, a problem which Dante, Voltaire and Tolstoy do not seem to have encountered. More recently they have taken to complaining that a similar unilingual sectarianism has sprung up among smaller linguistic groups who feel threatened. At both levels the writers are guilty of betraying their obligation to communicate.

Today more senior bureaucrats and business executives are multilingual than writers. The corporatist élites are therefore inheriting by default the right to decide what will be in the language of our international agendas, whether they deal with politics, business or culture. See: **CORPORATISM** and **DIALECTICS**.

BABY SEAL   A superior form of animal life which holds animistic power over the European imagination.

Many civilizations have wrapped themselves in skins to assume the qualities of a particular animal. Chiefs, warriors, indeed European kings have often worn the hides of courageous or powerful beasts such as the lion, the wolf or the buffalo. Rabbits and hyenas do not attract them.

The principal characteristics of the baby seal are the purity of its whiteness, a face eerily reminiscent of the infant child and its lack of intellectual pretension. Since Europeans seem to admire their own intelligence and have never developed a religious fetish for brown, grey or black seals, it can only be assumed that they identify with this animal's infantile whiteness.

The adoration of the infant seal is a reminder that colour is more than artifice. Other species, usually endangered, have mobilized a limited élite in their defence. Only the baby seal—always in ample supply—has moved millions of people of all ages and backgrounds. These people believe in the absolute value of the life of each member of that particular species.

To the question "Surely all animals, like all humans, are equal?" the answer is that of Napoleon the pig. "All animals are equal, but some animals are more equal than others."[1]

The same English man, woman, child whose eyes fill with tears before the photograph of a baby seal is indifferent to the genetic manipulation of the sacred chicken whose entrails decided public policy for our ancestors. Science, for the sole purpose of producing larger breasts, has created physically challenged birds, who could make a living in a topless bar had they not been left so top heavy and with so little brain that they can't walk let alone dance. And what of the

French, who weep for the baby seal over dinners of artificially swollen goose livers. The divine goose of our Greek heritage has a large wooden tube shoved down its throat and is force-fed to death to produce *foie gras*. In defence of the Italians, it must be said that by locking young calves in pens so small that they become bloodied invalids, they have turned their backs on the Old Testament temptation of the Golden Calf. They have rejected idolatry in favour of *fegato alla Veneziana.*

But a nagging doubt remains that idolatry is idolatry whether a calf or a seal is worshipped. The important thing for the adored one is to establish the difference between being god and being food or clothing. The baby seal has succeeded in doing this and may therefore be a great deal smarter than it looks.

BACON, FRANCIS   The English Cartesian. See: DESCARTES.

BAD NEWS   Those who have power always complain that journalists are only interested in bad news. "But if the newspapers in a country are full of good news, the jails are full of good people."

Elsewhere, bad news comes as light relief from the unrelenting rightness of those with expertise and power. They insist that they are applying the correct and therefore inevitable solution to each problem. And when it fails they avoid self-doubt or a public examination of what went wrong by quickly moving on to the next right answer. Bad news is the citizen's only available substitute for public debate.

BAD PEOPLE   In public life bad people, like bad money, drive out good. Only a constant effort by the citizenry to favour service over ambition and, in policy, balanced complexity over manipulative simplicity can draw the good forward.

It is far easier to gain and hold power for those who seek
only power. Self-interest is not constrained by the distracting
difficulties of trying to serve the public good. Unless society
has a respect for public service so strong that it amounts to
an unwritten obligation, a large number among those who
present themselves will be the unreasonably ambitious and
the emotionally damaged seeking to work out their INFERI-
ORITY COMPLEXES and other problems in public.

This difficulty has always been with us. In his definition of
Fatherland, Voltaire complained that "he who burns with
ambition to become aedile, tribune, praetor, consul, dictator,
cries out that he loves his country and he loves only himself."[2] Yeats returned to the subject in "The Second
Coming"—"The best lack all conviction, while the worst/Are
full of passionate intensity." What is this lack of conviction?

Relatively well balanced, disinterested people make an
important private sacrifice by giving time to the general
good. They also have trouble believing that their contribution could be important. This is not false modesty. The
energy of political ambition is like a tornado which clears
out those who don't have it. The particular problem of our
courtier-ridden society is that its standards are those of pure
power and of money.

In 1993 the departing director of the French secret service, Claude Silberzahn, laid out for his agents their three
principal areas of work. The first two were the rise of "ethnic
intolerance" and the "extraordinary and frenetic quest for
money in all its forms...by the political and economic élites,
as if money had no smell...when often it is dirty, doubtful
and illicit."[3] This atmosphere repulses most people.

More balanced citizens may have strong convictions about
the public weal and public service. But they are less likely to
be obsessed by the exercising of power. The Federalist
Papers, in arguing for the new American constitution,
argued for checks and balances which would neutralize the
power of factions and so draw the best citizens out into the
public process. But the ultimate checks and balances are not
constitutional. They are the approval and disapproval of the

citizen. So long as we reward raw ambition and the skilful manipulation of power, we will continue to draw those whose interest is self-interest. See: BANALITY and CARLYLE.

BALANCE   See: HUMANISM.

BALLROOM   There are four architectural periods:

Pre-1850: Situated one floor above ground level (the *piano nobile*) in a palace, chateau or large house. Vaulted ceilings were succeeded by flat painted ceilings. Used for dancing. A mainstay of the Jane Austen–Leo Tolstoy novel.

1850–1945: Situated on the ground floor of hotels and commonly decorated with classical columns and gold leaf. The floors were sprung for dancing, but they are now most often used by businessmen's lunch clubs to listen to speakers or for charity functions. A fixture of Edith Whartonesque fiction.

1946–1970: Situated on the fortieth floor (the penthouse) where they revolve. These rooms are decorated with oil-based materials in primary colours. They are usually empty. Sometimes used in feature films to depict modern life.

Post-1970: Situated in hotel basements beside the garage. These cement rooms seat 2,500 people when all the partitions are folded back. They are used for BUSINESS CONFERENCES and AWARD SHOWs. Thanks to the division of society into thousands of specialized groups, they are always full. The basement ballroom has replaced the opera house, which itself replaced the royal palaces as the place in which the élites legitimize themselves. They exist in a post-literate vacuum. See: CORPORATISM.

BANALITY The political philosopher Hannah Arendt confused the meaning of this word by introducing in 1961 her brilliant but limiting concept, "the banality of evil." In the late 1980s and early 1990s a minor political figure, Brian Mulroney, released the term by demonstrating that it could also reasonably be understood to mean the evil of banality. See: CARLYLE and SPECIAL RELATIONSHIPS.

BANKERS Pillars of society who are going to hell if there is a God and He has been accurately quoted.

All three Western religions have always forbidden the collection of interest on loans. When Samuel Johnson defined the banker in the eighteenth century his status was clear: "One that trafficks in money."[4] Their venal sin of usury continues to sit high on lists of scriptural wrongdoing, which raises the question of why bankers—the money-market sort excluded—tend to be frequent church-goers. The respect in which they have increasingly been held over the last two centuries has paralleled the growth of economics based on long-term debt, which has spread into every corner of society, from governments and corporations to the poor. The more money owed, the more the lender is respected, so long as the borrower intends to pay it back.

But what effect does this have on the moral position of bank employees? Few modern bankers are owners. Except through their salaries they do not profit from interest payments. Are they or are they not among the damned? Perhaps they should themselves be seen as victims of usury, having little choice but to lend their lives to the usurious process in order to feed their families. Yet for the borrower, these employees are the human face of usury.

The clearest situation for bankers would be if God didn't exist. They would then be morally home-free and could go to church in a more relaxed frame of mind. See: DEBT.

BARONS: ROBBER, PRESS, ETC. Individuals operating in

spite of—or perhaps thanks to—a severe inferiority complex transformed into megalomania.

As Andrew Carnegie and John D. Rockefeller demonstrated, the robber variety can find some inner peace through the semi-physical therapy of having people make and do things. A select few may even come to resemble the sort of mediaeval barons who bullied King John into signing the Magna Carta. The press sector offers less scope for improvement. Devoid of practical therapeutic tools, it leaves the mentally unstable to pontificate publicly while using their power to bully others into silence. So long as the widespread ownership of newspapers prevents them from limiting the public's general freedom of speech, these unhappy individuals provide others with the welcome distraction of colourful comic relief. See: INFERIORITY COMPLEXES.

BEES   In his *Philosophical Dictionary* Voltaire points out that bees seem superior to humans because one of their secretions is useful. Nothing a human secretes is of use; quite the contrary. Whatever we produce makes us disagreeable to be around.[5]

The bee's social organization also invites comparisons. If the queen were to be removed and the drones were able to convince the worker bees to go on working while they stepped in as MANAGERs, what would happen to our supply of honey?

BIOGRAPHICAL FILMS   Since attention to historical detail ruins filmed drama, the essential property of biographical cinema is that it improves in quality by not telling the truth.

These films, whether describing the lives of American presidents or criminals, French generals or Russian kings, are among the major beneficiaries of the "big lie" idea. As a result they have helped to create a modern mythology which erases the Western idea of intellectual inquiry and returns to the pre-intellectual tradition of mythological gods and heroes. This is the context in which portraits of John Kennedy, James Hoffa, Al Capone, Napoleon and so on can most easily be understood.

BIOGRAPHY   Respectable pornography, thanks to which the reader can become a peeping tom on the life of a famous person.

Biography has increasingly replaced the novel as the most popular form of serious reading. While in the eighteenth and nineteenth centuries the novel provided the reader with a reflection of him or herself, today the biography encourages the gratuitous pleasures and self-delusion of voyeurism. See: **AUTOBIOGRAPHY**.

BIRTH CONTROL PILL   Responsible for a sense of loss and even failure among people who came of age in the 1960s, the birth control pill produced a twenty-five-year-long holiday from reality. For the first time in history, sex had no consequences. It was what it felt like. Nothing more.

Then a rising tide of new venereal diseases appeared, culminating with AIDS. And part of the feminist movement began to argue that the pill reflected a male desire for convenience, while another part replied that it gave women control. They no longer had to berate men to take precautions. And suddenly, like a ghost from the past, the condom was back. For the rest of their lives the sixties generation will live in an atmosphere of regret—some over the good times lost forever, but most because they didn't take advantage of a once-in-eternity opportunity. See: **ORGASM**.

BLOOD (1)   A mythological and almost always invisible liquid.

Apart from a banal utility as the fuel of life, its real value lies in what is called the blood line. Purity of line justifies all actions which are dependent on paternity, tribalism and nationalism. Blood lineage makes certain groups better lovers, others more individualistic, others more honest, others quite simply nicer. It fuels their creative genius. Makes them courageous and inspired warriors.

These are the burdens, which each individual must bear, as copulation interweaves with history. They cannot assume individual responsibility. Individuals are not even responsible for their own claims of superiority which lead them to murder, rape, exploit or dominate others. Such acts can only be attributed to paternity or tribalism.

Unfortunately, modern medicine has still to catch up with these self-evident truths. It remains unable to prove paternity, let alone racial purity. Laboratories can only reduce blood to a few broad types common to most races. Fortunately, the demonstrable fact that certain tribes are better lovers or more individualistic and the clear understanding that particular groups deserve to be raped and murdered removes the need for scientific proof of the blood line.

BLOOD (2)   The most probable explanation for the fundamental practicality of women versus the endemic romanticism of men is that women, from twelve years old to their mid-fifties, must handle their own blood as it pours from their bodies one week out of every four.

The signs of male mortality are much more abstract. Only war guarantees them a regular confrontation with blood, which may explain the romance of organized violence.

Men have always presented themselves as clear-headed and practical versus the female who is enveloped in a romantic mist. This is an early and persistent example of the DICTATORSHIP OF VOCABULARY. See also: TOUGH.

BLUE JEANS   One of the most successful impositions of voluntary visual conformism in the history of the world. Curiously enough, the primary attribute of this particular piece of clothing is meant to be a rejection of conformity in the name of individualism.

BORING The scientific community speaks about its work in a cool and disinterested manner. To present an exciting profile would be unprofessional. Any excess of emotion would suggest a lack of neutrality and therefore a tendency to read what they want in the facts rather than reporting what they see. Scientific objectivity must therefore appear to be boring.

Scientists are well aware that their work is neither boring nor objective. If it were, very few discoveries would be made.

Social science, being falsely empirical, is triply obsessed by the obligation to present itself as the objective interpretation of observed reality. Since the more or less hard edges of scientific inquiry are not involved, social scientists are free to be more categorical about truth, reality and what they call facts. They therefore seek to be more boring than scientists. See: DIALECTS.

BRETTON WOODS A system for international financial management and stability which was put in place by the Allies, minus the Soviets, in 1944 and destroyed in 1973 by President Richard Nixon without consideration being given to a replacement.

Nixon hoped in this way to solve some short-term American economic problems by re-creating the sort of financial disorder in which the largest power would be best placed to benefit. It could be said that this was the single most evil act undertaken by an elected leader in the postwar period. Other leaders should not be discouraged, however. The opportunity to do worse is perpetual. See: DEPRESSION.

BRIEFING BOOKS The protocols of power in the second half of the twentieth century.

Whoever structures and/or writes the argument, which

each book disguises as objective fact and disinterested analysis, ultimately controls the decision-making process. Briefing books are rarely read by those who receive them, but are referred to as if they contained Holy Writ. Where once a single collection of Testaments was sufficient, thousands of these contemporary gospels are now presented every day in every sector in every country. They assert brief moments of artificially constructed absolute truth. See: FACTS.

BUDDHISM (TIBETAN) The most popular form of Buddhism in the West because it has the least Buddhist content.

Like Christianity, Buddhism contains many schools. Some concentrate on providing their priests, preachers or monks with a living, usually by appealing to the least noble instincts in the population. The Tibetan approach combines Buddhist form with content dominated by the worst of animism.

Tibet is a country in which poverty was and remains the rule, where the monkhood has always been the equivalent of a privileged élite. For centuries religion has been the sole export and only source of hard currency. So a select group in each generation of monks would walk down out of the mountains to chant and teach in richer places. China was their primary source of income. The difficulty was that the sophisticated Chinese élites weren't particularly interested in the Buddha's argument.

The aristocracy and the Mandarins were already committed to the complex ethical system of Confucius, thanks to which the empire could be administered. What they wanted from these rather crude but mysterious mountain monks were light entertainment and amusement. Like a miraculous glove adjusting to the hand it needs to fit, the Tibetans complied by drawing upon their childhood memories of superstition and magic.

With the Chinese invasion of the 1950s most of the monks were either locked into the country or locked out. For those on the outside life continued as it always had, except that they travelled West instead of East. In the process they discovered that, as with the pre-revolutionary Chinese élites, our equivalent had a taste for mystical circus entertainment.

They also discovered that the rich Westerners, who were dissatisfied enough with their lives to approach a Buddhist teacher, were nevertheless attached to their money and belongings. They were often willing to finance the monks, but not to become devoutly poor themselves. Although Buddhism is primarily about giving up desires and attachments to the tangible world, these monks have diligently worked to demonstrate that Westerners are an exception to the rule. The monks have developed an anti-materialistic way of materialism to help us through our lives. Providing we're willing to do a bit of chanting and fasting, we can have our cake and eat it. Reflecting on the glovelike approach of these holy men, it is difficult not to believe that our modern concept of the service industry was originally a Tibetan invention.

BURKE, EDMUND   An unfortunate prisoner of the twentieth-century ideological prism, forcibly confined for the last sixty years to the Right, although for the preceding one hundred years he was considered one of the great voices of reform, which constantly sought justice and social balance.

Burke appears to be the victim of a peculiar long-standing cooperation between the intellectuals of Right and Left, in which all thinkers are reduced to a caricature in order to be fitted into a closed dialectic of extremes. For a long time the idealogues were unable to do this to him. His practical ideas of justice bore no relationship to the building-block abstractions of modern ideology.

Burke was not an isolated observer of real events, but an elected member of parliament, the leading strategist of the Whig opposition as well as its most eloquent spokesman. When he spoke, he didn't have the privilege that most modern philosophers take for granted—that they can constantly lay out ideal scenarios as if these are practical options. The complexity of Burke's message comes not from his philosophical line but from the effects of sitting on the parliamentary bench in a senior position dealing with reality on a daily basis. In that sense, Burke's trail resembles Thomas Jefferson's.

By picking out particular political events, almost any political group is able to deform the constant line of his career and claim him as their spiritual ancestor. As for Burke's enemies, they have concentrated on the practicalities of his daily political life in order to suggest that he was a hypocrite on the important philosophical questions.

By the early twentieth century, the reduction of Western political ideas to two reflecting opposites was almost complete. It suddenly seemed easy to ignore his long and passionate struggles for justice in America, India and Ireland so as to concentrate on what interested the ideologues—his "anti-revolutionary" stand during the French crisis that began in 1789.

The French Revolution was and remains the deflowering orgasmic event of the modern Left and Right. To have opposed it was to oppose the idea that a single overwhelming act—revolution—could solve the problems from which society suffered. From the 1790s on, the ideologues had found that Burke's opposition constantly interfered with their matrix. His had been the loudest voice raised in disinterested opposition at the time, and perhaps the only one which carried serious intellectual weight. Over the succeeding decades, as philosophers attempted to set down their opposing interpretations of the event and therefore its long-term implications, the memory of Burke's non-conforming voice seemed to become louder and ever more annoying. At the height of the Western ideological split in the 1930s they simply locked him up as an anti-revolutionary voice on the Right.

That this meant discounting most of what he had said and written was a curious thing to do to a man whose life and considerable public power were based entirely on his words. "The only way in which you can find Edmund Burke guilty of authoritarianism," Conor Cruise O'Brien has written, "is by choosing to ignore everything he ever said, as a result of arbitrarily deciding that he didn't mean any of it."6

While Burke saw Americans as victims of the power held and abused by London, and while he continued to lead the movement in England which supported their cause, he also resisted the colonial opposition to the Quebec Act. Americans hated it because it gave citizens' rights to the French-Canadian Catholics. They hated the idea that any power would be given to a rival religion and language.

Subsequent mythology has presented the colonial revolt as a simple affirmation of citizens' rights, but the short list of American demands always included the removal of the rights of another group of citizens to the north. Burke also opposed a move to give the Americans representation in Westminster because it would have meant seating elected slave-owners.

Two decades later, when he was—according to twentieth-century ideologues—acting like a man of the Right by opposing the French Revolution, Burke was also working and voting with a small minority in parliament to abolish the slave trade. Through much of this period he was pursuing an exhausting campaign to see Warren Hastings punished for his violence, autocracy, racism and corruption in India. His efforts won him formal admiration, but also profound enmity in most circles of power for having stood in the way of England's *raison d'état.* London wanted control of India by whatever means. Burke disturbed a façade of respectable action by forcing parliament to deal with India and the Indians as a real place and real people.

The theme that ran through each of these Burkian interventions was his opposition to the abuse of power, particularly dressed up as an intellectual abstraction, and his belief that some sort of public equilibrium was possible. He did not propose as an alternative either unlimited individual right or the religion of the market-place.

The NEO-CONSERVATIVEs' claim that Burke is their inspiration can be dealt with by reading a few of his words while thinking of their market and social Darwinism:

> Freedom is not solitary, unconnected, individual, selfish Liberty. As if every Man was to regulate the whole of the Conduct by his own will. The Liberty I mean is social freedom. It is that state of things in which Liberty is secured by the equality of Restraint... This kind of Liberty is indeed but another name for Justice...but whenever a separation is made between Liberty and Justice, neither is, in my opinion, safe.[7]

Most of those who today claim to be his spiritual descendants are precisely the sort of people he spent his whole life fighting. If he could be brought back to life to meet with his current disciples, the probability is that he would refuse to sit down in the same room with them.

Burke's arguments—his definitions of ethics and values—remain central to the events that have shaped our struggles over communism, capitalism, justice, nationalism, colonialism and religious freedom. If, as many believe, the standard arguments used in our society have come to an impasse, then the explanation probably lies not in recent events but in an intellectual wrong turn taken some time ago. The campaign to misrepresent a non-ideological thinker like Burke is among the best evidence we have of that wrong turn. See: DIRECT DEMOCRACY and ELECTORS OF BRISTOL.

BUSINESS CONFERENCES   Aside from being a waste of the shareholders' money, these gatherings of executives can pose serious economic threats.

Conferences have a theme, official or unofficial. There will be a topic or a new method or a new market which will dominate all talk. The conference-goers can then return

home enthusiastic about the latest Asian opportunity or production cost-saving process or diet book. This shared enthusiasm justifies the conference. It rarely has much to do with
economic reality, common sense or particular interests.
Conferences create business fashions and carry whole industries off in odd and often counter-productive directions.

The higher the quality of these gatherings—those sponsored by business newspapers or business schools, for example—the more dangerous they are. National and
international gatherings which do not have a concrete purpose are the most dangerous because they are desperately
solution-oriented. Important people gather to discuss the
state of the world and of their industry and the relationship
between the two. The participants' status as powerful people—that is, their egos—requires that progress be demonstrated. A theme or an attitude, no matter how unfocused,
must emerge in order to prevent doubt setting in while they
are all locked together in meaningful meetings.

The annual gathering of business and political leaders at
DAVOS in Switzerland has the highest profile and the least
purpose. It is the most susceptible to a fashionable idea
which can then reverberate around the world and give cre-
dence to the sense of importance felt by the participants
about themselves. See also: ASPEN INSTITUTE.

BUSINESS SCHOOLS   Acting schools which train experts in
abstract management methods to pretend they are capitalists.

The graduates of these institutions have dominated
Western business leadership for the last quarter-century.
This corresponds exactly with a severe economic crisis in the
West, which has included runaway inflation, endemic unem-
ployment, almost no real growth, record levels of bank-
ruptcy, and a collapse in industrial production.
Manufacturing, the sector which they have been trained to
manage, has suffered more than any other.

This raises two questions:

1. Is there any indication—practical, statistical, philosophical or financial—that training future business leaders in specialized management schools has benefited business or the economy?
2. Has this new élite—approximately a quarter of the university population[8]—been able to communicate to society any convincing program for ending the crisis?

Not surprisingly, an education which above all teaches the management of structures is impervious to failure. Those within the structure continue to define the economy's needs in their own terms and so seek out successive new generations of business school graduates.

In 1993 the Harvard Business School reacted to growing criticism of its methods by announcing a new curriculum. In the future students would "focus less on specific disciplines and more on combining skills to solve problems."[9] But it is precisely their obsession with problem-solving that is the heart of the problem. To organize the training of business leaders from the point of view of the corporate executive is rather like training athletes to compete from the point of view of the team's office manager.

The outside observer might conclude dispassionately that these schools should be shut down or their methodology revolutionized. The graduate will argue, like the World War I staff officer, that failure could be turned into success if only there were more of his own kind in positions of power. Just one more wave of bodies heaved out of the trenches for a charge and the war will be won. See: **MANAGER**.

C

CALM A state of emotion which is overrated except in religious retreats. It is used principally to **CONTROL** people who are dissatisfied with the way those in authority are doing their jobs. When individuals show annoyance, the person in power or with privileged information or expertise will make them feel they are not calm enough to deal with the situation rationally. A lack of calm suggests a lack of courage, intelligence or professionalism.

Calm was the quality most admired by World War I generals in themselves and in their troops. Since then, calm incompetence has risen to become a quality of high professionalism. A loss of calm in a catastrophe is seen to be worse than cowardly; it indicates a lack of breeding as well as inappropriate amateurism. Outsiders are amateurs.

The cliché of calm as a virtue was captured in Rudyard Kipling's "If you can keep your head when all about you..." But Kipling was far too smart to mean that people should be victims of incompetence or mulishly stubborn or blindly loyal to either their professions or their class. He was talking about deft, razor-sharp coolness; a fast, flexible mind capable of admitting error and adjusting to circumstance; a talent for reaction to crisis with white-heat action or invisible subtlety.

The Captain of the *Titanic* was no doubt pleased that his male passengers in first class remained calm as they waited to drown. Had they been less controlled, they might have found some small satisfaction in passing their time by throwing him overboard. See: PANIC.

CANADA

1. So complicated that nobody knows how it works, which causes Canadian social scientists to talk about it all the time, which causes foreigners to say it's boring because nothing ever happens.
2. The most decentralized country in existence, which causes Canadians to complain constantly about the power of the central government.
3. Administered under the third oldest constitution in the world, which causes Canadians to insist that it has never worked and must be changed.
4. The only major country in which the two leading western cultures have managed to live peacefully together for several centuries, causing Canadians to insist that they cannot live together.
5. Burdened by the laziest élite of any developed nation; people who have made their fortunes by selling off the country's resources and by working for more energetic foreigners. They are most comfortable on their knees, admiring those from larger countries who have purchased them.
6. A country where 95 per cent of the land is north of the major cities, which causes its urban inhabitants to treat their hinterland as an embarrassing and backward region, while pretending that they themselves are situated hundreds of miles to the south, somewhere between New York and FLORIDA.

CANNIBALISM   A few years ago over dinner in St. Tropez, a retired colonial doctor in his nineties began recounting his experiences with cannibals in the Cameroons. He had been twenty-one. We were up on a terrace looking across the great bay with the lights of other towns ringing the shore.

His account turned entirely on the administrative problems which the phenomenon produced. Was it a crime? By whose law? Who was to be punished? A whole village would have consumed the body. Were they therefore, in European terms, accomplices to the murder? This was his first colonial job and he had been left as the sole civil authority over hundreds of square miles. In this district the villages were isolated from one another.

I eventually interrupted to ask what seemed to me a key question. How did they cook their humans? The doctor stared at me as if he didn't understand.

"Grilled or boiled?" I asked again.

With an energetic enunciation of contempt—the sort of energy which was common in language before electronics cooled it—he replied, "Boiled of course! Boiled!"

Sensible civilizations, which have not been deformed by urban fashions, are unanimous about the healthiest way to cook meat. Some may grill it after it has been boiled. But all will boil it. This removes excess fats and other unhealthy enzymes as well as tenderizing the flesh. Only the most basic savages grill or barbecue their meat. Interestingly enough, this universal early human understanding has been confirmed by contemporary chemists who have discovered that the grilling process causes a molecular rearrangement which is bad for the eater and may contribute to cancer.

According to the colonial doctor, no particular religious or social mythology was involved in these incidents except that villagers did not eat their own. But if they were short of food and a stranger happened to travel through the area, they might well kill him and boil him. In the course of each year two or three cases would be brought to his attention and each of these led to interminable complications. See: CROISSANT.

CAPITALISM A concept which has moved beyond the stage of sensible discussion.

Capitalism can be a useful social tool or a weapon of

unabashed human exploitation. Which it will be depends entirely on the way it is regulated. Capitalism itself contains no ethical values. Those who use it decide by their actions whether it is a force of good or evil.

Each economic system does tend to be more at home in certain circumstances than in others. Capitalism is happiest in a non-democratic society.

Not that any old dictatorship will do. Two types in particular can be disastrous. The first is the bureaucratic sort, when a nation is dominated by a state religion or ideology, as in the former Soviet Union. Second are the personalized dictatorships, where all financial dealings must run through the hands of the dictator, his family and friends.

Capitalism thrives in the evolved authoritarian dictatorship. There the streets are calm, dissent is discouraged, disorder repressed. Little time is wasted over politics, debates, elections and tiresome, inefficient legislatures. For decades at a stretch the same ministers and policies remain in place. The firm hand all of this suggests must, however, be benevolent. Individuals must have the freedom to make money and spend it as they wish, believing that so long as they don't challenge the system, they will be permitted to live out their lives in peace, keep their wealth and pass it on to their children.

The glory days of the Industrial Revolution came in England before a series of parliamentary reforms had created anything resembling a fairly elected assembly. With the rise of mass democracy during the late nineteenth century, the capitalist system began to stall, then decline, and has never recovered. In France, capitalism's greatest moments came under two benign dictators: Louis-Philippe and Louis-Napoleon; in Germany it prospered happily under Kaiser Wilhelm.

In the United States the capitalist system was first established under slavery. Its moment of glory came in the last quarter of the nineteenth century and the first quarter of the twentieth, when the workforce was flooded by immigrants who either were not yet citizens or were still politically

passive. Slavery still functioned in its legal form of segrega-
tion. Capitalism complained a great deal from 1932 to 1968;
the period during which public participation was most
evenly spread and government paid most attention to the
needs of the whole populace. It regained a sense of optimism during the 1970s and 1980s when voter participation
fell to 50 per cent in presidential elections and far lower in
those for Congress. This period coincided with a rise of public disgust for the political process, a decline in labour-union
membership and intense deregulation.

Capitalism was reasonably content under Hitler, happy
under Mussolini, very happy under Franco and delirious
under General Pinochet.

This is not what the early philosophers of capitalism had
expected. The tempering of man by commerce as imagined
by Adam Smith and David Hume has not happened. The
once-popular view that democracy blossomed thanks to the
rise of capitalism can now be seen in perspective. Their parallel rise isn't one of cause and effect, as their ongoing difficult relationship continues to demonstrate.

These misunderstandings aren't surprising. Remarkable
men writing in the eighteenth century were trying to guess
what the new economic whirlwind would bring. We now
have the advantage of experience.

Even Max Weber in the early twentieth century was convinced that bureaucratic capitalism, along with public
bureaucracy, would be forces for efficiency, speed and preci-
sion. We now know that he was wrong. The large corporations use their structures and their wealth to protect
themselves from their own failures, but they are ineffectual
when compared to smaller owner-managed companies.

These visible experiences have been clouded for us by the
self-serving public relations of the business schools, which
continue to feed the structures, and the kidnapping of people like **EDMUND BURKE** and Adam Smith by the **NEO-CONSER-
VATIVE** ideologues. They present Smith as an apostle of
unrestricted trade and unregulated markets. In fact his was a

relatively moderate, balanced position which included public regulation to curb the excesses of capitalism.

We can now see how some of the miscalculations were made. For example, many of those who imagined the new American Republic had the Venetian Republic in mind as a model. They saw **VENICE**'s economic organization as a solution to their problems. They scarcely bothered with its underlying principles which excluded such elements as individualism, a responsible citizenry, free speech and democracy. It was an almost perfect **CORPORATIST** dictatorship.

The great American philanthropist industrialists—such as Carnegie and Rockefeller—were in some ways naïve descendants of the Venetian tradition. They seemed to promise a society led by economic daring. Alongside their economic infrastructures, which became those of the nation, they left wonderful monuments to culture. But their sort of robber **BARON** leadership, no matter how creative, undermined the possibility of a citizen-based state.

What these experiences indicate is that democracy and capitalism are not natural friends. That doesn't mean they must be enemies. But if allowed free run of the social system, capitalism will attempt to corrupt and undermine democracy, which after all is not a natural state. Democracy was a gradual and difficult creation against the stated desires of the natural sectors of power (authoritarian, military, class). It requires constant participation and can only be maintained by the toughness of its citizenry.

A functioning democracy nevertheless needs to create wealth. It therefore needs some balance of capitalism. By carefully defining the limits permitted to that phenomenon, responsible government can allow the process of wealth creation to succeed. This doesn't mean that democracy can create ethical capitalism. That would be to impute values where none exist. Democracy can, however, lay out rules of procedure which are based in ethics. Capitalism is then surprised to discover that it can produce wealth within the rules of the democratic game, providing that they are perfectly clear and designed with the creation of wealth in mind. See: **CORPO-RATISM** and **FREE**.

CARLYLE, THOMAS   There is a certain pleasure to be had in picking out unpleasant individuals from the past and blaming them for whatever has since gone wrong. Unfortunately this is an inadvertent way of embracing the Heroic or Great Man view of **HISTORY**.

As the nineteenth century advanced, so the battle between the forces of democracy and dictatorship gathered strength and they repeatedly engaged each other. Thomas Carlyle's role was to round up all the anti-democratic ideas careening about in a society dependent on great men—ideas largely inspired by the Napoleonic adventure—to make an integrated theory of civilization. *On Heroes, Hero-worship and the Heroic in History* appeared in 1841, the year Napoleon's body was brought back to Paris in triumph.

Carlyle's concept had an enormous impact. He had packaged what the anti-democratic elements in society had been trying to express. He was not the first to evoke the Great Man theory. Hegel preceded him. Friedrich Nietzsche, Léon Bloy, Max Weber and Oswald Spengler followed close behind. But it was Carlyle who neatly wrapped up the whole theory in an intellectually respectable yet populist manner.

> For, as I take it, Universal History, the history of what man has accomplished in this world, is at bottom the History of the Great Men who have worked here. They were the leaders of men, these great ones; the modelers, patterns, and in a wide sense, creators of whatsoever the general mass of men contrived to do or to attain; all things that we see standing accomplished in the world are properly the outer material result, the practical realization and embodiment, of Thoughts that dwelt in the Great Men sent into the world.[1]

One of Carlyle's most effective tricks was to roll famous dead poets, philosophers and martyrs together with generals and dictators into a single Heroic class. In his chapter on Dante and Shakespeare he insists that "in man there is the *same* altogether peculiar admiration for the Heroic gift, by what name soever called..."[2] Twice he speaks of Napoleon while discussing Dante. They are part of the same Heroic family.

Of course the Florentine poet was a genius who made an important contribution to our civilization. But Dante never sought craven worship from others. He would have detested Carlyle's fawning attitude. There is nothing worshipful in the way he wrote of the famous dead men he met in *The Divine Comedy*.

In Carlyle's analysis of Napoleon, the Great Man's flaws are treated as mere "smoke and waste."[3] This contrasting of the Hero and his weaknesses is central to our contemporary "personality" debates. And it continues to play its role as a mechanism for removing the citizen's sense of his or her right to judge their leaders on matters of importance.

> To me, in these circumstances...'Hero-worship' becomes a fact inexpressibly precious; the most solacing fact one sees in the world at present. There is an ever-lasting hope in it for the management of the world. Had all traditions, arrangements, creeds, societies that men ever instituted, sunk away, this would remain. The certainty of Heroes being sent us; our faculty, our necessity, to reverence Heroes when sent: it shines like a polestar through smoke-clouds, dust-clouds and all manner of down-rushing and conflagration.[4]

Conventional wisdom has it that the last world war liberated us from these sorts of Heroic attitudes. But even a cursory examination of contemporary political debate reveals that we are still caught up in Carlyle's dream of Heroic leadership.

That word—LEADERSHIP—can be found in every sentence which addresses the state of our civilization. Leadership. The lack of leadership. The need for leadership. The cause of our problems. The solution to our problems.

Carlyle was an anxiety-ridden man. He lost his Calvinist faith as a young man and spent the rest of his life desperately looking for something or someone to give himself to. He hated his own uncertainty and feared above all to doubt. In his thirties he was already writing "Doubt of any sort cannot be removed except by Action" and action required an authoritarian figure to lead the way. Action to what purpose was not a question he asked. That was the responsibility of the Heroes who would take him and us in hand and lead the way: "I say find me the true Könning, King or Able man and he *has* a divine right over me."[5]

The philosophers who propose Hero-worship are men filled with self-loathing and fear. They worship power and the men who wield it. Carlyle is hardly a name present in our daily conversation and yet it was he with his disturbed psyche who most successfully inserted into modern society our fear of doubt, worship of action and need for Heroic leadership. See: HEROES.

CHICAGO SCHOOL OF ECONOMICS   A great centre of contemporary SCHOLASTICISM. The economists working there and produced by it are as important to the stagnation of useful thought as the Schoolmen of the University of Paris were at the height of the Middle Ages.

Like that of the Paris scholastics, their mastery of highly complex rhetorical details obscures a great void at the centre of their argument. They also share a tactical genius for exporting their conceptual definitions to less important centres around the world. The result is a pleasing symphony of international echoes imitating their calculations and cadences and so confirming their correctness, even when their policies bring economic disaster. The percussion section of Chicago's orchestra is the Nobel committee for economics. Each golden medal is like another congratulatory parchment presented at the end of an elaborate theological debate.

But what of content? There isn't much. What of Friedrich Hayek and Milton Friedman? These minor Thomists preach little more than inevitability and so counsel passivity.

What they call libertarian economics is a remarkable revenge of the scholastics on the men of the Enlightenment, who had theoretically destroyed them. Peel away the tangle of intellectual leaves from the Chicago School and what remains is a great clockmaker god who has set the world ticking. But the conclusion of the Enlightenment was that god's indifference left humans free to organize the world as they wished. Chicago has so deformed this idea as to invert it. The great clock has been turned into an absolute, all-encompassing system. Better than an ideology, the world is its own absolute economic truth. We must remain passive before its majesty.

This is a denial of Western experience. It is nonsense which simply comforts the power slipping increasingly into the corporatist structures.

Strategic thinking can save a great deal of time wasted over tactics. A large number of America's economic problems, and those of the West, could be solved by shutting down the Chicago School of Economics.

This would not prevent the academics employed there from preaching their essentially anti-social and amoral doctrines. They would be gathered up with delight by the hundreds of imitation Chicago Schools. The purpose of closure would be simply to disentangle a tendentious ideology from its unassailable position within contemporary power structures. The same sort of liberating shock treatment was applied to European civilization in 1723 when the Society of Jesus (Jesuits) was disbanded. The effect was to set free the ideas of the Enlightenment. See: BRETTON WOODS, DEPRESSION, FREE TRADE, GROWTH and REGULATION.

CHILDREN   See: FACTORIES and WAR.

CITIZEN   The individual is essentially a citizen.

This is a reality inherited from Athens. We have little choice but to accept it since democracy cannot function in any other way. It is possible to hop along in a one-legged manner with citizens voting from time to time but refusing to participate and being denied most of their obligations. The result is a superficial, even dishonest, system and a population constantly dissatisfied with itself.

If the individual is not first a citizen, then the obligations and privileges which go with that status are effectively lost and the person ceases, to all intents and purposes, to be an individual. See: SOCRATES.

CIVILIZATION   The single and shortest definition of civilization may be the word LANGUAGE.

This is not to suggest that images or music are of lesser importance. It is simply that they have more to do with the unconscious. They are somehow part of metaphysics and religion. Civilization, if it means something concrete, is the conscious but unprogrammed mechanism by which humans communicate. And through communication they live with each other, think, create and act. See: DOUBT.

CLASS   Although class has never existed in North America and is a thing of the past in Europe, there are large numbers of exclusive travel agencies which organize paying weekends in English country houses as guests of the baronet and rent out *piani nobile* in Italian *palazzi*. These and the profusion of romantic chateau hotels remind us that in an egalitarian society today's duchess is tomorrow's landlady. And as Mrs. Simpson demonstrated, today's landlady may well be tomorrow's duchess. Everyone has an equal right to inequality. The basic rule for men seeking social promotion through marriage is to ignore titles, manners and houses until they have established clearly whether the lady is sweeping her way down the stairs or up.

CLAUSEWITZ, CARL VON   Clausewitz is to military strategy what **DESCARTES** is to philosophy—an excuse for those who hold power to treat as inevitable that which mediocrity and received wisdom cannot overcome.

This nineteenth-century strategist is often blamed by twentieth-century generals and military commentators both for the advent of total war and of war used as a continuation of civil policy. That Clausewitz recommended neither would seem to suggest that they feel the need for a scapegoat to justify strategies which, in the absence of purpose and shape, have mistaken administrative structures, technology and prolonged violence for resolution.

CNN   A privately owned reincarnation of the Voice of America, except that government funding and an official foreign policy commitment have been replaced by a brilliantly simple financing system.

The CNN formula is to report on public affairs in the manner of a local American commercial television station and to broadcast it around the world. This means choosing a few high-profile international events, which are then reduced to a visual form resembling that of tabloid headliners, all reported from the U.S. point of view. These suggestions of internationalism are then interspersed with soft documentaries on minor topics, such as the closure of a naval base in South Dakota or the spread of a new venereal disease among blind drivers in California.

The secret to CNN's success is the marriage of satellite technology with the power of the American myth—in other words, modern **PROPAGANDA**. And propaganda can be profitable as well as useful.

The Voice of America was not entirely without merit and neither is CNN. In a single moment of journalistic glory during the Iraq War, CNN surprised the international news-gathering community when it left a journalist in Baghdad, thus providing the only counterpoint of information in the most controlled war story of modern times.

By 1993 it had sunk back down to its natural level. This meant covering the parliamentary revolt in Moscow with portentous declarations of its own importance, but mainly without leaving their studio. Their message to the world was a faithful reflection of the American president's.

COLLECTORS   In 1983 a junior Paris bank employee failed to turn up at his office. The police forced the door of his apartment only to find it blocked by what turned out to be a solid mass of garbage, which filled the entire apartment to within less than a metre of the ceiling. They found the bank employee lying under a blanket in a little dip on top. He had died in his sleep.

What they publicly categorized as garbage was actually old shoes, old clothes, abandoned suitcases, rags, empty bottles and scrap-paper. The apartment was so full that the collector was obliged to eat, bathe and change elsewhere. To get out the door he had to shift a whole section.

Each item had been cleaned, washed and brushed before being added to the collection. He was forty-nine and died of undetermined natural causes. It may have been gasses emanating from his clothes and newspapers.

To collect objects is an obsession which can either be positive or negative. The positive collector believes that he or she is doing it for pleasure—his own or that of others. The negative personality mistakes his collection for immortality and thus for power.

There is an infectious joy in positive collectors. In an almost childish way they often give their lives over to the pursuit of beauty, like Nabokov with his butterflies. In this obsession they are not creators but detectives, and they know that yet more wonderful objects are to be found hiding somewhere ahead; hiding because everyday life can be cruel to beauty and so it is often lost or forgotten. These collectors are the agents of our collective memory. Their weapon is not money (although they often need it). They work with intuition and a good eye. They are the true creators of our public collections.

Museum curators are sometimes collectors. But more often they are the technocrats and accountants of creativity. Not obsessed by beauty, but by identifying precise styles. One of their principal jobs is to seduce aging negative collectors and then convince them to will their objects in the right direction. This is a macabre profession which involves soliciting old men incontinent in bed with their best objects hidden underneath as if they can be carried with them through death, and old women in apartments they rarely leave, surrounded by their debris of historic beauty.

These collectors and curators clarify the past. By exposing the sense and pleasure of creations they can make history useful. But their museums play an increasingly confused role—larger and larger, basements and warehouses stacked high with objects never put on show, curators battling for ever more pieces. André Malraux pointed out that the very idea of the museum is only two centuries old; that they have served to separate art from its function and so to free beauty.

But is it free without function? Can beauty even exist without function?

The practical effect of our emphasis on treating objects as something to be appreciated is that our society spends far more on collecting, cleaning, restoring and identifying than it does on creating. Those fascinated by new technology are more likely to be interested in the archaeology of beauty than in the creation of it. To hand so much of our aesthetic sense over to collectors and curators—scavengers and pathologists—seems to indicate that we are confused about what beauty can mean if it doesn't have a purpose.

COMEDY The least controllable use of language and therefore the most threatening to people in power.

In class-based societies a great deal is made of accents and linguistic formulae. Civilization is then defined as the verbal elegance needed to avoid engaging with other people. Language in such cases is designed to glance off the edges of all important subjects. Comedy is reduced to the harmless elegance of deft and amusing wit.

In contemporary society, respectability is tied to expertise. Subjects are controlled by those who know how to talk about them properly. These DIALECTS of expertise are both obscure and SERIOUS. They require the gravity of the insider. The effect on public debate is to transform any levity into irresponsibility. Almost everyone then feels they must use responsible language when they talk about public questions. Individuals far from power and from specialized language try to mouth the formulae of the economists when they talk about debt, as if they were all Cabinet advisers.

In this atmosphere comedy is excluded and reduced to base entertainment intended to distract the non-expert. Television situation comedies are examples of this. Comedy is converted into moralizing belly laughs which reinforce the authority of the controlled, serious, specialized language.

Real comedy doesn't give a damn about respectability. It belongs neither to a class nor to an interest group and expects to mock power and those who hold it.

Intelligent mediaeval kings kept court fools to remind them of the natural limits on their unlimited power, but also to prevent the swirling clouds of courtiers from binding them up with obscure servility. The novel first found its role as the most effective device for questioning established power, truths and language through satire, which was often wicked and vicious. Swift, Voltaire, Cervantes, Rabelais and Fielding refused to engage according to the rules. Instead they mocked the established order by removing its protective armour of dignity.

Salman Rushdie has said that the worst thing about the conundrum in which he finds himself is that everyone has forgotten *The Satanic Verses* is a comic novel. Being taken seriously is the kiss of death. He also points out that when Mohammed captured Mecca in 630 after fleeing eight years before, he was remarkably forgiving. Few people were punished and only two writers were executed. However, both of them were satirists.[6]

In classical thought people imagined confrontations between the wise man and the tyrant. Often the wise man used satire and wit to keep his life while speaking out.

But how could contemporary philosophers play that role, locked as they are in obscure SCHOLASTIC studies? The profession has never recovered from the heavy hand of Immanuel Kant.

Part of their role has been picked up by burlesque comics. Some of them carry sharp social knives, but most seem isolated from the mechanisms of power. And the men of power have themselves discovered comedy. Stalin and Mussolini were great practical jokers of a deadly sort. The false Heroes of modern politics have discovered their jokester privileges. The president of the United States is always presenting funny hats to senators or having himself tackled on football fields by entire teams of courtiers. This is comic PR—a return to the humour of royal *noblesse oblige*. It stands comedy on its head by making it serve the interests of power.

But how can comedy have any power in a technocratic society? The drabness of modern intellectual discourse and the insistence on specialist knowledge are the barriers which writers must penetrate in order to liberate language and with it our ability to communicate. Comedy remains one of the last weapons we have. Above all, the writer has to resist the seductive call of respectability which dresses itself in myriad forms from professorships to prizes, honorific titles, medals and the siren call of art for its own sake, which leads us to take ourselves so seriously.

If writers and readers feel they must act in a respectable manner, then comedy is dead. And what is true for the writer is true for the citizenry. There is no reason why all of us—except perhaps the head of government and those in charge of financial policies—should worry about sounding responsible every time we open our mouths. Gravity is a lot less useful than irresponsible inquiry. See: **EXISTENTIALISM** and **SERIOUS**.

COMPETITION   An event in which there are more losers than winners. Otherwise it's not a competition. A society based on competition is therefore primarily a society of losers.

Competition is, of course, a very good thing. We cannot live in a complex society without it. On the other hand, if the principal relationship between citizens is based on competition, what has society and, for that matter, civilization been reduced to? The purpose of competition is to establish which is the best. The best may be defined as any number of things: the fastest, the cheapest, the largest quantity. It may even be the highest quality. Unfortunately the more competition is unleashed, the more it tends to eliminate quality as something too complex to be competitive.

The point of competition, if it is left to set its own standards, is that only the winners benefit. This is as true in economics as it is in sport. And a society which treats competition as a religious value will gradually reduce most of the population to the role of spectators. Democracy is impossible in such a situation; so is middle-class stability. That is why the return to increasingly unregulated competition over the last two decades has led to growing instability and an increasing gap between an ever-richer élite and an ever-larger poorer population.

We appear unable to decide what sort of competition we are referring to when we treat it as a religious truth (see: **HOLY TRINITY–LATE TWENTIETH CENTURY**). After all, competition must be a relative term. Everyone means something different when they talk of it.

Competition in a middle-class society must include the costs of a middle-class infrastructure. In a Third World society these secondary costs are almost non-existent. Thus if a middle-class people compete without the benefit of a formal handicap against slaves (to take the most extreme example), the slaves will be more competitive.

Hundreds of other factors create hundreds of other levels of competition. That's why in serious competition, such as hockey or football, there are strict regulations controlling time, movement, numbers, dress, language. Unregulated competition is a naïve metaphor for anarchy. See: **LEVEL PLAYING FIELD**.

COMTE, AUGUSTE   Having invented sociology, he bears some responsibility for society's return to a persistent belief that human behaviour can be quantified—as it was in the Middle Ages with the statistical weighing of sins. Behaviour can then be altered in a manner satisfactory to the value system established by the quantifiers—rather in the way sins could be wiped out through the calculation and sale of indulgences. See: **AUTOBIOGRAPHY** and **FREUD**.

CONFESSIONALS   Business schools, law schools, medical schools and schools of public administration have recently taken to teaching ethics with some enthusiasm. This has come in response to the widespread public perception of unethical behaviour by the élites—in particular by the corporate leadership—during the 1980s. The public's scepticism and the eagerness of the élite schools to appear to be doing better are signs of a general crisis of confidence in the rational élites.

However, the general thrust of what is taught in these schools remains unethical or is simply detached from ethics. The market-place, for example, is presented as a form of pure competition enshrining rational and necessary values such as efficiency, productivity and profit. Ethics taught in this context is reduced to a non-competitive sacrifice or something which may have to be dealt with in order to facilitate management.

What does it mean to throw in an hour of ethics on Friday

afternoon, except a return to the weekly confessional visit in a society organized to encourage sin? We teach ethics to make people feel better by making them feel guilty. Perhaps that's why the chapel at the Harvard Business School was financed by the graduates of Michael Milken's year. See: **ETHICS**.

CONRAD, JOSEPH   The essential modern writer. He demonstrated that the novel could have a third century of relevance if the story was transformed into metaphysics disguised as reality.

Many of those who have continued to believe that the novel is central to public communication have gone out of their way to acknowledge Conrad as a spiritual godfather. Ernest Hemingway, F. Scott Fitzgerald, Graham Greene, André Malraux, J.M.G. Le Clézio, and Gabriel Garcia Marquez among others.

Their conviction can be opposed to the prolongation of the art for art's sake movement, which has paralleled the West's obsession with specialization. Rather like doctors who devote their lives to a single organ, this school of writing has tried to divide fiction into a multitude of water-tight compartments. Their use of language is divisive and given to what might be called literary dialects which resemble the rigid **SCHOLASTIC** dialectics of the Middle Ages.

Conrad's most obvious strength was that of a Pole coming to English as an adult. While other writers were struggling with the baggage of their respective literatures, Conrad enjoyed virginal freedom. Just as his life at sea forced a certain practicality upon him, no matter how dramatic the circumstances, so the uncharted waters of English turned him into a practical explorer of the language. And his emotional freedom from any particular nation, with their interests and prejudices, made him a natural Universalist. When he wrote about power or ambition or hypocrisy or courage, he wrote about the things themselves in a way which has rarely been accomplished.

CONSULTANTS In an attempt to discredit **SOCRATES**, the **SOPHIST** Antiphon attacked him as follows:

> Socrates, you decline to take money for your society. Yet, if you believed your cloak or house or anything you possess to be worth money, you would not part with it for nothing.... Clearly, then, if you set any value on your society, you would insist on getting the proper price for that too.... Wise you cannot be, since your knowledge is not worth anything.

Socrates replied:

> Antiphon, it is common opinion among us in regard to beauty and wisdom that there is an honourable and a shameful way of bestowing them. For to offer one's beauty for money to all comers is called prostitution.... So is it with wisdom. Those who offer it to all comers for money are known as sophists, prostitutes of wisdom.[7]

See: **ACADEMIC CONSULTANTS**.

CONSUMPTION

"You can never get enough of what you don't really want."

Eric Hoffer[8]

The problem with markets dependent on consumption is that the consumer cannot be relied upon to know what he or she wants.

Consumers are unreliable. The producer must constantly try to outguess them. This is risky and tiring. Above all, in a stable middle-class society, people don't need or want enough goods to support an economy built upon their desire to consume. They already have a great deal. There is only so much room in their houses. Their family size shrinks as their class level rises. The middle-class mentality inevitably admires restraint and care and seeks quality goods which last and can be repaired.

It is therefore more rational to simply decide what people should want, then tell them they need it, then sell it to them. This three-step process is called consumption. See: **PROPAGANDA.**

CONTROL, BEING IN   Ideal of managers and housewives. The enemy of creativity and growth, whether economic, social or individual. One of the most destructive characteristics of modern society.

What is it exactly that they are trying to control? See: **FEAR** and **MANAGER.**

CONVENIENCE   Thanks to flags of convenience and Third World fleets, the world of shipping—No! Don't skip this!— has been the first sector to attain the Utopian ideal of free trade.

Most goods that cannot be shipped by road or rail continue to move by boat. Only information can travel by the air waves and only small, light, high-cost goods by air itself. What could be more fitting? The first sector to achieve a truly open market in the new global economy is the one whose business it is to make the global market function.

The result has been the virtual elimination of the merchant marines of developed countries. The new merchant marines belong to corporations which sail under flags of convenience or are domiciled in large Third World countries.

Flags of convenience are truly Utopian because they permit the avoidance of all national regulations. They are issued by small countries which do not care what happens on the ships carrying their flag. Ownership is usually structured through off-shore financial mazes in order to escape completely from restrictive regulations.

The now enormous Third World merchant marines have simpler structures. A Filipino ship will probably have a Filipino captain and crew. They are able to compete against the flags of convenience because the Filipino government either encourages them to operate in a competitive manner or turns a blind eye to the way they function.

How are competitive shipping rates achieved by either system? Lower maintenance and safety standards keep expenses down. The crews are protected by no civilized regulations. At best they are treated as raw labour to be paid wages that are a mere fraction of those in developed countries. They can also be hired, fired and treated on a day-to-day basis exactly as the captain wishes. Since many of the crews are national units from Third World countries, the practical effect has been the creation of small floating slave gangs. Having gradually outlawed socially unacceptable standards on our own ships, we promptly sabotaged our fleets by sending and receiving our goods on those which adhere to eighteenth-century standards.

There is nothing to prevent us from creating an effective international registering system which only accepts ships that meet agreed-upon standards. Competition could then revolve around reliability, speed and service instead of depending on the lowest possible cost, achieved if necessary by the use of slave labour. Unregistered ships could be excluded from our ports.

But our governments suffer from an old syndrome—"If we don't use cheap labour, other countries will." This formula has been used over the centuries to justify everything from the slave trade and child labour to intense pollution and selling arms to all comers. It is the most banal of excuses for doing wrong.

Our governments listen to the corporations, who quite simply have goods to ship and want to do so at the lowest possible cost. They say this is because the market-place must establish value and they believe that this can only be done through the free market, competition and efficiency. The shipping industry has proved that this is possible and shipping is central to trade and trade brings prosperity for everybody.

That the Western fleets have been destroyed in the process and ugly systems of exploitation re-established is beside the point. Government interference would mean an artificial market-place and the return of organized sailors with middle-class pretensions. When this happened between the 1930s and 1960s sailors in the merchant marine became so rich that they could easily have been mistaken for degenerate playboys. See: **FREE TRADE**.

CORPORATION   Any interest group: specialist, professional, public or private, profit-oriented or not. The one characteristic shared by all corporations is that the primary relationship of individual members is to the organization and not to society at large.

In a corporatist society, the corporation replaces the individual and therefore supersedes the role of democracy. In their own relationship with the outside world, corporations deal whenever possible with other corporations, not with individuals. The modern corporation is a direct descendant of the mediaeval craft guild.

CORPORATISM   Among the most important yet most rarely used words. Better than any other it describes the organization of modern society.

Corporatism is the persistent rival school of representative government. In place of the democratic idea of individual citizens who vote, confer legitimacy and participate to the best of their ability, individuals in the corporatist state are reduced to the role of secondary participants. They belong to their professional or expert groups—their corporations— and the state is run by ongoing negotiations between those various interests. This is the natural way of organizing things in a civilization based on expertise and devoted to the exercise of power through bureaucratic structures.

One of the characteristics of a strong movement within a civilization is that it persists throughout long periods of history. Each time it fails to win or hold on to power, it will submerge into the general stream of events for a time and then resurface as if from nowhere, disguised in a new, more attractive form.

The early, practical corporatist organizations—the mediaeval craft guilds—were imitated in the organization and specialization of the Catholic religious orders. These two experiences produced the original corporatist states, the Republic of VENICE first among them. The whole concept was pushed by a growing intellectual rivalry between democracy and corporatism and a conscious intellectual movement in favour of corporatism.

Hegel, who was treated almost as "the official philosopher" during his time teaching philosophy in Berlin (1818–31), believed that "the real is the rational and the rational is the real." He considered "a corporative state as more rational than democracy...citizens should participate in the affairs of the State as members of subordinate wholes, corporations or Estates, rather than as individuals... Representatives should represent corporations or Estates rather than the individual citizens precisely as such."[9] It isn't surprising that the almost social-democratic policies of Bismarck in the second half of the nineteenth century were produced out of an essentially corporatist society.

The surface argument of corporatism has always been that democracy is inefficient, ineffective, corrupting, subject to whims and emotion. Corporatism, on the other hand, presents itself as professional and responsible. It promises to deliver prosperity by helping those who know how to do their jobs properly and in concert.

These claims resurfaced in the 1920s in Italy. And if Mussolini's cumbersome corporatist structures didn't function, corporatism itself did. In both Italy and Germany the relationships which were able to work quite happily under a dictatorship were those between expert groups. Even the academic community worked away happily on the theoretical structures of this new anti-parliamentary national contract.

Since 1945 we have downplayed the corporatist aspect of both the Nazis and the Fascists. Instead we have demonized those two regimes into simple manifestations of evil. Such false simplification obscures the fact that they were proposing—or rather reproposing—a complete and complex alternate to democracy.

The Second World War was about many things, but at its heart it was a battle between two concepts of civilization—the one based on individualism and democracy, the other on corporatist authoritarianism. Theoretically the democratic individualists won. Yet since 1945 corporatism has advanced with even greater strength and now has a real hold on day-to-day power. Somehow we seem to have lost World War II after all.

The first superficial corporatist resurgence came in the form of endless social contract negotiations during the 1960s and 1970s. Unions, management organizations and governments sat down to do deals in order to ensure the smooth functioning of society. This was presented as a new efficient form of government tailored to the new complex industrial state. Parliaments were seen as too cumbersome and inefficient to deal with their problems. Mediation and arbitration became greatly admired skills. Everyone seemed to have forgotten that these were precisely the arguments used by Mussolini. The new efficient process reached its chaotic conclusion in Britain, where elected governments of both the Left and the Right were held to ransom and eventually destroyed by these interest groups.

Meanwhile the professionalization of the national élites was reaching a complexity never before seen. Each group and sub-group, public and private, was educated and organized in a self-protecting manner. Their ethos was defined according to their specialist purpose. Since the end of World War II people with education and position have seemed to become their professions.

The old corporatist idea has re-emerged with sparkling new sophistication. It had learned from the heavy-handed attempts of the 1930s not to attack democracy itself but to attack the function of politics and the inefficiency of the system. Organizations which actually speak for the interests of groups now actively present themselves as the defenders of populism.

The success of such senior executive organizations as the American **ROUND TABLE** and the Canadian Business Council on National Issues in shaping national policies by speaking out as if in the national interest is remarkable. They are taken by many to be more disinterested than the people's elected representatives, yet all they have done is develop policies which serve their interests, dress them up in disinterested arguments, then use their money and their access to public authorities to press their agenda.

The force of their arguments is so great that elected officials who oppose them have often ended up sounding interested. More precisely, the interests of the citizenry have come to be treated as if they were romantic self-interest. The interests of the corporatist groups are now reported as if they were the measure of effective social action.

The practical effects of such a change can be seen throughout society. A disturbing example is the apparent powerlessness of the elected authorities before the disorder brought on by deregulation of the financial sector.

More all-encompassing has been the rapid growth of **ARMAMENTS** production and sales between 1960 and 1990. In this period of peace arms became the most important industrial good sold in the world. Those who oppose this lunacy tend to talk about the military industrial complex. Thus, by sticking to old-fashioned myths of capitalism and conspiracy, they miss the key point. The production and sale of these goods is almost entirely the result of cooperation between public and private professionals employed in several sectors (corporations)—senior bureaucrats, senior executives, senior officers and university economists.

A less dramatic but more insidious illustration has been the change in the legal status of the corporation. The **JUDGEs** have bit by bit given corporations the status of the individual. Once it has been decided, in a society structured around law, that corporations are people, then mere individuals are at such a disadvantage that they have little choice but to become corporations.

That is why the rational élites tend to see themselves primarily as a part of their corporatist group. But this also explains the rise of the personal corporation. Why would individual citizens feel that operating through the structures of a personal corporation gave them an armour-plated defence unless they lived in a corporatist society?

A final example illustrates the inevitable death of disinterested public policy in a society dominated by corporatist groups. The insane can play no useful role in such an efficient society. Over the last twenty years their position has seriously declined back towards the assumptions of the nineteenth century. As James Hillman points out, "criminality and psychic breakdown" are once again being confused. "The poor, the misfits, the ill, the crazy and the criminal are again held in the same compounds, like the hospices in the Middle Ages." In Idaho the mentally ill are regularly jailed and fingerprinted before being examined. "The largest de facto mental hospital in the United States is the Los Angeles County jail..." Thirty-six thousand of its prisoners are mentally ill.[10]

The methods of Ross Perot are those of the classic populist corporatist. He continually attacks the constituted democratic system and claims a direct link with the citizenry—a link which he says can be expressed through direct consultations in REFERENDA. He claims that he is attacking democracy on behalf of the people, yet he promises to govern through a National Advisory Panel of one hundred—a group of leading, expert citizens who represent the spectrum of interests; that is to say, of self-interests. The man he has most hated was President Bush, whose career had been built upon serving various interest groups.

But perhaps the purest example of a corporatist political success is the Italian businessman-politician, Silvio Berlusconi. From a complex financial background, which includes the now illegal P2 Lodge, he captured newspapers, television stations and publishers to represent the interests of his companies. He then created a political party made up in good part of his employees and used his various interest groups to run a highly successful political campaign in the general elections of 1994.

President Clinton, who can make serious claims to have reinvolved the citizenry, at first glance seems to operate in a very different world. And yet he is obliged, in order to govern, to make heavy use of lobbies and interest groups.

These groups function as almost independent states. The large banks and industrial corporations are so complex that their presidents are often reduced to glorified princes who read what is written for them, travel in a cocoon, fulfilling predetermined activities. It is perhaps in Germany that this isolating process has gone farthest in creating potentates parallel to the state.

The question which the various democratic systems will have to address over the next decade in order to survive is whether they can draw the members of the hundreds of corporatist groups out of their structures. So long as they continue to define themselves by their expertise, the democratic system cannot function. And there can be no question of society turning its back on these enormous élites. There is no second string of citizens to replace them. It is a question of convincing the individual that their primary obligation is to society as a whole.

Corporatism has been for some time the only real threat to democracy. That explains why our corporatist élites never discuss it.

COSMETIC SURGERY   Cosmetic perjury.

COURTIERS Instantly recognizable. Unchanged throughout history. These individuals live in the half-light, chasing power without purpose. Prestige without responsibility. They travel in the shadow of those who have responsibility.

There are more courtiers in Western society today than perhaps at any other time in any other society. More even than in imperial China. It isn't simply the crowds of WHITE HOUSE STAFF or their equivalents around the presidents and prime ministers of other countries who count in this class. There are the lawyers, consultants, PR experts, and opinion-poll experts. They exist throughout the public and the private sectors and yet are no more than a superficial decoration.

A corporatist society itself turns every technocrat who wishes to succeed into a courtier. Such highly structured systems find it almost impossible to reward actions over methods. And the corporation excludes the idea of individual responsibility. They are breeding grounds for those who seek power through manipulation.

The popular image of the courtier involves elaborate court dress. But the Jesuits were the most successful manipulators of power and they appeared in an anonymous uniform, similar to that of our discreet contemporary technocrats.

CRITICISM, POLITICAL Favourite reply of those in authority to those who question their actions: "It's easy to criticize." Alternate reply: "Anyone can criticize." This is often followed by: "And what would you have done in my place?" by which is meant "if you're so smart." A more complex variation is: "You have to be TOUGH to do the right thing. Leadership isn't a popularity contest."

These denigrations of criticism have become such a generalized chorus that we often feel embarrassed, even guilty, when the need arises to say something negative.

Yet those we criticize chose freely to seek positions of authority. We are the *raison d'être* of the entire system. We are also the employers of those in public office and in the public service. Why should we accept from them a discourse which suggests contempt for us and for the democratic system?

What's more, it is not easy to criticize. It is extremely difficult. We have to question experts and insiders in areas in which we are not expert. This involves constantly out-guessing them, because they keep back much of the information we need in order to decide what we think. The problem is that any facile idiot with a bit of power can avoid giving an honest reply by putting on an important air and protesting that criticism is easy. See: BANALITY.

CRITICS Delightful people. Perceptive. Fair. Disinterested. Even-handed. Charming.

In the unlikely case that one of them should mistakenly dislike something, the creator of that book, play or film should be intelligent enough to accept with good grace that even Solomon can be wrong. But he remains Solomon. See: CRITICS, BAD.

CRITICS, BAD Extremely rare. When, from time to time, they slip into the ranks of CRITICS, specific uncontrollable characteristics are usually responsible. For example, in the field of literature:

1. They have written a book on the same subject and theirs is better.
2. They have not written a book on the subject but as experts in this area—more often than not TENUREd professors— had they done so theirs would have been better. It is that desire to make it better which has delayed theirs and not, as cynical outsiders might imagine, the comfortable and banal life of academic continuity.
3. They are academics who, whatever their literary ambitions, own the subject in question. Specialization does not mean, as the eighteenth-century thinkers imagined, the

communicating of knowledge. Rather, it means control over knowledge. If the writer of a book successfully communicates, he is untrustworthy and therefore not serious.
4. They are about to publish a book on any subject. The purpose in reviewing someone else's book is to sell their own. This is most easily done by attacking the book under review in order to advance their own intelligence.
5. They are drunks, don't drink but should, didn't have time to read the book or, worst of all, review for money. Reviewing is paid less than Third World factory labour and any reliance on it for income may unbalance the mind.

CROISSANT   Islamic symbol of paradise in the shape of a quarter moon. As an act of religious denigration during the Turkish invasion of Europe, Austrian bakers reduced the croissant to a breakfast bun.

In 1683 the Turks were laying siege to Vienna for the second time. Inside the walls life went on as best it could. The town bakers, as always, worked through the night until one evening, in the silent darkness, they heard the sounds of tunnelling under the walls. They gave the alarm, the Muslims were foiled and the city saved, as well as Christendom. The authorities honoured the bakers by commissioning the creation of a symbolic pastry. It was known as a Wiener Kifferl.

This Austrian specialty gradually made its way to Paris; perhaps in the kitchen of one of the Austrian/Spanish princesses who became queen of France. Over the centuries it slowly metamorphosed into a symbol of Parisianism. The eighteenth- and nineteenth-century victories of political centralization carried the croissant, along with the rather stark northern accent, a certain type of education, a particular interpretation of history and a taste for **WHITE BREAD** throughout the nation, where they were waved in an insulting manner as the flags of Parisian superiority over the heads of provincials. Before long, French men and women everywhere had convinced themselves that the croissant and, failing that, sticks of tasteless white bread, were their quintessential breakfast.

With the internationalization of culture as a symbol of nationalism, francophiles around the world took to eating croissants with enthusiasm. Among them were the Islamic élites from Morocco through to the Middle East, who tended to be educated—depending on colonial patterns—in either Paris or London. These habits have continued, but for most of them it is France which has fulfilled their idea of Western culture. As a result they have joined with well-to-do Americans, Latin Americans and Japanese who with every nibble at their croissants *au beurre* feel they are indulging in the inconsequential pleasures of Parisian life, when in fact they are joining with the Austrians in the denigration of their own religion. See: DESSERT.

CURE   The notion that we can be cured is above all obsessional. To the extent that doctors become active agents of this obsession, the cure becomes a focus of unspoken hysteria.

Take the treatment known as blood-letting. It was standard medical procedure for at least 2,300 years—from Athens to the middle of the nineteenth century. Just as new medical methods began to undermine its credibility in the early 1800s, a French doctor, François Broussais, proved yet again by the judicious use of statistics that bleeding a patient could cure a whole range of diseases, from the plague and cancer to nervous disorders and headaches. The argument as always was based on the theory that disease is caused by "an excess of blood." This excess can be drawn off either by slitting open the skin (venesection) or by applying leeches. In 1833, 41 million leeches were imported into France for that purpose.

The obsession was over by 1850 and doctors could say that our civilization had PROGRESSed beyond that sort of treatment. But the popularity of bleeding had never had to do with the presence or absence of progress for the simple reason that it had never worked. Of course it often produced a short-term superficially beneficial effect. Whatever agitated a patient—fever or convulsions—the removal of blood calmed him for the simple reason that he was weakened.

In this way tens of thousands of people were killed by medical practitioners. Between the 14th and 15th of December, 1799, George Washington was effectively murdered by his old friend Doctor Cräik. He was bled four times. In fact, the first time was at his own insistence before the doctor arrived. People were bled the way women's breasts have been lopped off for the last fifty years. That they died of cancer anyway didn't seem to discourage anyone.

This mechanistic approach reached its apogee in the twentieth century's world of drugs. There are now some 30,000 different medications behind the counter. After the remarkable breakthroughs of the 1940s and 1950s, doctors took to declaring that the world was cured.

The surgeon-general of the United States in 1969: "The war against infectious diseases has been won."[11] These words were no sooner out than malaria, cholera and gonorrhea, all three theoretically beaten, began to mutate and so escaped the control of most drugs. As if from nowhere, dozens of new, drug-resistant viral infections appeared, as did AIDS.

Researchers and doctors see themselves as locked in a war on disease. Even if this doubtful military analogy is accepted, they have been using bad military strategy. To cure is to eliminate. A good general knows that trying to eliminate the enemy simply causes the next war. Disease, like war, is never more than a small part of an unlimited interlocking pattern. That's why at the centre of any stable victory is some sort of peaceful coexistence.

Neither diseases nor the diseased exist in isolation. It is the isolation of our specialists, locked up inside their narrow sectors, which makes them believe that a disease is a phenomenon with natural limits. See: **HUMANISM** and **DEATH**.

CYNICISM An effective social mechanism for preventing communication.

Cynicism is found in people who see themselves principally as members of a class or ideological group and not as individuals. It indicates a lack of self-confidence. Through an appearance of world weariness it attempts to suggest the possession of inside knowledge. The cynic knows and can't be bothered to tell those who are ignorant.

Since no real discussion is possible, the cynic's group-attitudes cannot be questioned. Cynicism is thus an aggressively superior attitude which aborts debate in order to disguise inferiority.

As a result, the eighteenth-century idea that wrongdoing was caused by ignorance has been reversed. Instead, the possession of expert knowledge is regularly used to argue that only the naïve don't understand why it is necessary and even good to do wrong. This approach has been particularly popular in the NEO-CONSERVATIVE movement as a way of justifying economic policies which produce suffering.

D

DANDRUFF   The ANSWER is usually vinegar. To some problems there are solutions.

What we call dandruff is often the result of a PH imbalance on the skin, which shampoo exacerbates. Wash your hair with a simple non-detergent shampoo, soap, olive oil, beer, almost anything. Rinse. Then close your eyes and pour on some vinegar. The extremely cheap but natural sort—apple cider, for example—is probably best. The smell will stimulate interesting conversations in changing-room showers and your explanation will win you friends. Wait thirty to sixty seconds. Rinse it off. The smell will go away. So will your dandruff.

All dermatologists, pharmacists and pharmaceutical companies know this simple secret. They don't tell you because they make money by converting dandruff into a complex medical and social problem. By most professional standards this would amount to legally defined incompetence or misrepresentation.

Dandruff shampoos that promise to keep your shoulders and even your head clean are harsh detergents and may promote baldness, which ought to constitute malpractice.

DAVOS (THE ANNUAL CONFERENCE OF THE WORLD ECONOMIC FORUM)   Tucked safely into the Swiss Alps, a consecrated temple of tomorrow's conventional wisdom for political and business leaders.

Once a year in the depths of winter two thousand businessmen, academics, politicians and civil servants gather there under the gaze of three hundred journalists. The consultants speak up in the hope of winning clients. Politicians attempt to impress lenders. Businessmen glad-hand like salt-tax collectors, happy to be there and filled with world-saving ideas.

Davos is a slightly ludicrous attempt at something worrying—an international assembly on the corporatist model. See: INDOLENCE.

DEATH Something which has happened—although this has not been statistically verified—to everyone who has lived, with a few disputed exceptions. As neither Christ nor his Mother nor the Buddha ascended bodily in the presence of licensed medical practitioners, it could be argued that while not everyone is dead, everyone who has lived has eventually died. In a world filled with risk and speculation, death remains one of the few things which can be relied upon. It is more inevitable even than birth, since we cannot say that everyone who could have been born was born.

In its struggle to preserve the human body, modern medicine has achieved what we now call miracles. Still, it hasn't saved anyone from death, just postponed the appointment. These admirable delays are generally treated as the greatest accomplishments of modern civilization. Lives have been saved, we say, when we mean prolonged. That small slip of the tongue betrays the great cliché—that we do not want to die.

Our growing technical sophistication seems to have had a negative effect on the reasonableness with which we face it. Where once death was treated with a certain bluntness, as part of family life, we have fallen back on childish denial. We don't die, we pass on, we decease, we are the beloved, people are sorry to hear about us. To hear what? There has never been an era in which death was such an unacceptable topic of conversation. Humans have never so planned their prolonged lives and taken so little into account their termination.

Among the possible explanations for this change is the decline of organized religion. However, more compelling is modern society's obsession with *function*. The overwhelming importance now attached to what people do is the natural product of a society which defines itself by its systems and structures. These systems have no meaning in themselves, but they function as if they were eternal. Like medicine with lives, they prolong conscious limitation out of sight.

Millions of people, either old or terminally sick, lie in hospitals with tubes up all their orifices, waiting. Apparently they are not waiting for death. If they were, they would probably want to free their bodies of machinery and be transported to a place where they might prepare to take leave of their family and friends and then consider their life as it was lived and then consider the approaching bridge or cliff.

Conscious thought isn't greatly admired in a civilization devoted to systems. Active consciousness is seen as a form of rebellion. And yet what possible harm could self-doubt do when the doubter is no longer strong enough to walk, let alone preach?

Neither current education nor the life that follows is designed to prepare the individual for that inner conversation. The sight of millions of self-doubting diers—*compos mentis* or not—would sow doubt among those still proceeding through their stages of specialization and promotion. Besides, care of the human body is a specialist profession to be handled as part of a continuous process. To remove individuals from that system before it has finished with their bodies would be to suggest either that process is less important than this civilization says it is or that the medical profession is not doing its job properly. See: **HOBBES** and **SOCRATES**.

DEBT, UNSUSTAINABLE LEVELS OF   National debts are treated today as if they were unforgiving gods with the power to control, alter and if necessary destroy a country. This financial trap is usually presented as if it were peculiar to our time, as well as being a profound comment on the profligate habits of the population. The reality may be less disturbing.

1. The building up of unsustainable debt loads is a commonplace of history. There are several standard means of resolving the problem: execute the lenders, exile them, default outright or simply renegotiate to achieve partial default and low interest rates.
2. There is no example of a nation becoming rich by paying its debts.
3. There are dozens of examples of nations becoming rich by defaulting or renegotiating.

    This begins formally in the sixth century BC with Solon taking power in debt-crippled Athens. His organization of a general default—"the shaking off of the burdens"—set the city-state on its road to democracy and prosperity. The Athens which is still remembered as the central inspiration of **WESTERN CIVILIZATION** was the direct product of a national default. One way or another most Western countries, including the United States, have done the same thing at some point. Most national defaults lead to sustained periods of prosperity.
4. The non-payment of debts carries no moral weight. The only moral standards recognized in Western society as being relevant to lending are those which identify profit made from loans as a sin. Loans themselves are mere contracts and therefore cannot carry moral value.
5. As all businessmen know, contracts are to be respected whenever possible. When not possible, regulations exist to aid default or renegotiation. Businessmen regularly do both and happily walk away.

    The collapse of the Reichmann financial empire— larger than most countries—is a recent example. The family was able to turn around, walk away and almost immediately begin a new life, promoting the biggest property development in the history of Mexico.

6. There are no general regulations dealing with the financial problems of nations simply because they are themselves the regulatory authority. There is however
   well-established historic precedent. Mexico effectively
   defaulted in 1982–83, thus regenerating its economy. The
   reaction of Western lenders has been to treat these crises
   as special cases. The sort of thing that only happens to
   Third World countries. That's nonsense.
7. The one major difference between private and public
   debt is that the public sort cannot be based upon real collateral. This makes default a more natural solution to
   unviable situations.

   The question of national collateral was fully addressed
   in the eighteenth century when it became clear that an
   indebted people could not owe their national rights
   (their land and property) to a lender. The citizen's natural and concrete rights took precedence over the
   lender's abstract contractual rights.

   One of the most peculiar and insidious aspects of twentieth-century **CORPORATISM** has been an attempt to reverse
   this precedence. The managerial imperative suggests that
   national debts can be indirectly collateralized in several
   ways. Governments can be forced to sell national property
   to pay debts (**PRIVATIZATION**). They can also be pressed to
   transfer ownership of national property to lenders, as has
   been done in the Third World.

   There is also the threat that defaulting nations will be
   treated as international pariahs. This is a strange argument since it doesn't apply in the private sector (see 5). It
   is also an idle threat, as Mexico has demonstrated (see 6).
8. Debts—both public and private—become unsustainable
   when the borrower's cash flow no longer handily carries
   the interest payments. Once a national economy has lost
   that rate of cash flow, it is unlikely to get it back. The
   weight of the debt on the economy makes it impossible.
9. A nation cannot make debts sustainable by cutting costs.
   Cuts may produce marginal savings, but savings are not
   cash flow. This is another example of the alchemist's

temptation.

Mrs. Thatcher spent a decade trying to slash the British national debt. She had the advantage of being able to use North Sea oil income for this purpose. The result was a damaged industrial sector, economic stagnation and endemic unemployment.

The payment of debts is a negative process which can only be a drain on investment and growth. The more successful major repayment programs are, the more the economy will be damaged.

10. Strong nations weaken their own economies by forcing weaker ones to maintain unsustainable debt-levels. For example, in spite of enormous efforts on all sides, the Third World debt has continued to grow. In 1993 it was $1.6 trillion. This costs them far more in interest payments sent to the West than the West sends in aid. The practical effect is to make economic growth impossible. The Third World thus constitutes a dead weight in our own ongoing DEPRESSION; a barrier to renewed cash flow.

11. Civilizations which become obsessed by sustaining unsustainable debt-loads have forgotten the basic nature of money. Money is not real. It is a conscious agreement on measuring abstract value. Unhealthy societies often become mesmerized by money and treat it as if it were something concrete. The effect is to destroy the currency's practical value.

12. An obsession with such false realities and with debt repayment indicates a linear, narrow, managerial approach to economics. The management of an economy is the profession of finance-department technocrats, economists and bankers. Their approach is quite naturally one of continuity. This is a means of denying failure.

To treat money or debt as a contractual matter—therefore open to non-payment or to renegotiation—would mean treating the managerial profession as of secondary importance and unrelated to fundamental truths. What sensible people might see as originality or practicality, financial experts see as a threat to their professional self-pride.

13. Does all of this mean that governments should default on their national debts? Not exactly.

    What it does mean is that we are imprisoned in a linear and managerial approach which denies reality, to say nothing of experience. Money is first a matter of imagination and second of fixed agreements on the willing suspension of disbelief.

    In other words, it is possible to approach the debt problem in quite different ways.

14. There have been changes which limit our actions in comparison to those of Solon or Henry IV, who negotiated his way out of an impossible debt situation in the early seventeenth century and re-established prosperity. First we have to recognize and protect the investment made by citizens directly (government bonds) and indirectly (bank deposits) in the financing of national debts. Second, there is the new and unregulated complexity of the international MONEY MARKETS, which now constitutes an important corporatist element.

15. Our central problem is one of approach. For two decades governments have been instructing economists and finance officials to come up with ways in which the debt can be paid down and interest payments maintained.

    No one has instructed them to propose methods for not paying the debt and not maintaining interest payments. No one has asked them to use their creativity in place of *a priori* logic.

16. Were the members of the Group of Seven (G7) each to pool their best economists and give them a month to come up with modern versions of default, we might be surprised by the ease with which practical proposals would appear.

17. There are two simple guiding points:
    A. The appearance of continuity is easily achieved in

default scenarios through paper mechanisms which can be categorized as "debt retirement."

B. What is difficult for a single country in contemporary circumstances is easy for a group, particularly if that group speaks for the developed world. See: ETHICS.

DECONSTRUCTIONISM A generalized denial of CIVILIZATION can't help but be a voice of evil.

To insist that language is in contradiction with itself or nothing more than a system of self-serving formulae or essentially meaningless is to argue that human communications have no ethical, creative or social value. Fortunately deconstructionism can also be seen as a school of light comedy. After all, to argue that language has no meaning is to eliminate your own argument. The deconstructionists may after all simply be suffering from an acute lack of IRONY.

Jacques Derrida and his disciples protest that what they actually mean is that language never means exactly what it says. If so, they have come rather late in life to what has always been a given between writers and readers. Besides, their protest is disingenuous, since through simple observation we can see that the practical intent of deconstructionism is to demote the communications of the writer and the citizen to the level of naïvety if not idiocy and to insert the critic or professor as the essential intermediary. This is a prime example of how intellectuals create ANTI-INTELLECTUALISM.

In fairness it must be assumed that these thinkers are better intentioned than their writings make them appear to be. Individual deconstructionists may well think of themselves as socialists or liberals or conservatives or something else. But since their argument undermines the value of public discourse, they can't help but be the servants of whatever anti-democratic forces are at work. These days the deconstructionist argument is a great support to both CORPORATISM (in which language is a secondary tool of self-interest broken up into obscure dialects) and those on the ideological extremes whether of the left or the right (where language is propaganda).

Most deconstructionists are academics. It is remarkable, given their belief in the meaninglessness of language, that they have so little trouble assigning A's, B's and C's to their students.[1] Perhaps this is a hint that their whole argument is an insider's joke. With hindsight, of course, the same can be said of the intellectual arguments used by Hitler and Stalin.

Note: Deconstructionists tend to insist that the proper term is deconstruction, not deconstructionism. That is, they do not want to be treated as an ism. They hate being deconstructed. See: SCHOLASTICISM.

DEMOCRACY   An existential system in which words are more important than actions. Not a judgemental system.

Democracy is not intended to be efficient, linear, logical, cheap, the source of absolute truth, manned by angels, saints or virgins, profitable, the justification for any particular economic system, a simple matter of majority rule or for that matter a simple matter of majorities. Nor is it an administrative procedure, patriotic, a reflection of tribalism, a passive servant of either law or regulation, elegant or particularly charming.

Democracy is the only system capable of reflecting the humanist premise of equilibrium or BALANCE. The key to its secret is the involvement of the citizen. See: REFERENDUM.

DENIAL   Characteristic reflex of a technocrat. Since actions are the result of solutions arrived at by experts there can be no ERROR. Error is replaced by a linear succession of right answers. This requires the systematic denial of error when each preceding answer fails to do its job in spite of being right.

The contaminated blood scandals of the late 1980s and early 1990s involved a series of errors in several Western countries by various medical authorities who failed to screen properly blood donations for HIV infections. The universal methods of the medical profession (corporation) produced the same initial approach in each country. This involved errors, which in each case were rigorously denied, which led to further damage being done to uninformed patients, which led eventually to public inquiries which ought to have been extremely damaging to the medical corporation and caused them to rethink their general approach to communication and error. Instead, they went into an emergency state of denial and were able to muddy the waters enough to limit the damage to unfocused outrage.

The denials or lies were exactly the same in Canada, England, France, Germany and the United States. The desperation to be seen to be right in all cases was more important than the lives of patients.

This mania for denial has marked policies ranging from the economy to defence. It constitutes an assertion that expertise and the corporatist structure are more important than reality. See: DIALECTS.

DEPRESSION   A form of economic disaster common throughout history. In 1973 the word was deleted from all Western languages and replaced by the term recession.

There are three reasons for this rebaptism:

FIRST, depressions have been fixed in the public imagination with images drawn from the collapse of 1929–39. Yet the West has been stricken by a series of modern depressions since the mid-eighteenth century. They have all been products of both the industrial revolution and the new financing methods, yet each has looked quite different. There is no reason for them now suddenly to begin looking alike.

Society's structures have changed radically since 1929, in an effort to eliminate through regulation the worst of the economic instabilities which had brought on the crisis in the first place. People believed that regulation was necessary because time after time, from the eighteenth century onward, the market-place had proved itself devoid of the characteristic of sensible self-regulation. It could only regulate itself through boom and bust cycles, which led not to a gradual levelling-out, but to recurrent depressions.

The changes begun in 1932 were also intended to eliminate the extreme social inequities—or rather iniquities—brought on by the crisis. However effective the new regulations, there would always be economic highs and lows. But that didn't mean children had to be in soup-kitchens. This idea of social reform through regulation was actually a return to the pre-capitalist view of society as a conscious whole. It was no longer acceptable to think of society as no more than an abstract economic mechanism in which some were winners and others losers who might fall as far into despair as the market found useful.

If the Depression which began in 1973 has appeared far less dramatic than the preceding one, it is thanks to the balancing effect of regulation.

SECOND, the pseudo-scientific approach to economic reality leads the economists and their more powerful half-brothers, the business school professors, to believe that they are constantly managing real situations. This is a delusion filled with paradoxes. For example, the ideologues of the market-place see themselves as managing detail within the great inevitable flow of competition. The truth about modern economists is that their macro visions are rarely more than inflated versions of their micro science. This isn't unusual in a society dominated by technocratic systems. Contemporary military strategy, for example, is rarely more than a blow-up of tactics.

The economy is now seen as a series of details, and the experts believe they can measure their way. They resemble a sailor who sets his course, without a compass or a sea-anchor, from the trough of the waves, by calculating his way up to the next crest.

THIRD, the themes of contemporary leadership contain a strange combination of mythological optimism (which promises continual progress towards a better world) and virtual inertia brought on by slavery to micro-economic systems.

Thus, those with power feel obliged to promise big solutions, while in reality they seldom move beyond the obscure briefs of their experts.

To admit to the existence of anything as uncontrollable as a depression would be to admit failure, which is tantamount to declaring that you have no right to power. As a result the political, administrative and academic élites insist that, since 1973, we have suffered from a series of recessions. Recessions differ from depressions in length and severity, so there is a strong feeling that they can be managed. The word depression is feared because it suggests a profound social imbalance which is beyond management. If a depression were to exist, the élites would have to engage in serious self-criticism. They would have to reconsider how the economic system functions. Our élites are not trained or chosen to think of themselves in those terms. They are sometimes falsely Heroic; but in reality they are themselves a micro phenomenon.

The Western refusal to respond intelligently to the crisis has been as blatant on the Left as on the Right. At the annual DAVOS gathering in January 1993, the fashionable economist Lester Thurow declared that we are not in the great Depression, but in the great Recession. This left the false impression that our only need is to stimulate the economy. But stagnation is the characteristic of Act II in a depression tragedy. Act I involves crisis and collapse; Act II stagnation; Act III brings regeneration either through a cataclysmic fire or through the discovery of a new approach. That discovery lies inevitably in the root causes of the crisis—Act I.

Yet we remain stubbornly in Act II. After all, the most important trade good remains an artificial industry—armaments—which continues to dominate the high-tech sector. Public funding, that is TAXATION, remains at an impasse. An abstract, ideological obsession with EFFICIENCY and COMPETITION continues to undermine our social economic structures. The international money markets—a monstrous and unregulated descendant of South Sea Bubble–style speculation—remains so powerful that it can overwhelm any economy, whatever its health or productivity. Western governments are still unwilling to deal with the implications for competition, employment and money flows of the **TRANSNATIONAL CORPO-RATIONS**, even though passivity means that national and even multinational policies are meaningless. The profession of economists remains fixated on the virtues of the service industries without bothering to identify the highly contradictory elements which this term contains. And they are unwilling to make sense of the relationship between their technical tinkering and their abstract theories on debt and inflation. More to the point, they continue to see economics as a mathematical abstract rather than a manifestation of civilization.

How can we have solid economic recovery when the dominant economic schools do not begin from the assumption that there are 270 million people in Western Europe and 300 million in North America and that all of these people must somehow be involved in the economy? If ignored, they become expensive, even destructive dead-weights. Such disembodied and abstract theories can only weaken society and incidentally its economy.

All of these problems could have been focused on before 1973. Yet, no sooner had the crisis begun, then most were abruptly seen as strengths and thus encouraged to become crutches for the ailing system in place. To suggest that now all we need do to ensure recovery is stimulate or educate or single out potential areas of growth is to act as if economies only exist as superficial appearances.

With a little disinterested common sense it is possible, however, to identify a handful of key phenomena which, if not entirely responsible, account for much of our crisis.

1. The failure of our managerial **ÉLITE**s, whether public or private, which throws doubt on our assumptions about organization, leadership and higher education (see: **MANAGER**).
2. Our belief that technology has purpose and direction and therefore needs no guidance.
3. The inability of our élites to examine what will, can and

must happen to traditional ideas of **GROWTH** in an advanced industrial society.

4. As a result, the conversion of our economics to dependence on inflationary, non-growth activities such as the **MONEY MARKETS, ARMAMENTS** production, mergers and acquisitions and **PROPERTY DEVELOPMENT**.

5. As a further result, an explosion in public and private **DEBT** accompanied by a simplistic, linear belief that we must strip ourselves naked in order to pay those debts.

6. The re-opening of the nineteenth-century file on unregulated competition. This was initiated by the transnational corporations who are making use of cheap unprotected labour in the Third World to undermine the **STANDARDS OF PRODUCTION** inside the developed nations (encouraged by an ideological approach to the practical mechanism of free trade).

7. And all of this has been worsened by a determination to treat our ills with the symptoms of the disease.

Depressions do eventually come to an end. Sometimes this takes a decade. It can just as easily take five. Usually they burn themselves out like fires, consuming in the process both the problems that started them and much of society's fabric. Sometimes this fire takes the form of war, sometimes poverty and ruin. Recovery is then based upon rebuilding and is dependent upon the willpower of the citizenry. The depression of 1973 will end, but so long as we deal with it through abstraction, denial and desperate positivism, the phenomenon will go on mutating, shifting and re-emerging. See: **REGULATION** and **SEVENTY-THREE**.

DEREGULATION The airline industry fought for this privilege. It was a necessary freedom, they said, to strengthen competition, thus strengthening companies, which would lead to the creation of more companies, and that to more flights flying to more places, leading to overall lower prices for the consumer.

The result has been competitive chaos, leading to continuous bankruptcies, leading to a constantly shrinking number of companies, leading to less real competition and therefore to fewer flights to fewer places at higher prices. Between 1990 and 1993 the American companies alone lost $11 billion.[2]

It should be noted that two events in this deregulatory period ought to have guaranteed success for the industry. After two peaks in oil prices, the real cost of fuel has steadily fallen. And the explosion in mass tourism over the last fifteen years has led to a massive increase in the number of passengers.

The air carriers tried to save themselves from the catastrophic effects of deregulation by concentrating on executive travel. The technocracy was growing, wanted to fly to do business, and had to pay full fare because that is the way large organizations work. The result was an ever-expanding third or middle class of travel called Business or Executive. The increased cost of sending businessmen on this class was assumed by their shareholders and was therefore a dead weight on the general economy.

The effects of deregulation on personal travel were particularly negative. During the years of regulation, travel had been relatively simple for the passenger. And simplicity is a real form of efficiency. There were two classes; most people, including most corporate employees, used Economy class. There were some bargains, principally aimed at family tourism which was planned well in advance.

The collapse of real competition under deregulation led to those forms of false competition typical of oligopolies. There was an explosion in the area of special deals, promotions and packages. The result was a travel jungle which continues to waste the traveller's and the airline company's time. This has led to a confusion of money-losing promotions aimed at winning the loyalty of customers, who see fewer and fewer reasons to be loyal in a disordered market.

Free-air-mile plans have been among the most costly aspects of this false competition. Of course, they aren't free.

The companies have to cover the costs by charging more per ticket to their paying customers. The principal beneficiaries of this system are the various technocrats—particularly the corporate executives—whose flights are paid for by their companies, a pleasant fact which does nothing for competition or an increased choice of destinations. Quite the contrary. The more the executives get personal free air miles, the more the airlines must charge for the Business-class tickets bought by the corporations. This system doesn't increase paid-for travel, cuts into the profits of both the airlines and the corporations who use them and involves complex management costs.

The overall effect of special deals and bonuses has been to reduce competition to the level of the old "free glass at the gas station" routine. But passengers don't want free glasses, bigger meals, special tags, cards, waiting-rooms or even toothbrushes. What they want is a simple way to fly to the maximum number of places with the maximum choice of flights in acceptable comfort and dignity with minimum fuss at a reasonable price. This is a description of real competition which experience has now demonstrated can only be produced by thoughtful and tough REGULATION.

DESCARTES, RENÉ   Gave credibility to the idea that the mind exists separately from the body, which suggests that he didn't look down while writing.

The credible certainties Descartes sought were not of the body, but of method. His obsession with doubt was not to explore the unknown, as Socrates might have put it, but to remove doubt. To answer absolutely.

In this he and Francis Bacon were on exactly the same track. Bacon's scientific attitude was a source of power. These two profoundly modern intellectuals both claimed to have escaped the *a priori*. Each, in his own way, is the inspiration for the modern technocracy whose *a priori* truths are disguised by theoretically neutral methods. See: GANG OF FIVE.

DESELECT A passive but transitive verb which indicates that an individual has been RATIONALIZED.

DESSERT Years ago the wonderful Yvonne of the restaurant Tante Yvonne, rue Notre Dame des Victoires, in Paris, was asked to name the greatest dessert. She replied instantly.

"*Chichis*! The second stand on the left coming out of Marseille."

Chichis are made of chick-pea flour and water with a little orange-flower extract added for taste. The batter is squeezed out of a large pastry bag into a vat of boiling oil in a great curl resembling a very long sausage. It is then drained, rolled in sugar and cut into four pieces. If you buy four, the left-over tail-piece (the *bada*) is thrown in. The four *chichis* are individually wrapped in brown paper cones. The *bada* is not. *Chichis* are cooked to order, so on a Sunday afternoon there is a long line-up, particularly at the second stand on the left, which, after the recent arrival of a new stand, is now the third. See: MONARCHS.

DESTINY The product of mysterious inevitability and human passivity, both presented as unshakeable tenets of something which can't quite be identified.

A half-century ago the idea of destiny seemed moribund, except among communists and a dwindling group of religious believers. Now, carried aloft by the natural truths of ECONOMICS and the linear logic of CORPORATISM, destiny once again determines our lives.

Some 2,500 years ago the joint dictatorship of destiny and divine will was first broken by Athenians like Solon and Socrates. Their specific enemy was the Homeric mythology under which the shape of men's lives was decided in advance. At best or worst they might be marginally altered if the gods intervened. The great contribution of the Athenians was to argue that humans could, within the limits of a larger reality, continually re-create their own destiny.

They couldn't do this from nothing or in spite of everything or in isolation from the world, but they could act. Their destiny was not sealed from birth. Western civilization begins with that conviction. The idea of the conscious, responsible individual is born with the defeat of fate and passivity.

Two and a half millennia later, the largest and most sophisticated élite ever to have existed—some 30 per cent of our populations—in possession of more knowledge than the élites of earlier history could have imagined, have convinced themselves and their civilizations that the Athenians were wrong, after all. Most things are inevitable. They were wrong. We were wrong. We've wasted 2,500 years.

This recrudescence of primitive mythology involves a modernization of the forces before which we must bow in submission. The gods and destiny have transformed themselves into the forces of specialist expertise and the marketplace. However it describes itself, the Homeric dictatorship is back in place.

Language, argument, conscious choice—all fundamentals of a functioning democracy—are thus reduced to mere distractions. The anger, confusion, frustration which citizens feel today arises from the sense that their real attributes have evaporated, and that they live in a society where they are rewarded principally for their cooperation, which is to say...passivity.

DIALECTS Formerly variations in language produced by geographical isolation, dialects are now the variations encouraged by specialists to prevent non-specialists access to their professional territory.

For those who belong to these professional guilds or corporations, not being understood is one of their few individual powers. The rules of professionalism—often spelt out in their contracts of employment—prevent them from speaking freely. What is the one subject on which a nuclear engineer cannot be frank in public? Nuclear engineering. Thus experts are silenced in the area where they in particular have something to offer the community.

They compensate by reconstructing their castrated individualism around the power of not communicating. The power of retention. Wilful obscurity does little for public debate. It creates a fear of outsiders who try to understand and an acceptance of ignorance in areas outside of their own dialect. If you don't want to be interfered with, you mustn't interfere with others. The insiders, as Vaclav Havel puts it, end up characterizing "every attempt at open criticism as naked terrorism."[3]

They would defend themselves by arguing that the explosion of knowledge has made areas of specialization too complicated for public language. But none of us really wants to know where to put the bolts on a nuclear reactor. And we don't need to know.

Specialist language can be dealt with in two ways. It can roll gradually, in a process of honest popularization, from the inevitable complications of the expert towards general communications. The citizens are then free to penetrate as far down the road of verbal specialization as they care to. Or the specialists can establish their dialect as a general barrier—a rite of passage—and so reduce public language to a cacophony of distracting information and opinion, none of which is related to the use of practical power.

Isolated in these dialects, the experts cut themselves off from the collective imagination, which is what feeds each domain with ideas and energy. Like a small provincial aristocracy cut off from the metropolis by its own standards of propriety, they are ultimately victims of inbreeding. See: ORAL LANGUAGE.

DICTATORSHIP OF VOCABULARY The moment a word or phrase begins to rise in public value, a variety of interest groups seek either to destroy its reputation or, more often, to co-opt it. In this latter case they don't necessarily adopt the meaning of the word or phrase. They simply want control of it in order to apply a different meaning that suits their own purposes.

Words thus are not free. They have a value. More than any commercial product they are subject to the violent competition of the emotional, intellectual and political market-place.

Moral and ideological crusades fuel this desire for control over words. They are kidnapped for the cause and strung up like flags. Others then feel obliged to use them in order to indicate that they are in tune with the times. **DEREGULATION. EFFICIENCY. FREE TRADE. GLOBAL ECONOMY.** Their meaning really doesn't matter. The important thing is not to be caught without them. And then, like transubstantiation and the dictatorship of the proletariat, their day passes, the market in their use collapses and the pressure to capture a new vocabulary reasserts itself.

DICTIONARY   Opinion presented as truth in alphabetical order.

The social stability that has settled over the West in the last half-century tempts those who define language to confuse their powers of analysis with a power to declare truth. In the disguise of description they offer prescription. This is done in a dissected, dispassionate manner as if simply reporting on use.

Serious dictionaries give a selection of the successive true meanings of each word over the centuries. Some seem to forget definitions which they themselves have provided in earlier editions. Others give a fairly thorough selection of historic examples, but their choices contain attitudes.

Is it true, as almost every twentieth-century dictionary asserts, that **TRUTH** is "consistent with" or "conformity to" or "in accordance with fact or reality"?[4] Or is this an ideological position? If it is true, then how are we to explain the ability of facts to produce several truths on the same subject and the inability of some or all of these truths to conform with reality as people see it? What then is the relationship between facts and truth or facts and reality?

Dictionaries legitimize the process which has already half

persuaded citizens that language does not belong to them because it does not reflect what they see or think. Languages which do not provide the forms of meaning needed by the populace are on the road to becoming anthropological remains.

This is not a DECONSTRUCTIONIST exercise. There is no linguistic conspiracy. Nor is language always a reflection of special interests. Nor must it be an embodiment of whatever ideology is temporarily on top. To the contrary. There are great volcanoes of linguistic energy in any society which has not become moribund. They are constantly exploding—often through ORAL LANGUAGE—in order to shatter or readjust the established order of received wisdom. If a language isn't dead it must be an argument.

Earlier dictionaries were passionate arguments about truth. Chambers, Diderot, Johnson and Voltaire weren't certain they were right. But they were certain that the church scholastics who had preceded them were wrong. As the twentieth century moves towards its end, there are fewer and fewer people who believe that facts add up to truth. This means that there are fewer and fewer people who simply accept received wisdom. In that sense, our era increasingly resembles the eighteenth century. It is therefore quite natural that dictionaries should again become arenas of debate.

DIRECT DEMOCRACY   An appealing idea which has been unworkable for more than two thousand years. This makes it a favourite with political groups whose basic instincts are anti-democratic.

Twenty-five hundred years ago in the Athenian *agora* and *ekklesia* every citizen could speak and vote on every question. This didn't include women or slaves, but compared to any other civilization of that or later times right up to the modern era, this was the most open and participating of societies. And Athenian democracy did work. It worked better than its competitors and inspired what has come to be known as Western civilization. However, there were only

40,000 voters, 5,000 to 6,000 of whom took part regularly.

The Athenian model could still work—in smaller towns, for example, or in specific areas such as school boards—if people were willing to commit the equivalent time and energy. This kind of PARTICIPATION would mean making politics as important in their lives as family and careers and far more important than private pleasures.

Those who promote direct democracy talk a lot about small towns, but are not really interested in them. What they are fascinated by is the mythological theme of the small town. They like the big picture, where the undercurrent of discontent includes millions of people. They like big themes—race, language, freedom, security, debt, efficiency, individualism. These emotion-laden abstractions are almost impervious to sensible public discussion. They can be activated through the exploitation of pain. History, after all, inflicts emotional wounds on us all. The proponents of direct democracy scratch away at these in order to increase the sense that a personal wrong has been done. If these wounds can be made to bleed profusely enough, the sensible, practical nature of the population will be destabilized.

Over the last half-century the direct democracy argument has come from an increasingly strange right wing which somehow manages to combine a romanticized version of local nationalism with practical support for NEO-CONSERVA-TIVE economic policies. In other words, their language evokes a small, naturally unified group, while their policies assume that the ugliest sort of competition will hold sway and therefore be free to sweep away that group's interests. The contradictions are so flagrant that cause and effect are lost in the confusion.

The new Right claims the citizen is being excluded from public affairs. They are right. However, instead of coming to terms with the real causes of this exclusion, they exploit it through false populism. They condemn the slow mechanisms of public debate in large complex societies. This process of serious deliberation can't help but be awkward and filled with doubt, lost time and errors. Yet, this inefficiency can transform itself into an expression of the public interest.

The false populists will seize upon any moment of failure as if it were a breakdown of representative democracy. They seek to hijack it through more direct mechanisms which, because they eliminate consideration and indirection, are fundamentally judgemental and authoritarian. What they seek are more easily controllable structures.

The REFERENDUM has always been one of their favourite tools. The complexities of the real world, long-term practical evolutions and working relationships are transformed abruptly into an abstract clarity involving a yes or a no. Technology has since added dozens of new techniques. The old Heroic rallies have grown, with the development of electronic communications, into advertising or propaganda; that is, a one-way illusion of debate. Electronic town hall meetings have been created to simulate direct democracy through televised debates with "representative" audiences who ask "populist" questions. New technology makes direct votes on endless subjects possible. We are at the beginning of a sustained push by authoritarian movements in favour of these systems. As with referenda, they make real debate almost impossible, but facilitate large emotional swings of the sort that demagogues are best at creating.

The old-fashioned demagogues have been given a new lease on life by their marriage to technology. What they share with this communications technology is a devotion to the linear. Questions are asked, then answered. Problems are posed, then solved. And when they are not answered or solved, the conclusion is that the system has failed.

Direct democracy seems to push the citizen forward by emphasizing the importance of casting a ballot. Of course the vote is essential to the democratic process, but it is not the purpose. Consideration, reflection, doubt and debate were the primary purpose of the Athenian *agora* and *ekklesia*, as of representative assemblies over the last few centuries. These four processes are the body of the democratic sentence. The vote is merely the punctuation. The body of the sentence, if properly expressed, makes it almost inevitable that sometimes there will be an uncertain question mark, a careful period or sometimes a determined exclamation. Without the body, these signals are clear and even exciting, but meaningless. Direct democracy is all punctuation, but denies functioning language. See: DOUBT, ELECTORS OF BRISTOL and IMAGE.

DIVORCE The deconstruction of SEX and PROPERTY.

Since the unification of these two *non sequiturs* through marriage deforms reality, separating them again several years later can't help but be as unpleasant as any other part of the DECONSTRUCTIONIST movement. The mysteriously recurrent idea that divorce will convert contractual enemies into natural friends belongs to the fantasy genre of fiction. See: ORGASM.

DOUBT The only human activity capable of controlling the use of power in a positive way. Doubt is central to understanding.

The ÉLITEs of organized societies define leadership as knowing what to do. The citizenry are not so certain. Their response is to doubt, consider and deliberate. That is, to question, contemplate and weigh carefully.

Most human activities are divided into three stages. The act of doubting is the second and is the only one which requires the conscious application of our intelligence.

The first stage consists of the reality by which we are faced. This is always a confusing mixture of situations out of our control, attitudes clouded by received wisdom and a variety of cure-all solutions. The third stage is what we call decision-making. In a rational society this is supposed to be the result of having a solution produced by the correct answer. Decision-making is, in fact, an overrated business, rarely more than mechanistic. It, in turn, is followed by a minor, passive business—the management of the decision taken. Given our obsessions with LEADERSHIP and right ANSWERS and our fear of doubt, we have been slipping into treating this managerial stage as if it were of primary importance.

Doubt is thus the space between reality and the application of an idea. It ought to be given over to the weighing of experience, intuition, creativity, ethics, common sense, reason and, of course, knowledge, in balanced consideration of what is to be done. The longer this stage lasts the more we take advantage of our intelligence.

Perhaps this is why élites move so quickly to limit doubt and consideration. Those who gain power almost automatically seek to leap from reality to solution, from abstraction to application, from ideology to methodology. This is as true of contemporary rational society as it was of those dominated by religion or monarchies. Deliberation is mocked as weakness. Consideration is rushed through, if possible eliminated. The effect is to reduce the intelligence of the citizenry to received wisdom, unconscious or secretive procedures and mechanistic actions.

Healthy democracies embrace doubt as a leisurely pleasure, and so prosper. Sick democracies are obsessed by answers and management and so lose their reason for existence. But, above all, doubt is the only activity which actively makes use of the human particularity. See: ERROR and HUMANISM.

DUAL USE Rhetoric for the 1990s invented by the armament's technocracy to replace TRICKLE-DOWN ECONOMICS.

Both phrases are designed to persuade non-specialists that arms production is an inherent part of the civil economy, which it isn't. Although the purpose of both is identical, each is based upon a different geometric model.

TRICKLE-DOWN ECONOMICS should be seen as an equilateral triangle in which concentrated, purposeful military spending spreads out like a waterfall, to provide financing and innovation across the broad base of the civil economy. Dual-use economics, on the other hand, turns the equilateral triangle on its side, first one way, then the other. The result is that the purposeful spending of the civil economy flows like a powerful river into the military and the purposeful spending of the military like a river into the civil.

In more sex-oriented conversations the term dual use can be replaced by a second key new rhetorical phrase—"cross-fertilization."

"Dual use," as John Polanyi, the Nobel chemist puts it, "is no use at all."[5] It is bad economics and bad strategy. If the direction of civil production is limited by military needs it is stymied. If the nature of armaments is limited by "market requirements," then the basic purpose of arms and armies—to protect and to win—is weakened.

However, the purpose of dual use is, as a close adviser to the American secretary of defense puts it, to "...move decisively towards a fully integrated industrial base to meet future U.S. economic and national and security requirements."[6] This is to include the total integration of civil and military R and D in order to produce "generic, dual-use technologies that have the potential to support both commercial and military requirements." Military controls and standards are to be removed from arms production and replaced by the tension of the market-place. If the economic ideas being put forward here bear no relationship to reality, the strategic concepts are even more farfetched. The intent is "...to promote an arms acquisition culture that is compatible with the demands of the commercial market-place." Wouldn't they be more useful if they were compatible with the demands of the battlefield?

In late 1993, early 1994, the term "dual use" abruptly appeared on the lips of every armaments expert in Germany, France, England, Russia and the United States.[7] All declared that this was the solution to both the economic crisis and tighter military budgets. The simple fact of who is using it makes this anonymous little phrase one of the most important economic concepts of the decade. It doesn't seem

to matter that this is exactly the same policy that has provoked inflation, government debt, economic stagnation and
unfocused over-arming for the last three decades under the
name of TRICKLE-DOWN ECONOMICS.

E

ECONOMETRICS A seductive combination of facts and faith, it is not so much a sub-category of economics as a schismatic sect.

Economics sprouted from the same intellectual roots as WEATHER FORECASTING—rarely accurate but devoid of memory, thus cheerful about being wrong. When economists begin to confuse the well-being of humans with the proving of theories (for example, the market-place is always right or private enterprise is evil), they may actually have become a destructive force resembling maddened weathermen, who call upon the population to fight their way through a hurricane in order to reach the eye of calm at the centre.

This manic phenomenon can be identified by the rise of untempered OPTIMISM and pessimism and is characterized by the repetition of religious formulae. Thus "the debt must be repaid" or "the recession is over" will be chanted in the way priests once repeated "the devil must be defeated" or "Christ is risen," by which they meant "You also will rise from the dead."

There are many intelligent economists who, when faced by the real social needs of real people in real societies, attempt to be both practical and imaginative. The importance of imagination is that while the people and their needs are real, economics is created with illusions, which for the purposes of daily life must be treated as real. This is why large theories are so dangerous. They mistake conventional illusions for reality and so treat the people and their societies as abstractions.

Unfortunately the practical and imaginative economists have been increasingly frustrated by the rise of econometrics, the premise of which is that society can be reduced to the elements of accountancy. And since numbers are the face of god, it follows that all will be well.

This has been the dominant school since the 1970s—so dominant that even sensible economists find they must conform to the conventions of numerology if they wish to be heard. And yet they know that in the real world numbers are what numbers do. They are not real and are rarely useful. Economics based on econometrics resembles King Canute, sitting on his throne out on the bared beach and ordering the ocean not to rise. This is one of the explanations for the arbitrary division of the 1973 DEPRESSION into a series of recessions, each of which has been ordered to end.

ECONOMICS   The romance of truth through measurement.

An understanding of the value of economics can best be established by using its own methods. Draw up a list of the large economic problems to have struck the West over the last quarter-century. Determine the dominant strand of advice offered in each case by the community of economists. Calculate how many times this advice was followed. (More often than not it was.) Finally, add up the number of times this advice solved the problem.

The answer seems to be zero. Consistent failure based on expert methodology suggests that the central assumptions must have been faulty, rather in the way sophisticated calculations based upon the assumption that the world was flat tended to come out wrong. However, streams of economists are on record protesting that they weren't listened to enough. That the recommended interest rate or money supply or tariff policy was not followed to its absolute conclusion.

This "science" of economics seems to be built upon a non-scientific and non-mathematical assumption that economic forces are the expression of a natural truth. To interfere with them is to create an unnatural situation. The creation and enforcement of **STANDARDS OF PRODUCTION** are, for example, viewed as an artificial limitation of reality. Even economists who favour these standards see them as necessary and justifiable deformations of economic truth.

Economic truth has replaced such earlier truths as an all-powerful God, and a natural Social Contract. Economics are the new religious core of public policy. But what evidence has been produced to prove this natural right to primacy over other values, methods and activities?

The answer usually given is that economic activity determines the success or failure of a society. It follows that economists are the priests whose necessary expertise will make it possible to maximize the value of this activity. But economic activity is less a cause than an effect—of geographical and climatic necessity, family and wider social structures, the balance between freedom and order, the ability of society to unleash the imagination, and the weakness or strength of neighbours. If anything, the importance given to economics over the last quarter-century has interfered with prosperity. The more we concentrate on it, the less money we make.

ECONOMIST, THE   A magazine which hides the names of the journalists who write its articles in order to create the illusion that they dispense disinterested truth rather than opinion.

This sales technique, reminiscent of pre-Reformation Catholicism, is not surprising in a publication named after the social science most given to wild guesses and imaginary facts presented in the guise of inevitability and exactitude. That it is the Bible of the corporate executive indicates to what extent received wisdom is the daily bread of a managerial civilization. See: **MUSSOLINI.**

EDUCATION, PUBLIC   The single most important element in the maintenance of a democratic system.

The better the citizenry as a whole are educated, the wider and more sensible public participation, debate and social mobility will be. Any serious rivalry from private education systems will siphon off the ÉLITEs and thus fatally weaken both the drive and the financing of the state system.

That a private system may be able to offer to a limited number of students the finest education in the world is irrelevant. Highly sophisticated ÉLITEs are the easiest and least original thing a society can produce. The most difficult and the most valuable is a well-educated populace.

What happens when those who have power concentrate on their own training is hardly surprising. A study in 1993 suggested that almost half of America's adults were functionally illiterate.[1] This explains why ENGLAND and the UNITED STATES, having made such essential contributions to the rise of democracy, have ever greater difficulty making their systems work.

What remains incomprehensible is the apparent failure of public education throughout the West. Teeth gnash every day over the effects of electronic communications and weakening family structures. Yet all we do is fiddle with the content of courses and agonize over teaching methods.

Specialists in the science of education hold great sway. They are the management consultants of the adolescent mind. But the quantity of teachers is constantly being reduced, as are the budgets for general education. If such things as television and social disorder make it difficult to capture and hold the attention of students, then what and how they are taught is of little importance. What matters is the intensity put into teaching them.

We could do worse than to reduce classes from the typical twenty to thirty students down to ten. This would mean hiring more teachers and our public budgets tell us there is no available money. A more important point is that there'll be even less money in a society of functionally illiterate citizens.

How much does an unemployed teacher or an unemployed, university-educated potential teacher really cost the state if integrated accounting methods are used? There are the direct social costs; the loss of a long-term investment in their training; the removal of their powers of consumption from the economy, and of their contribution to property values. Does all of that add up to less than the salary of a teacher? This is not a question which our systems of public accounting can entertain. They refuse any sort of inclusive weighing of our profit-and-loss situation.

The conclusion of our sophisticated system is that we cannot afford to educate properly our citizenry. We know that this is a suicidal and lunatic policy position. What we are doing, therefore, is passively accepting the conclusion of lunatics. See: ÉLITE EDUCATION.

EFFICIENCY A skill of tertiary importance which can be useful if kept to its proper level and closely controlled.

Efficiency is also, of course, a very good thing. It would be foolish to waste time and money unnecessarily. On the other hand, what is actually necessary? What unnecessary?

The question that must be asked about efficiency is whether it should be treated as a driving force in a civilization or even in a society or even in an economy? Or is it no more than one of those useful little tools which can help us all to do better if it is used appropriately?

Those who preach the HOLY TRINITY of competition, efficiency and the market-place tell us that only the most efficient competitors will win in the new GLOBAL ECONOMY. Yet we can see from our own experience that those who become obsessed by efficiency often go bankrupt. The reason is simple. The market-place—if allowed to function in a reasonable manner—will try to favour better products. These are produced to some extent by competition and are to some extent reflected in low prices. But above all, they are the result of creativity and imagination, neither of which is efficient.

The great capitalists and the great companies make good use of efficiency but in such a manner that it must follow in the baggage train. If it is allowed to become a form of leadership, efficiency will go straight for the throat of imagination and strangle it until no breath of life remains. Then the economic problems will begin.

If efficiency must be carefully controlled in order to be helpful in business, that principle is doubly true in other areas such as government and the arts. In places where the primary function is reflection, the intent being to search for solutions—legislatures, for example—efficiency is quite literally the enemy of the public weal. See: INEFFICIENCY.

ELECTORS OF BRISTOL, ADDRESS TO THE   A fundamental statement on how representative democracy ought to work.

Elected for Bristol in 1774, Edmund Burke immediately laid out in a speech to his electors the extremely difficult balancing act he would try to maintain, constantly weighing their opinions and local interests against his judgement of what was responsible action in a national assembly:

> It ought to be the happiness and glory of a representative to live in the strictest union...with his constituents. Their wishes ought to have great weight with him...their business unremitted attention. It is his duty...to prefer their interest to his own.
>
> But his unbiased opinion, his mature judgement, his enlightened conscience, he ought not to sacrifice to you...or to any set of men living.
>
> Your representative owes you, not his industry only, but his judgement; and he betrays, instead of serving you, if he sacrifices to your opinion.[2]

This is not a neat recipe. It's not even a structural guide. Burke is making a humanist statement about the impossibility of formulae or ideology in a healthy democracy. He is saying that the responsibility of the representative, like that of the citizen, is to maintain a sensible and ethical BALANCE.

ÉLITE More common than a lumpenproletariat.

Every society has an élite. No society has ever been without one. There is therefore little to be gained by worrying a great deal about the creation or protection of an élite. They protect themselves and someone is always ready to take their place.

The thing élites most easily forget is that they make no sense as a group unless they have a healthy and productive relationship with the rest of the citizenry. Questions of nationalism, ideology, and the filling of pockets aside, the principal function of an élite is to serve the interests of the whole. They may prosper far more than the average citizen in the process. They may have all sorts of advantages. These perks won't matter so long as the greater interests are also served. From their point of view, this is not a bad bargain. So it really is curious just how easily they forget and set about serving only themselves, even if it means that they or the society will self-destruct. See: **EDUCATION, PUBLIC.**

ÉLITE EDUCATION Something in which the élites are personally interested.

Those already in responsible positions feel the need to fund the training of their successors. The rising power of specialist groups increasingly ties this training to what is called utility. In order to attract money from and for these groups, universities are now reorganizing themselves to serve directly a variety of specific interests. The thousand-year struggle to create independent centres of learning and free thought is rarely mentioned.

Those faculties unable to adapt—including most of undergraduate education—are increasingly of marginal importance, as are such things as reflection and inquiry, including, of course, pure science. Anything that concerns basic intellectual training or the use of the imaginative capacities isn't considered much use.

In other words, élite education is very effective at sucking up a good part of the funds which its graduates administer.

This leaves public schools and liberal arts institutions to scramble about for whatever remains. See: **INTELLIGENCE**.

ENGLAND   The only remaining purely ideological nation.

The English pride themselves on their peaceful common sense and take great pleasure in accusing the Europeans of intellectualism and a vain addiction to the abstract. On the other hand, the English also pride themselves on being the only truly ironic race, which may explain why this intellectually divided and militaristic people insist so on their practicality. It may also explain their devotion to gardening and pets.

These are strange characteristics to find in a nation which once made such essential contributions through literature and politics to the very idea of the modern individual, to the development of democracy and to **HUMANISM** itself.

Public decisions on this half-island are taken by the forcible reduction of complex issues to false clarity so that everyone must choose sides. Even the details of everyday life—clothing, accents, innocuous opinions—are broken down into ideological positions. These are sometimes called class differences, but when class no longer reflects utility, it has mutated into **IDEOLOGY**. The result is a highly structured form of rational conformism from which relief is sought through the celebration of the irrelevant but amusing eccentricities of a small minority.

Since ideology incapacitates leadership, most of the successful fighting, talking and doing is done for them by the Irish and the Scots. The best tailors, however, are English. See: **EDUCATION, PUBLIC** and **NANNYISM**.

ERROR   Error is the result of a peculiar human strength: the ability to act in an unprogrammed, that is illogical, that is conscious, manner, by thinking and communicating unconventional thoughts. To err is a sign of intelligence.

In science, error is still recognized as a permanent characteristic of progress. Why then is the same not true in politics or business? Errors that lead to altered policies are the building blocks of civilization.

A society that punishes error—as Western civilization increasingly does—discourages individual responsibility. The false HERO, who obscures the real activities of power behind a screen of meaningless activity, is more likely to survive in high office than an individual who is honest about what he is doing and whose errors are therefore visible. But if those in office must hide their mistakes in order to keep power, those errors are more likely to be repeated.

Take the stubborn attempts over the last two decades to revive the economy by the repeated use of high interest rates in order to strangle inflation. While inflation had been repeatedly, though only temporarily strangled, the result has not been a revived economy. It didn't work the first time, nor the second nor the third. And yet it remains the official anti-inflation policy. Those who criticize are accused of being soft on inflation. But the solution to non-inflationary GROWTH is not high interest rates. Why not admit it and look for a fresh approach? Instead, with every repetition of this old-fashioned, sadistic policy, the economic hole in which the West is stuck grows deeper.

The inability to admit error is a problem at every level of society. As a result, fads seem to sweep ever more dramatically through industries and professions. When reality abruptly reasserts itself and the junk-bond market collapses, no one can be blamed. A few scapegoats may be found, but there was no error because all the experts were and remain in agreement.

The only place in which errors are used actively is in intellectual debate. Innovative thinking is greeted not with enthusiasm and open argument, but with a strangely desperate attempt to deflate all new ideas by demonstrating that they contain errors. Thus instead of being used as a force for improvement, modern criticism tends to become a support for received wisdom.

Our fear of error comes in large part from our specialist society. The very existence of the specialist is dependent on his or her ability to be seen to be right in matters of their own expertise. In this way they deny their own reality, limit their own progress and misuse the responsibility society has given them.

The best way for a society to escape this crisis would be to re-examine its severe attitude towards competence. The specialists—particularly the intellectual specialists—are among those least likely to achieve that re-examination in order to free themselves. Their best chance lies with the population as a whole, who can't help but notice the unreal absence of real error. They now spend a great deal of time looking for ways to convey their disbelief in an aggressive and practical manner. See: IDEOLOGY and INTELLIGENCE.

ETHICS A matter of daily practical concern described glowingly in universal terms by those who intend to ignore them.

Even the most ordinary action contains an ethical question, which must either be respected or denied. This is different from the phenomenon of power, which even at its most banal is usually applied as part of a larger, all-inclusive design. Those who hold and exercise such power may not see themselves as part of a formalized intellectual movement, but the signs of its existence include an arbitrary definition of INTELLIGENCE and a system of rewards only marginally related to accomplishment. In contemporary society this typically takes the form of APPLIED CORPORATISM.

And so power becomes an applied abstraction. That's why those who have it spend so much time trying to render ethics irrelevant by elevating them to the status of an ideal.

It takes less effort to push a little old lady off the sidewalk into oncoming traffic than it does to go around her. It is unlikely that anyone will notice, so there is little risk of punishment. In fact, it's more efficient to kill her than to step out of her way.

Some people do this. Others, afraid of being caught, do not. Both see the law as a means to control mankind's unruly or unethical nature.

A third group includes those in positions of power who consider the law and its enforcement to be the principal barrier between order and mayhem. They fear that without the law everyone might begin pushing little old ladies off sidewalks. Their distrust of the population must be an expression of their own unspoken fear that without effective restraints they and anybody else would do the same. Given the opportunity, **HOBBES** would probably have shoved a little old lady into the traffic.

A fourth group, which may include as much as 90 per cent of the population, perhaps 95 per cent, includes those who, even without witnesses, do not push little old ladies off sidewalks. They don't even consider it. They simply step aside.

The first two groups believe that ethics are a matter of measurement. The third do not believe in ethics and so replace them with a rationally organized antidote to **FEAR**. The fourth simply seems to understand that ethics are a matter of personal daily practical responsibility. They seem to know this irrespective of education, religion, whether reason is a conscious fact or not and whether or not they have access to sidewalks.

At the heart of modern power is a rational structuralism which reduces the essential human relationships to contracts.

As anyone who works in a sophisticated organization knows, to treat ethics as a practical reality is to invite punishment. To be ethical is to choose not to get ahead. A corporatist society cares about structures, corporate loyalty and systems of efficiency. All of this is bound together by contractual relationships, as is epitomized in the late twentieth century by the writings of John Rawls.[3]

Our worship of secrecy as an attribute of power further rewards amorality. How can we treat ethics as an essential quality of the citizen if, for example, participation in public debate by those citizens with expert knowledge of the subject is effectively forbidden by employment contracts? (See: **DIALECTS**.)

Our problem is thus not one of teaching or enforcing ethics. Nor is sanctimonious idealism of any particular use.

Ethics being a matter of practicality, they need to be included in our systems so that citizens can treat them as they normally would—as a standard aspect of everyday life. See: HUMANISM.

EXECUTIVE The corporate executive is not a capitalist but a technocrat in drag.

The members of the massive class which manages our joint stock companies have fallen into the delusion that they are capitalists, not employees. Yet they own no shares or only a small quantity bought with money borrowed from the company at low or deferred interest rates. The delusion grows stronger every year. In 1960 the average pay after tax of the CEOs of the biggest corporations in the United States was twelve times the average wage of a worker. By 1990 it was seventy times. Executives also benefit from impressive benefit packages, paid for by the shareholder, which in politics would be termed corruption. And they hector the public and their workers in particular about the capitalist ethic. They seem to feel that these workers are too expensive, lazy and non-competitive. This must be true or the managers would not be paying themselves so much more than their poorer employees. See: MANAGER.

EXISTENTIALISM When you strip away the details, existentialism simply means that we are judged by our actions. We are what we do, not what we intend. This is a humanist philosophy. A philosophy of ethics. Individual responsibility is assumed and therefore demanded. This is the exact opposite of the great rational ideologies in which the structure assumes responsibility and the individual is rewarded for passivity.

What began as a relatively straightforward argument, when introduced in its modern form by Kierkegaard in the middle of the nineteenth century, became confused after

World War II at its moment of greatest popularity and then sank into disrepute.

There were several problems. Two of the worst were created by Jean-Paul Sartre, the theory's best-known spokesman. First he tried to mix the idea of personal ethical responsibility with Marxist determinism, which included obligatory political violence. It made no sense at all. Then, in an amusing but lunatic extension of this contradiction, he pushed forward the writer and convicted criminal, Jean Genet, as an example of extreme existentialism. This created the impression that in existentialism the intensity of an act was in itself a value—murder, for example. Intentionally or unintentionally Sartre had confused ethical responsibility with NIHILISM. Worse still, he had slipped into a view of existentialism as pure action. It was the sort of approach guaranteed to attract adolescent boys contemplating suicide and other false friends.

What was lost in all of this excitement and drama was that existentialism by any other name was a continuation of the Christian argument in favour of salvation by good works as against salvation by divine grace. In Buddhism and Islam this is even more clearly put. Everyone in a Buddhist society except monks is judged by the universe (not by others) on the basis of the merit they have earned in doing good works.

Existentialism is not therefore Kierkegaard's invention. And that is the real reason for its difficulties in Western society. We, after all, have organized ourselves so that individuals are judged not by their acts but by their access to information and control over structures. Our place in the system determines what we are. If we undertake actions which can be attributed directly to us, our power is likely to suffer. This has nothing to do with whether we are right or successful. In a world of technocrats and courtiers, actions which are visibly successful in their own terms have about them an egotistical ring for which the individual will eventually be made to pay.

Also lost was Sartre's real argument. His genius was poorly served by his tangents. And yet he was a genius and for those who wanted to see, he was demonstrating that existentialism is an argument—that language is argument and argument is action. That is why freedom of speech is central to democracy. Speech is a more concrete action than any specific governmental policy. In fact all of the basic guarantees necessary for democratic government—freedom of thought, speech, assembly, personal security whether it be tied to dignity, safety or well-being—are existential values.

F

FACTORIES Children love factories.

They don't have to go to school. They sometimes earn as much as two or three dollars every day and are often allowed to work as much as seven days a week. What wonderful pocket-money to buy toys or empty cardboard cartons, which make ideal roofs for the family home. In most factories there are also games of risk to play—not falling into machinery, not getting your fingers squashed. What with the doors locked shut and the solid, windowless walls, it's snug and warm inside, particularly in the hot season.

A lot of paternalistic well-to-do adults, usually foreigners, would like to stop children working in factories. That's because these lazy grown-ups can't compete. They're afraid of the global economy. They keep their own children locked up in schools. It's far more fun to be allowed to play in a factory. See: **LAGOS**.

FACTS Tools of authority.

Facts are supposed to make truth out of a proposition. They are the proof. The trouble is that there are enough facts around to prove most things. They have become the comfort and prop of conventional wisdom; the music of the rational technocracy; the justification for any sort of policy, particularly as advanced by special-interest groups, expert guilds and other modern corporations. Confused armies of contradictory facts struggle in growing darkness. Support ideological fantasies. Stuff bureaucratic briefing books.

It was **GIAMBATTISTA VICO** who first identified this problem. He argued that any obsession with proof would misfire unless it was examined in a far larger context which took into account experience and the surrounding circumstances. Diderot was just as careful when he wrote the entry on facts for the *Encyclopédie*:

> You can divide facts into three types: the divine, the natural and man-made. The first belongs to theology; the second to philosophy and the third to history. All are equally open to question.[1]

There is little room for such care in a corporatist society. Facts are the currency of power for each specialized group. But how can so much be expected from these innocent fragments of knowledge? They are not able to think and so cannot be used to replace thought. They have no memory. No imagination. No judgement. They're really not much more than interesting landmarks which may illuminate our way as we attempt to think. If properly respected they are never proof, always illustration. See: JURY.

FAITH   The opposite of dogmatism. Individual responsibility and persistent inquiry have been founded upon faith since SOCRATES:

> If I say that it would be disobedience to God to "mind my own business," you will not believe that I am serious. If on the other hand I tell you to let no day pass without discussing goodness and all the other subjects about which you hear me talking, and that examining both myself and others is really the very best thing that a man can do, and that life without this sort of examination is not worth living, you will be even less inclined to believe me. Nevertheless, that is how it is.[2]

Socrates' defence before the jurors trying him for his life is thus that the maintenance of faith in any system requires an enormous and constant individual effort. It can't help but be conscious, **EXISTENTIAL** and subject to anguishing **DOUBT**. Modern scientific inquiry is equally dependent on the marriage of uncertainty with faith in the value of knowledge.

Dogmatism replaces faith with the power of structure. We are spared the effort of consciousness and the strain of living with doubt. We can relax into the certainty of a church structure, a corporate interest or an ideological package, each with its fixed dogma.

The defenders of dogmatism, in an approach which has not varied over the centuries—from the Jesuits through to the technocrats—have made great use of scepticism and cynicism. They attempt to assimilate this with Socrates' examined life, but its purpose is the exact opposite. While Socrates sought to provoke each individual into believing that it was worth questioning everything, the sceptics seek to silence the individual by denigrating her faith in inquiry.

FALSE HERO   The only thing worse than a **HERO**.

False Heroes are now endemic to public life. They are the public-relations version of **CARLYLE**'s Hero, before whom we were to abase ourselves in orgasmic adoration. Whatever relationship there was between heroism and the hero is replaced by a marriage between politics and popular entertainment. Even serious public figures feel obliged to disguise themselves in this way.

The most accomplished False Hero yet produced has been Ronald Reagan. He did not "Win one for the Gipper," he acted out the role. He did not fight for freedom as a World War II bomber pilot, he made training films for pilots. He didn't ride out onto the prairies to struggle against the elements for individualism. He put on make-up and waited on his studio nag for cameras to turn. He fought alongside no troops. His life did not include acts of personal courage intended to benefit others. There may have been acts of private courage. We cannot know this.

Many decent unheroic leaders have been obliged to send others into risk or to their deaths. If they are honest with themselves they use this power with care and take care that their language remains moderate. President Reagan spoke from film scripts. Sometimes they had actually been used in films, sometimes they came from the cinema of his imagination. He spoke of war and courage as if he had done what he asked his soldiers to do. It seemed that if necessary he would personally lead them into battle.

The False Hero is dependent on an impenetrable wall separating illusion from reality. That separation is part technology, part advanced propaganda-cum-public relations. Thus Ronald Reagan was able to base his presidency upon fiscal responsibility, while he was one of the most profligate chief executives the United States has ever had. He preached law and order while his policies produced ever-higher levels of civil violence. He claimed to rule for individualism while his laws, above all, served small sections of the community.

He was, however, what many people consider to be a man of great charm. The question is what value should be given to whether a leader is polite, happily married or good-looking? Charm, conventional wisdom says, will take you a long way. How far and at what cost?

FASHION

1. A self-destructing paradox. In order to be fashionable you must avoid everything in fashion.
2. A relatively harmless use of the herd instinct.
3. Always right. Female models have continued into the 1990s swallowing cotton balls soaked in olive oil to reduce their hunger, although in the late eighties their lives were complicated by the return of breasts to fashion. Many of the girls felt obliged to have implant operations. The result has been a striking contrast between melonlike protuberances which stick out unnaturally from whippetlike ribcages.

Ever sensitive to the larger meaning of conflicting social trends, designers have, in effect, invented motherly anorexia. Camera images are kinder to geometry than they are to the natural line and so this fashion has been a great success. (See: TASTE.)
4. As demonstrated by the young boy who called out in the street when the emperor passed, FREE SPEECH is anathema to fashion of any kind.

FAST FOOD, PHILOSOPHY OF   See: MCDONALD, RONALD.

FEAR   In light of our upcoming disappearance from the world, this is an endemic human condition. The exacerbation and manipulation of fear is used by dishonest people to gain or hold onto power. HOBBES made the dishonest respectable by arguing that it was inevitable. See: PANIC.

FIRST CLASS   Should a plane crash, those seated at the front are almost guaranteed a clean death. Their passage to the next world is eased by a decent last meal, unlimited alcohol and enough leg room to meet their end with dignity.

The middle classes sitting behind in full economy with their knees pressed neatly up against their throats know that they will have to wait longer to die. They may even be condemned to survive in some horribly maimed condition. As for the lumpenproletariat in the cheap seats at the back, they stand a reasonable chance of walking away from the wreckage in good health, thus being denied release from their vale of tears on earth.

The most galling aspect of this system is that by dying first in First Class, people whose only qualification is wealth find themselves at the head of the line for entrance to heaven or hell. And that at a moment when, given the size of contemporary airplanes, there is bound to be a crowd. See: DEATH.

FLORIDA Former American state. Latin Americans are now locked in a long-term struggle with Canadians for control. The Latin Americans are driven by their need for financial and political stability, the Canadians by theirs for warmth and a place to die. The ultimate weapons of the Latin Americans are politically based para-military groups and organized crime financed by drug money. The Canadians have set up a professional hockey team.

FOREIGNER An individual who is considered either comic or sinister. When the victim of a disaster—preferably natural but sometimes political—the foreigner may also be pitied from a distance for a short period of time. See: **SUPERIORITY**.

FREE The most over-used term in modern politics. Evoked by everyone to mean anything. Samuel Johnson once spoke of patriotism as the last refuge of scoundrels. Evocations of what is free and of freedom have now overtaken patriotism.

This has led to a limitless series of oxymorons which have somehow become respectable: free air miles; **FREE TRADE**; the twinning of free men and free markets when history demonstrates clearly that free markets do best under sophisticated dictatorships and chafe under the limitations imposed by democracy (see: **CAPITALISM**); free love; free glasses at gas stations; free offers and in general a free ride.

The problem with this word "free" is that it has two contradictory meanings. One refers to political freedom or liberty and has an ethical value. The other refers to an imaginary state of being in which there is no effort and no cost. Freedom is thus confused with the gambler's idea that you can get something for nothing. That is why Johnson's scoundrels are attracted to it. See: **DICTATORSHIP OF VOCABULARY**.

FREE SPEECH Not a pleasant or an easy thing, but perhaps the single most important element in any democracy, free speech is afflicted by two widely held, contradictory opinions. The first is that we have it; the second that it is a luxury.

How can you have something which exists only as an **EXISTENTIAL** act? You can declare its inviolability in constitutions and protect it with laws. You can invoke it until you are blue in the face. But freedom of speech is only maintained at sufficiently high levels through constant use.

The exhausting effort which this requires involves a willingness to listen combined with a desire to be heard. Listening means taking into account, not simply hearing what people say. And being heard means being exposed to criticism, even ridicule. That is one of the reasons our élites, who have little desire to be heard as individuals, refer to it as a luxury.

The perfectly natural reflex of those who have power is to try to limit freedom of speech. They do this in an ongoing almost unconscious manner, whatever their particular political opinions. The more structured the society, the more this happens through social convention by euphemism and **POLITENESS** and indirectly through laws and contractual arrangements which make no reference to the thing that they are limiting.

For example, employment contracts almost automatically make the employee's expertise and opinions the property of the corporation. There are also libel laws, which apply a strict interpretation of "the facts" to those areas of public debate in which the people most likely to sue are precisely those who hold back the facts. The court process puts them under no obligation to explain, but focuses on those who seek information and try to use free speech. There are vast and complex laws of secrecy which remove whole areas of public interest from the public domain. And of course there is *raison d'état* which removes the citizens' right to discussion in their own best interests.

A new method of limitation involves arguing that free speech, having been won in the absolute, can now be treated as a luxury. What people need above all, the argument runs, is prosperity. With the physical well-being and stability that brings, people have the time and energy to engage in free speech. It follows, *sotto voce,* that the more unsuccessful those in responsible positions are at running the economy of a country, the less the citizenry should use their free speech.

The "property first" argument is based on a common interpretation of Western history in which the growth of trade and industry created a middle class that began to demand rights. It is a convenient point of view in a corporate society. It reduces the contribution of the citizenry and of HUMANISM to a secondary passive role. Instead it is technology and the market which created the edifice. Only then were the citizenry permitted to decorate the rooms.

This is a complete inversion of Western history. Solon was produced by an ethic of public service. And it was economic failure—not success—which provoked him and the citizenry to assume greater power. Socrates and the entire Athenian democratic debating system were the product of a stable, agrarian society. It was undermined and destroyed by the trading pretentions of the empire. Our contemporary concepts of equality, which implicitly include the right to speak out, come from early Christianity and the local assemblies of Northern European tribes. The Magna Carta was not an industrial product. Nor were the linguistic popularizers from Shakespeare to Dante. Nor was ERASMUS, who did so much to demonstrate that clear language could be used as a form of public power. Most of our ideas about democracy were firmly put in the public place a century before the industrial revolution got seriously underway. Although the American revolution included elements of taxation and trade, the urban trading classes tended to stay neutral during the war while those on the land, rich and poor, carried the military and political burden.

If economics played a central role in the rise of free speech, the benefactor was more accurately the Black Death than the industrial revolution. The plague so decimated Europe's population that greater concentrations of agrarian wealth were a result and established administrative systems broke down.

The point is not that industrialization played no role in the creation of the democratic system. But its role was secondary. An effect not a cause. We did not proceed from economic change to prosperity to democracy in order to finish off with free speech as a sort of luxurious gold leaf to cover the rampant part of an already completed structure.

It was the difficult and determined emergence of free speech in the seventeenth and eighteenth centuries which allowed us to formulate our ideas of democracy. In the process those who spoke out were sometimes killed or, failing that, often imprisoned or exiled. But a conscious verbal reverberation gradually unleashed the democratic process— sometimes through reform, sometimes through explosions. It was this affirmation of the citizenry which made it possible to imagine a different kind of economy and to set it in motion.

Within the West the same sort of historic inversion can be heard every day. Our CORPORATIST society takes pleasure in insisting on "responsible action." This is, in itself, an inversion of our concept of the responsible citizen. In a democracy, society's structures are responsible to the citizen who is the ultimate source of power. "Responsible action" suggests the opposite—the citizen must now limit the use of her power in order not to damage the structures in place. This amounts to the institutionalization of banalized *raison d'état*.

An irresponsible person is therefore someone who disturbs convention by speaking out. These are by definition people outside of the specializations, the professions and the corporate groups. Troublemakers. In an exaggerated version of middle-class propriety, the quasi-totality of our carefully trained élites see themselves as limited in their public words and actions by their obligation to administer society in a responsible manner.

Thus the structures and the education systems of the democracies have produced enormous élites which are unconsciously but profoundly anti-democratic. They may represent as much as 30 per cent of the population and occupy most of the positions of power. For them, free speech is an indulgence claimed by marginal outsiders and a luxury which responsible people put up with resentfully and only to the extent that they must.

FREE TRADE   An eighteenth-century theory of international economics limited by the primitive notions of what it was then imagined trade and capitalism might become.

The West has passed through and grown beyond the early industrial revolution and the high period of violent and unstable capitalism. In the process such old-fashioned methods as free trade and its alter ego, protectionism, have become increasingly impractical because of their destablizing effect on developed middle-class societies.

The tendency of those who have not evolved intellectually along with the practical evolution of their societies has been to convert free trade and protectionism into absolute abstract ideologies. Practicality can then be thrown out the window. Only a political debate of principles remains and the interests which lie hidden behind.

This ideological free trade imagines a world in which everyone benefits by specializing in their strong suits and exporting the results to each other. This idea arose as a breath of fresh air in the late 1970s, along with the **GLOBAL ECONOMY.** Of course, the same sort of argument had been put forward by Adam Smith in 1775 in *The Wealth of Nations* before being internationalized by David Ricardo in the early nineteenth century. Its moment of glory was the 1840s debate over the repeal of the British Corn Laws which protected English farmers by taxing imported grain. This was followed by a short period of what seemed to be limited success, depending on where you lived and what you produced. This in turn was followed by catastrophic market instability, recurrent depressions and widespread political violence.

The creaky old crudeness of the free-trade miracle can be seen in its obsession with specialization. Each person in a given place may not wish to devote themselves to coal-mining. They may wish to grow some wheat or research new medications, even if others in other places can do these things cheaper. Should the market be organized so that they cannot grow and sell their wheat or find the cure to a disease? The free-trade theory says yes. They must do only what they do cheapest.

But societies limited to one or two specialties are no longer societies. They are abstract production units and will suffer from the ills of overbred animals which have wonderful legs but weak lungs or a magnificent tail but no brains. Theories of generalized market-driven specialization leave everyone— in all classes—dangerously dependent on one or two goods. And the market is fickle. We can hardly blame it for that. With every shift in the patterns of market-driven production and consumption, whole societies can be thrown into despair.

We all know about the instability inherent in Third World countries dependent on the production of one or two commodities. Free trade, as presented in the last quarter of the twentieth century, aims to convert all of us into the equivalent of commodity producers.

Protectionism offers the exact opposite—the promise of absolute managed stability brought about by closing borders. In theory the result will be a cosy internal balance. But few countries are self-sufficient. The United States alone could perhaps close its borders and survive, but only if it came up with extra energy and water. Besides, few citizens want a society so managed that essential freedoms are negated.

People do sense that free trade and protectionism are political ideologies disguised as disinterested, economic inevitability. These days the leading free traders tend to be the CORPORATISTS, led by the executives of transnational corporations. They like a theory which permits their corporations to produce wherever production is cheapest and sell wherever prices are highest. It isn't their business if this is a self-defeating idea. After all, those paid least to produce are least likely to be rich enough to consume. And those who pay most to consume are unlikely to be able to do so if they're unemployed.

Today's protectionists tend to be led by the local corporatists; the unions and small companies. They like a theory which holds out the promise of all change being controllable. That this is impossible except in an isolated society with a nomadic or pre-agrarian economy doesn't seem to bother them.

While these organized interest groups argue, most people ask themselves why they must always be presented with religious options? Why must they identify the single pure truth in order to avoid an apocalypse? Is there any difference between Vladimir Lenin the communist, Mikhail Bakunin the anarchist and Milton Friedman the marketist? No. All three are ideologues.

Like other ideologies, that of free trade contains unspoken contempt for the individual citizen. It is a despairing response to the complexities of the real world and the politics of despair always replace choice with inevitability. Indeed despair is the natural tone of economists when they are selling their theories of salvation.

Since the early 1980s the explosion in the size of the international **MONEY MARKETS** has been advanced as a new factor justifying inevitability. But these money markets are largely paper inflation and are central to our problems, not a solution to them. Revolutionary changes in communication **TECHNOLOGY** are presented as an uncontrollable force. But communication has always been an essential enabling device of trade. However, it is not in itself trade, except to the extent that the materials of communication are bought and sold. Communications is merely machinery used or turned on, operated and turned off by human beings domiciled and working in specific places. The new version of the free-trade argument seems to be that we have regressed from being slaves of the market-place to being slaves of machines which are slaves of the market-place.

In 225 years of debate, there have been several attempts at extreme free trade and several at extreme protectionism. None have been successful. None have been absolutely applied. The most famous—that of Britain and the repeal of the Corn Laws in 1846—was concentrated on providing cheap food for the poorly paid peasants who had stopped producing grain to become workers. For Britain's industrial exports and imports all sorts of restrictions remained in place.

Free trade tends to be favoured by those who have power—as Britain did in the middle of the nineteenth century and as the transnational corporations do today. It is abandoned the moment their power slips away, as was the case with Britain. There is no proof that the period of freer trade actually permitted them to hold onto their power a moment longer than they did. Extreme protectionism can also appear to provide short-term pleasures, but it ends with isolation, immobility and poverty.

Civilizations do best when they engage in careful freedom and careful balance. Free trade in certain circumstances in certain areas can be a great boon for many people. In others, it will be a disaster and provoke disorder and suffering. Carefully and precisely used, protectionism can promote growth, particularly among some of the weaker parties in international competition. Used as a general principle it is a recipe for local exploitation. Free trade and protectionism, once stripped of their pseudo-religious-ideological disguises, are useful tools which can be balanced for general benefit and stability. See: IDEOLOGY.

FREEDOM An occupied space which must be reoccupied every day.

FREUD, SIGMUND A man so dissatisfied with his own mother and father that he devoted his life to convincing everyone who would listen—or better still, talk—that their parents were just as bad.

His movement eventually convinced millions of people that if they could understand why their parents and their childhood had made them so unhappy they would be able to live happier lives. This theory has been applied to unhappy people for three-quarters of a century. It does not appear to work. The pity is that consciousness is an all too rare human strength. Freud has unfortunately discovered an even rarer frivolous sort. Its main use has been to help novelists develop the voice of the inner self in their stories.

Jacques Lacan later refined Freud's theory by demonstrating that, in so far as French men and women were concerned, the founder's mother and father were a system. Carl Jung simply became bored with Freud's parents and turned to **ANIMISM**, a far richer source for the examination of the human psyche. See: **HAPPINESS** and **AUTOBIOGRAPHY**.

FRIENDSHIP   An imprecise emotion combined with loyalty.

In a specialist and **CORPORATIST** society friendship is often confused with shared ideas or tastes or skills or interests. But each of these involves the weighing of value and is therefore an evocation of self-interest. Friendship is the exact opposite. Or as Blake put it, "opposition is true friendship."[3]

G

GAMBLING, STATE-RUN   When governments raise money by acting as croupiers, the systems they manage are degenerate and are closer to their end than to their beginning.

The Burmese, for example, could always tell when a dynasty was close to falling; it would set up a state lottery.

Early in the 1970s, Western governments turned to licensed gambling to provide the funds which TAXATION no longer seemed able to raise. This initiative has been blamed on many specifics: the financial crisis, tax reform which drastically reduced the contribution of the large corporations, the cost of social programs. The combined result was a lack of money which turned into DEBT and that debt into chronic restraint.

From the moment a government encourages its citizenry to finance the state by gambling—which means by idle dreaming—instead of through creativity, work and productivity, that state is in an unacknowledged crisis.

The only nation to have prospered via gambling is Monaco, which is not a nation. It is a corporation specializing in tax avoidance presided over by a croupier prince.

GANG OF FIVE, THE   Machiavelli, Bacon, Loyola, Richelieu and Descartes. Between 1515 and 1650, these five rationalists invented the modern Western state.

This absolute statement deserves four caveats:

1. Historic theories are never quite true, but then neither is TRUTH, and some are true enough to be useful.
2. What about Luther? What about Calvin? There are always more names and no one is excluded who wishes to accept responsibility.
3. It isn't clear that any individual can be held responsible as the inventor of enormous social changes when millions of others are willing to live with them. Only the HEROic view of history, a rational deformation of true individualism, would assert that kind of personal accomplishment.
4. There is a victim in every gang—often the most imaginative and/or the one with least power. René Descartes is the victim here. The official version of the rational argument was quickly attached to his name and to one of his books (*Discourse on Method*—1637), so that whenever there has been a desire to castigate reason as arid or castrating, the critics turn on Descartes. In reality, the doctrine known as Cartesianism reflected a small part of his interests. He was a man who took pleasure in entertaining doubt and tried to embrace the humanist attitude. And yet. And yet there is that curious observation made by Voltaire about Descartes not looking up Galileo while visiting Italy and never quoting him, while going out of his way to cite Galileo's enemy, the Jesuit Scheiner, who did so much to block the scientist's work.[1] At the very least that is an interesting comment on the idea of rational certainty.

   In any case whole educational systems have identified Descartes as the source of rational methodology. Millions praise or demonize him. And he was part of the original gang, even if a victim of it.

The other four had a more revolutionary effect on our civilization because they combined their rational ideas with political and administrative responsibilities.

Niccolo Machiavelli was a courtier who lost his position when the Medici came to power in Florence. His writings (*The Prince*—1513, and *The Discourses*—1519) painted the picture of a government in which people like himself made society run in an effective and amoral manner by using the rational method. Morality was reduced to effectiveness and virtue redefined as strength of will or power. In Machiavelli's scenario the courtiers or technocrats would look after things behind the veil of the Prince (Machiavelli was writing in order to get his job back). The Prince would be called upon from time to time to apply his judgemental wisdom and if necessary to ensure ruthless executions and punishments which "terrify and satisfy" the people.

Loyola was a courageous and amusing Spanish courtier who turned to God after an unfortunate encounter between his legs with a cannonball. He invented the ultimate rational corps of public servants or courtiers and technocrats—the Jesuits (1539). As their leader, he became the Pope's chief courtier and directed the counter-reformation strategy, which was largely his invention. His education system remains the basis for all of our modern élite training. From the business schools to the government schools, the methodology is jesuitical.

Francis Bacon was an accomplished courtier who made his way to the top (minister under Elizabeth I and James I, including Lord Chancellor 1618–21) in part by betraying his patrons. He continues to receive a very good press in England as the practical and non-judgemental opposite of Descartes. In reality, he believed in an absolutist rule of law and a dictatorship of highly specialized experts as laid out in his Utopian novel *The New Atlantis* (1624). The English insistence that they are a practical people as opposed to the Cartesians across the Channel is based in good part on their fanciful opposition of Bacon to Descartes. As a result of this self-deception they remain the last truly ideological people in Europe while praising endlessly their own common sense. (See: ENGLAND.)

Cardinal Richelieu was a highly successful courtier who ran France (1624–42) behind the veil of Louis XIII, exactly as Machiavelli had prescribed. The shape of the modern, managerial nation state was laid out by Richelieu. While Machiavelli, Loyola and Bacon were addicted to behind-the-scenes manipulation, it was Richelieu who fully realized the modern use of secrecy as a central tool of advanced civilization. In 1627 (ten years before Descartes) he laid out a thirteen-point proposal for "a Rational Reorganization of Government."

The modern nation state, with its dependence on rational technocracy, is largely the creation of these four unpleasant, ruthless courtiers and one well-meaning, timid philosopher who was always careful not to offend those in authority. Four and a half centuries later, the contemporary middle and upper-middle classes are made up largely of employees who must survive in a culture of courtierism. To deny that there is an essential relationship between the two would be, quite simply, forgetful. See: **MEMORY**.

GATT   See: **IRRADIATION**.

GLOBAL ECONOMY   The modern form of ideology is economic determinism. It is presented as if neither the presenter (a coalition of interest groups) nor the receiver (the public) have any active role to play because the global economy is going to arrive whether they like it or not. In this way a complete ideological policy can be advanced without any discussion of its implications or any admission that it is an ideology.

The Global Economy is usually presented beneath four banners:

1. "The Global Economy is inevitable."

   But there has always been a Global Economy. Sometimes it has been more, sometimes less global. And there has been no technological or managerial breakthrough in the last three decades which makes this more or less so. Our remarkable advances in high technology communications are useful on the international scale just as they are locally. But they do not make local or regional rules irrelevant. For example, these technologies have not eliminated the power of national regulations inside countries. There is therefore no reason to believe that they must necessarily eliminate regulations between countries.

If there has been a fundamental change it is in attitudes. The question is whose attitude and why?

The second question is whether a Global Economy should be allowed to shape itself without any guidance or alternatively with the primary guidance of the large corporations in light of their corporate interests or with the primary guidance of those societies which produce and consume the goods.

The attitudinal change we are seeing seems to have originated in the managers of large corporations. It may have been produced by their realization that Western societies, based as they were on an ever-stronger middle-class contract, would always say no to an assault on that contract. The temptation of more and cheaper goods would be refused if it risked social stability. Thus the reinvention of the Global Economy permitted the large corporate structures—and their contracted consultants in university departments of economics—to reopen the entire dossier of early capitalism. Western civilization had just spent a century taming and training that ugly capitalism to act in a decent manner. This was done carefully in order to avoid removing the profit motive. Abruptly, the wild beast has been rereleased in the guise of inevitability.

2. "The Global Economy will produce more goods at lower prices."

Do we need more goods? Do we need cheaper goods?

We already have too many goods on the market and can easily produce more. Our problem is a lack of purchasers. The Global Economy reduces still farther the number of those who can buy. You can only be a consumer if you are employed.

As for cheaper goods, in absolute terms the lower the retail price, the lower the standard of living of the producers. This is because these goods are either produced by fewer people, leaving more unemployed, or by people paid lower wages. These savings theoretically decrease the retail price.

Would it not be reasonable to suggest that what the West needs is neither more nor cheaper goods, but a quantity of goods appropriate to the population at a fair or reasonable price—that is, a price which makes them affordable within a generalized middle-class social and economic system without undermining that system.

3. "To resist the Global Economy is to deny the Third World its opportunity."

Complete nonsense. The question is: Can the Third World only develop by going through the profound disorder and suffering endemic to early, unregulated capitalism? If our desire is to encourage economic growth in underdeveloped areas, there are far more effective and civilized ways of doing so.

The suggestion that by setting conditions on internationalization the West would be denying the Third World its opportunity, contains an unstated assumption: that the Third World will benefit from the Global Economy. But the creation of several million low-wage jobs in nineteenth-century conditions does not necessarily bring prosperity or development. This is more likely to bring social disorder with very real costs attached.

Given that an underlying principle of the Global Economy is that industry will continually move to the area of cheapest production, these Third World jobs will disappear from each location the moment there is enough local development to bring on demands for respectable work conditions.

There is an undeclared assumption in this notion of unfair Western denial: that some areas will benefit from the Global Economy. But it is not true that every economic system contains winners. Many systems are fundamentally negative and destabilizing. A few individuals will always prosper, and in this case some large corporate structures may benefit without even their employees prospering. But all societies will suffer. From what can already be seen, it is likely that acceptance of the Global Economy as currently presented will bring long-term poverty in the Third World.

4. "The Global Economy is the future."

The Global Economy is a nineteenth-century concept dressed up in high-tech and posing as the future. The fundamental question which this raises is, how can the developed nations protect a century's worth of social progress unless they agree to cooperate in regulating both the transnational corporations and the international money markets?

Passive acceptance of the Global Economy as an unregulated international demolition crew would mean a return to the past. Any use of the word "future," as a concept suggesting economic advancement, would require the consolidation of our social and economic progress over the last century by concentrating on new international agreements.

So far, the Japanese and the Europeans have treated the Global Economy as an ideological screen put forward by foreign special interests. They have therefore resisted its tenets. The American academic community, however, has tended to fall in line with its own corporate structure. As a result, the words "Global Economy" are more often than not used by Americans as if they represented a disinterested truth. This passivity is mimicked in countries such as Canada and Britain, where the influence of American acolytes is strong. So long as the ideology disguised in the words Global Economy has an institutional base inside Western civilization, any sensible resistance will be undermined. That is why the nineteenth-century disorder promised by globalization seems to be inevitable when in practical terms it is not.

GOD Either God is alive, in which case he'll deal with us as he sees fit. Or he is dead, in which case he was never alive, it being unlikely that he died of old age.

If God has always been a figment of our imagination, then, given organized society's distrust of the imagination, he must have been created for a reason. At best this figment was probably intended to provide us with a shared ethical relationship. At worst it was just an excuse for a small group of clerics to wield power in the name of an invisible person who could not interfere.

By acting as if he were dead without settling upon an existential alternative, we have invited a reign of negative confusion. This has encouraged charlatans and opportunists to propose complete replacements; that is, ideology.

The best way to avoid such confusion and the resulting exploitation is to ensure that God is replaced (if we are assuming that he never existed) not by a theory or a dialect or market forces or structure but by a generally agreed-upon ethical relationship. That, interestingly enough, is the central purpose of democratic society. The citizen has trouble remembering this because the ideologues and specialists who win power keep telling us that ETHICS, although worthy, are naïve. Who can blame them? Like all priests they want to be God and failing that to speak for him without the interference of free-standing values. See: IDEOLOGY and NIETZSCHE.

GROWTH   The assumption that prosperity is dependent on growth is an inseparable part of our obsession with COMPETITION, our confusion over DEBT and our exclusionary approach towards economics.

The dogma of twentieth-century economics presents growth as a divine expression of health. The stronger the growth, the greater the health.

Why this should be so isn't clear. Most civilizations have defined social well-being as either stability or modest growth. Even prosperity has usually been seen in those terms.

Instability, inflation, boom-and-bust—these phenomena, more than that of useful progress, have been associated with growth. Not that boom-and-bust cycles are of no value. Often they leave behind long-term infrastructures—railways, road networks, fleets of airplanes, urban development. But it would be a sign of congenital pessimism to think that civilization can only progress by lurching along irresponsibly.

Modern growth appeared first with a series of technological breakthroughs from the eighteenth century on. These provoked social and economic instability from which society eventually recovered, but at an encouragingly higher level of production. The eventual effect was the messy and unpleasant creation of a more balanced society.

Most contemporary economists insist that this untidy process is the inevitable cost of progress. They rarely talk about the uncontrollable social anger produced by each lurch of such economic determinism. Without a rapid increase in the overall standard of living, that anger could and often did lead to the overthrow of the élites in place.

The other detail often ignored is that, between these lurches, there was relative stability. For long periods in the nineteenth century, for example, companies sought a stable return, not growth.

Each abrupt lurch raises the question of how much production a society can consume. Theoretically there are no limits. It isn't simply that one person needs only so many objects or one country only so many factories or communications or apples. There is enough of a gap between rich and poor in the West that we could make good use of more production and consumption, providing that it was better spread throughout society. Instead the gap between top and bottom is growing as is the percentage at the bottom.

The question of consumption limits becomes interesting at the level where there is consumption. It seems that élites are capable of consuming only limited amounts of production before ceasing to function effectively. It is as if a single person can only control, own and wear so much property, so many objects and clothes. Beyond a certain quantity these inert elements no longer play a useful role in that person's life. They become a burden.

History indicates that most societies are eventually destroyed not by the laziness, incompetence or uncooperativeness of their poor or of their lower-middle classes or even of their middle classes, but by the failure of the élites to do their job. One of the factors which disables them is the imbalance between their sense of themselves as functioning individuals and the great weight of accoutrements with which their civilization has burdened them—from factories and investments, houses and clothing, to a paralyzing sense of social propriety and self-importance. One of the signs of this sickness is a conviction that the only solution to their sluggish and confused personal state is increased growth. And the more they consume, the more they see their situation as sufficient unto itself—as a personal right rather than a privilege which involves obligations to the society whose growth feeds them.

After the Second World War growth took on a new shape. It combined the continuing technological revolution with a need both to recover from the pre-war Depression and to rebuild Europe. To these three elements was added the sudden conversion of state **PROPAGANDA** into public relations.

A century and a half of gearing up political and military salesmanship spilled over into commercial advertising. And as the central theme in **ADVERTISING** was consumption, the underlying theme was the virtue of continuous growth.

The process of rebuilding after the Depression and the War began to peter out in the early 1970s. The Depression that began in 1973 awakened everyone to this problem and growth began fading mysteriously away. Rather than face this reality, we set about inventing mechanisms of artificial growth. Our two most successful illusions were **ARMAMENTS** production and financial speculation. Because we could no longer feed the mechanisms of useful growth, we began spinning ever more complex pieces of useless machinery and paper around and around. It was a return to the illusionary or inflationary economics of the early eighteenth century—the world of South Sea Bubbles and the John Law scandals.

There is of course still room for substantive growth. A revolution in communications and high technology based on increased production by fewer people is under way. So far the effect has been to undermine the existing economy. It can be argued that this is what happens each time we leap forward. However, in this case it comes at a time when we are already in overproduction and underemployment. Increased efficiency is only worsening our state.

A more sensible approach could turn this contradiction of development to advantage. Instead of increasing production, we could concentrate on improved quality and a better balance of consumption throughout society. For example, agricultural overproduction has already led to disastrously low prices and these to subsidies. The need is not for increased post-modern production but for a reduction in production, which could be compensated for through higher quality. (See: IRRADIATION.)

Equally there is no need for more cars or more televisions at cheaper prices. There is a need, however, to employ the labour we have so that they can earn enough to finance their own lives and join in the purchasing of the goods we produce. So long as a society capable of overproduction sees itself in Darwinian terms, new production breakthroughs will accentuate the problems we already have.

The availability of cheap foreign labour demonstrates the reality that large parts of the world are still susceptible to growth in the way the West was a century ago. The former Soviet Bloc, Asia and the developing world exist in situations very different to our own. Many economists believe that our future growth lies in selling to these people.

But (parts of Asia aside) they can only pay us for these mythological goods if they produce and sell an equal amount themselves—unless, that is, we further weaken our own economies by printing money we don't have to lend it to them to buy our goods.

Second, their need for real growth will not be satisfied if they become reliant on the West. Their need is not to buy goods from us. It is to produce goods themselves.

Third, while there is practical hope for growth over the next decade in parts of Asia and perhaps inside the former Soviet Bloc, the developing world is faced with a tragic long-term problem. During the 1970s and 1980s we attempted to jump-start their economies by force-feeding them with grandiose industrial strategies and vast loans. As a direct result their economies have collapsed, their populations have been destabilized, and their agricultural production has disintegrated, leading to recurrent famines.

The question which all of this raises is whether basing our economic hopes on growth is useful, healthy or even an historically accurate supposition. It may be that the key to dealing with our problems is to demote growth, at least for a period of time, to a secondary or tertiary position in our planning and replace it with a sophisticated concept of stability.

H

HAPPINESS A tired and twisted notion which has become an increasing embarrassment in a confused society.

Happiness rose to great social and political prominence in the eighteenth century, when it was used by most European philosophers as one of the essential qualities of a reformed society. It was legally consecrated at the highest possible level by Jefferson who, in the American Declaration of Independence, made it one of the citizen's three inalienable rights: "life, liberty and the pursuit of happiness."

Thanks to its philosophical and legal position, happiness has stayed at the forefront of social and political policy throughout the nineteenth and twentieth centuries. However, the meaning of the word has gradually changed.

Its Aristotelian sense was spiritual harmony. But Aristotle was the justifying genius of the **SCHOLASTICS** and spiritual harmony was one of the concepts which helped them to maintain a state of intellectual and social stagnation. It was no accident that the Enlightenment's attack on scholasticism included the reorienting of this word to give human harmony a more practical, active meaning. As a result, in the eighteenth century happiness came to include basic material comfort in a prosperous, well-organized society. As the Western upper-middle and solid middle classes gradually accomplished this for themselves, the word's meaning declined into the pursuit of personal pleasure or an obscure sense of inner contentment. Both the spiritual and the necessary material were forgotten. Few writers and public figures have dared to point this out or to suggest that, since the meaning of the word has changed, it no longer needs to be treated as a question of primary importance.

President de Gaulle responded to pressure from his ministers to give in to policies which might be popular in the short run, but were fundamentally damaging, by retorting that "happiness is for idiots." He wasn't proposing unhappiness or a loss of material comfort. Much of his time in power was spent creating social services and prosperity. Rather he was protesting the confusion of happiness with a state of mindless contentment. He was arguing against happiness and in favour of consciousness which, the world being what it really is, might not involve contentment, but would involve RESPONSIBILITY.

Nothing has happened in the last quarter-century to clarify this confusion. As economic and social conditions have gradually sunk, happiness, with its twisted meaning at the ethical and legal centre of our society, has seemed increasingly lugubrious and out of place. In a more practical world, there would be a formal process for retiring a word from active use until it finds itself again.

HAPPY BIRTHDAY   An international symbol of English-language culture.

With the gradual decline of those Western religious and liberal systems of belief which were central to the creation of modern society, only the debris of civilization remains. This is rich and complex matter, but it has no particular shape.

Public celebrations are the flowering of unquestioned traditions, and so in a civilization of debris few of them remain valid. Many of the mediaeval, Renaissance and early-modern ceremonies and pageants continued well into the twentieth century, when electronic communication finally put most of them to death. There was then an attempt to fill this void with celebrations manufactured for spectators by that same electronic communications industry, helped along by advertising experts. But the public still desires group expression and they understand this to mean events in which they, as individuals, participate and which they therefore share. Spectators are not celebrants.

Restaurants, until recently, were places of refuge for people excluded from the mainstream or seeking to escape it—poor students, aging unmarried men not rich enough to have themselves fed at home, richer men seeking sex not wives, and the proverbial artists leading their irresponsible lives. Over the last half-century, restaurants have risen in importance to fill the void left by the decline of the old public celebrations. They now provide the leading forums of public participation.

One of the restaurant's principal functions is to host birthdays. At this very moment, thousands of waiters and waitresses around the world are standing over slightly embarrassed clients and singing "Happy Birthday" to them in English. These employed choirs invariably substitute, wherever the words "dear Cathy" or "dear Sue" ought to be sung, the universal words "to you."

They resemble the professional mourners who not very long ago were regularly hired to weep at funerals. But why is it that they exclude the client's name? It is often spelled out in sugar on the cake the waiters are carrying and, if their singing were merely a commercialized gesture intended to satisfy the customer, then chanting out the name would be an easy way to earn more satisfaction and therefore more money.

But this is not an individual celebration. Given our inability to deal with DEATH, these singing waiters are the new professional mourners. The birthday client is being drawn into the great public process of continuity to which each of us belongs. The song "Happy Birthday" has evolved into an incantation sung endlessly throughout the West and beyond, in the way that the Christian mass once constantly echoed in Latin over the born, living, dying and dead twenty-four hours a day.

When Senator Benigno Aquino was murdered in suspicious circumstances on his return from exile to Manila in 1983, the Filipino government attempted to deal with national and international outrage by holding an inquiry. Mrs. Imelda Marcos was called to give evidence because her husband was suspected of direct or indirect involvement. Her appearance happened to fall on her fifty-fifth birthday. Everyone in the courtroom rose to sing "Happy Birthday."

HAPPY FAMILY The existence and maintenance of which is thought to make a politician fit for public office. According to this theory the public are less concerned by whether or not they are effectively represented than by the need to be assured that the PENISes and vaginas of public officials are only used in legally sanctioned circumstances.

The production of children is a basic animal function which involves no intellectual or ethical skills. The successful raising of children and the long-term maintenance of a contented marriage are mysteries so impenetrable that they have kept generations of poets, playwrights, novelists and social scientists continuously employed.

The relationship of marriage and children to the application of public policy is an even greater mystery. Nothing in history indicates that happily married leaders have been wiser, more humane, courageous, effective or intelligent, any more than personal moderation or respectability in themselves have led to good government. The list of happily married liars, thieves, cowards and monsters in public office is as long as that of the admirable drunkards and humane philanderers. The private lives of most first-class leaders seem to have been catastrophic.

Our modern insistence on a balance between private respectability and public policy therefore has nothing to do with leadership. Not only is it irrelevant to the democratic process, it may even be aggressively anti-democratic. Either the leader is an effective representative of the citizen's interests or he is a lifestyle model. If the latter, then we have slipped back into the traditional religious and dictatorial archetypes of noble sacrificial heroes, vestal virgins, wives of Caesar, saintly kings and virgin queens. In a democratic society, these are false standards which can't help but put the wrong people in office.

HAPPY HOUR A depressing comment on the rest of the day and a victory for the most limited Dionysian view of human nature.

HARD WORK The work ethic remains a popular explanation for the success of the West. This doubtful argument relies heavily on comparing humans to insects such as ants. Above all, the work ethic has a feel about it of low-level morality aimed at the poorer end of society.

There are lots of poor in the world who work all the time, often with great skill, and remain poor. On the other hand, large deposit banks, although non-productive, have been among the most profitable institutions over the last half-century. Their executives continue to work relatively short hours. The executives of large, publicly traded corporations work longer hours than the poor. And they compete with each other—not with other corporations—to work ever harder, by spending more of each day at their desks processing paper and developing relationships. This benefits their reputations and their careers. There is no proof that it has an effect on productivity or profits for the corporation.

Entrepreneurs are quite different. They usually have to work very hard in order to create their enterprise in order not to have to work hard later on in their lives. In other words, they create in order not to work.

To the extent that the West has succeeded, it is probably the result not of work but of innovation—not just technological, but social, intellectual, political, verbal, visual, acoustical, even emotional. In order to innovate some have spent a great deal of time thinking and experimenting, perhaps more than any other civilization in history.

Technological innovation in particular continues as if we were on an unstoppable roll. Yet our structures do not as a rule reward either thinking or innovation. And they don't reward physical hard work. What they do favour is a narrowly defined type of intense labour best described as white-collar slogging. See: INDOLENCE.

HARVARD SCHOOL OF BUSINESS   See: CHICAGO SCHOOL OF ECONOMICS and TAYLORISM.

HELL   The abolition of hell has created major problems in the maintaining of a general ethical standard. The eighteenth-century philosophers condemned the threat of hell as a cynical device used against the less powerful. But they regretted the loss of hell's real purpose, which was to deal with serious crimes, particularly those of the powerful and rich.

Voltaire in his dictionary noted that, "As soon as men lived in society they must have noticed that some guilty men eluded the severity of the laws. It was possible to punish public crimes. But how could you put a brake on the secret variety. Religion alone could provide that brake."[1]

The philosophers believed that law and disinterested administration would take care of this problem. However, the more complex and sophisticated the laws became, the more they actually protected the powerful. And once administration had been raised to the level of a moral value, those with power began to convert unethical behaviour into administrative regulations.

For example, it is common for senior managers to increase their income by a quarter to a third through what are known as "benefits." This is legalized fraud. It is common to hide serious errors in the public service behind security regulations. This also is legalized fraud. (See: DENIAL.) It is common to justify poverty and exploitation through reference to the rules of **COMPETITION**. (See: **HOLY TRINITY–LATE TWENTIETH CENTURY**.) The Encyclopaedists were already concerned about this in the eighteenth century. "The means for enriching oneself can be morally *criminal* even though permitted by law; it is against natural law and against humanity that millions of individuals are denied the necessary in order to feed the scandalous luxury of a small number of comfortable citizens."[2] Again the philosophers assumed that rational reform could solve this problem. And there have, indeed, been improvements. But recently the pendulum has begun to swing back. And this time exploitation is justified not by divine right or class privilege, but by expertise and law.

We have failed to replace hell with a viable code of ethics. That is because we slipped into a rational approach to society when we had intended to follow the road of **HUMANISM**.

HEROES   An illusion of leadership.

The modern Hero is the descendant of Napoleon Bonaparte. With the development of communications technology it has become possible to sell Heroic attitudes as being more important than actual heroism.

The Hero is the rational substitute for democratic leadership. To bypass the genuine complexities of the public place, technocratic expertise has been allied with the distracting excitement of leadership on horseback. By the late twentieth century this Napoleonic image had been refined to such attitudes as film-inspired Reaganite war stories, talking **TOUGH**, selling the leader's "character" via the mechanism of public relations and confusing the idea of the Hero with that of the celebrity.

Given that one of the roles of the Hero and the **FALSE HERO** is to distract the citizenry from their role, appearances are of primary importance. From 1800 to 1945 these false populists dressed up in military uniforms. This was the Napoleonic model, even though few of them were soldiers. After Hitler and Mussolini, the uniform was no longer possible.

A period of confusion followed as a new model was sought. It began to emerge in the 1980s through a blending of the B-movie actor with the entrepreneur. The need was for the concentration of a one-tone character role. The tough, decisive general was thus transmogrified into the tough, decisive businessman. The military uniform into the heavy, expensive, dark, double-breasted suit.

Reagan and Mulroney were early attempts at this image. It was perfected in Italy by the new prime minister, Silvio Berlusconi, former nightclub singer, wearer of five-centimetre heels, owner of a hair transplant, who advanced in public behind permanent make-up, even when greeting starving children rescued from Rwanda. He was, of course, an entrepreneurial Hero and wore the appropriate suit.

HISTORY   A seamless web linking past, present and future.

Contemporary Western society attempts to limit history to the past, as if it were the refuse of civilization. Individuals who hold power tend to see history only as mythology which can be manipulated to distract the citizenry, but is not useful in itself.

Among the different humanist areas of education, history has nevertheless survived best the pseudo-scientific reduction of non-scientific learning to theoretically objective standards. The other cornerstones of humanism—literature and philosophy—have been severely damaged by the drive to quantify and objectify everything in sight. Intellectual accounting is not a synonym for thinking. Driven by this vain search for objectivity, literature and philosophy have come to resemble the obscure and controlling scholasticism of the Middle Ages.

If the historical approach has been able to resist these trends, it may be because power structures require a comforting background of mythology and mythology requires a sweep of civilization. Thus, history is welcome as a superficial generalization viewed in a hazy distance.

Our technocracy is frightened by the idea that ideas and

events could be part of a large flow and therefore less controllable than expertise would like to suggest. For them, history is a conservative force which blocks the way to change and to new answers. In reality, history only becomes an active force when individuals deform it into a weapon for public manipulation. By that very process it ceases to be history.

The twentieth century has been dominated by a catastrophic explosion of ideologies of which communism and fascism have been the most spectacular. NEO-CONSERVATISM is a recent minor example. The fleeting success of these ideologies has been made possible in part by the denial of history—or rather, by freezing history into narrow bands of logic, the sole purpose of which is to justify a specific ideology.

This does not mean that history becomes a beacon of truth when it is separated from ideology. History is not about truth but about continuity, and not about a limited dialectic but about an unlimited movement. To the extent that ETHICS remain in the foreground, history cannot be grossly deformed. The ethics which Western civilization has attempted to push forward for two and a half millennia are scarcely a secret. If anything, they have remained painfully obvious as one set of power structures after another has sought to marginalize or manipulate them. It is in this context that ideology most typically seeks to fix our attention on a single, conclusive pattern which can be presented as inevitable and which therefore carries a deformation of ethics.

These destructive experiences illustrate the value of history as a guarantor of both stability and change. It is neither a conservative nor a revolutionary force. Instead, history is a constant memory and its value lies in our ability to make it a highly conscious part of our lives. In an age which presents abstract analysis—a method that denies continuity and memory—as the sole respectable method of exercising power, history is perhaps the sole intact linear means of thought. See: HUMANISM.

HOBBES, THOMAS   He was right about one thing—there is a solid relationship between authoritarianism and the difficulty humans have in dealing with their **FEAR** of **DEATH**.

What Hobbes put forward in *Leviathan* in the seventeenth century—that democracy was disorder and that societies could only function with strong leaders who used their subjects' fear of mortality—has turned into a recurring theme. Whenever we hear a pessimistic description of humanity or a call for strong **LEADERSHIP** or an obscuring vision of our approaching conversion into dust, we are hearing echoes of Hobbes's anti-democratic arguments.

We, the citizen guarantors of our own democracy, have taken to using a language which suggests that there is every reason to be pessimistic about our ability to choose policies and leaders wisely, to control our impulses and to participate intelligently in our civilization. This pessimism brings us back repeatedly to a perceived need for leaders, by which we seem to mean strong leaders—people who will run things for us. Curiously enough these self-destructive impulses also seem to be an integral part of a society which, more than any other in history, has been carefully constructed so that each of us can avoid facing the reality of our own upcoming death.

We are all familiar with the concept of the enemy within. Our tendency is to go on imagining that a good citizen is one who remains vigilant, ever on the lookout for the authoritarian enemy. But we have ourselves become that enemy by forgetting the implications of our own arguments.

HOLY TRINITY—CHRISTIAN   A pre-alchemist alchemist concept developed by early Christian administrators to soften the hard-edged simplicity of straight monotheism.

The three-in-one/one-in-three mystery of Father, Son and Holy Ghost made tritheism official. The subsequent almost-deification of the Virgin Mary made it quatrotheism. Twelve Disciples as semi-deities then made it sextusdecitheism. Finally, cart-loads of saints raised to quarter-deification turned Christianity into plain, old-fashioned polytheism. By the time of the Crusades, it was the most polytheistic religion ever to have existed, with the possible exception of Hinduism. This untenable contradiction between the assertion of monotheism and the reality of polytheism was dealt with by accusing other religions of the Christian fault. The Church—Catholic and later Protestant—turned aggressively on the two most clearly monotheistic religions in view—Judaism and Islam—and persecuted them as heathen or pagan.

The external history of Christianity consists largely of accusations that other religions rely on the worship of more than one god and therefore not the true God. These pagans must therefore be converted, conquered and/or killed for their own good in order that they may benefit from the singularity of the Holy Trinity, plus appendages.

HOLY TRINITY–POST-CHRISTIAN So far Nietzsche has been wrong about **GOD**. We have not managed to become Him in His place. Instead we have replaced God with a yet more abstract divinity based upon pure rational power.

Reason rose out of the generous humanist promise of the seventeenth and eighteenth centuries by climbing over the bodies of **HUMANISM**'s other constituent elements—common sense, intuition, creativity, memory and ethics. These elements, which by limiting reason make it positive, were not simply struck dead. They were converted into the enemy of the new divinity.

In their place a post-Christian Holy Trinity was installed. Organization or structure replaced the Father, **TECHNOLOGY** displaced the Son and the Holy Ghost gave way to information. The new priesthood was made up of technocrats. As the etymology of the word "technocrat" indicates, from the beginning they were to be specialists in power. Masters of structure. Modern courtiers. They would control the use of technology as if it were a natural extension of themselves, which it is not. And they would stand guard over information, each specialist category dispensing its specialist knowledge as it saw fit.

This is the underlying truth of our society. There are other factors. Complications. Reasons for optimism. But this is our basic religion.

HOLY TRINITY—LATE TWENTIETH CENTURY   The main tenet of faith in the last quarter of the twentieth century has been the promise of a rational paradise reached through devotion to competition, efficiency and the market-place. In this fashionable and remarkably intolerant Holy Trinity, the role of the Father is taken by competition, of the Son by efficiency and of the Holy Ghost by the market-place.

If these three mechanisms could be presented with both their strengths and their flaws, they would be valuable tools in a stable society. Treated as absolutes they quickly drag society into a confused and dangerous state where conventional wisdom is reliant on our denial of what we know to be wrong.

As with our earlier worship of saints and facts, there is something silly about grown men and women striving to reduce their vision of themselves and of civilization to bean counting. The message of the competition/efficiency/market-place Trinity seems to be that we should drop the idea of ourselves developed over two and a half millennia. We are no longer beings distinguished by our ability to think and to act consciously in order to affect our circumstances. Instead we should passively submit ourselves and our whole civilization—our public structures, social forms and cultural creativity—to the abstract forces of unregulated commerce. It may be that most citizens have difficulty with the argument and would prefer to continue working on the idea of dignified human intelligence. If they must drop something, they would probably prefer to drop the economists.

HUMANISM An exaltation of freedom, but one limited by our need to exercise it as an integral part of nature and society.

We are capable of freedom because we are capable of seeking the balance which integrates us into the world. And this equilibrium in society depends upon our acceptance of **DOUBT** as a positive force. The dignity of man is thus an expression of modesty, not of superior preening and vain assertions.

These simple notions are central to the Western idea of civilization. They are clearly opposed to the narrow and mechanistic certainties of ideology; those assertions of certainty intended to hide the fear of doubt.

Modern humanism appeared in Italy in the fourteenth century with Dante, Boccaccio and Petrarch. It was given philosophical form in the second half of the fifteenth century. Among those who reimagined its shape were Pico della Mirandola, who in his *Oration on the Dignity of Man* has God tell Adam: "I have placed you at the centre of the world so that from there you may see what is in it."

Most specialists devoted to the **HISTORY OF PHILOSOPHY** now describe humanism in highly technical terms as a movement which revived classical Greek and Roman texts and devoted itself to detailed studies of language and definition and translation. In this way they reduce a revolution to their own level of modern **SCHOLASTICISM**. But the original humanists were, above all, set on attacking the original scholastics. They sought out the classical texts not in a scholastic desire to study the past, but with a determination to use classical ideas against oppressive mediaeval rhetoric.

The humanist path was filled with writers seeking new ways to communicate with larger audiences in clear language. And the element of doubt was always there. In the early sixteenth century, Erasmus seemed often to stand alone as a moderate voice attempting to hold the religious extremists, Catholic and Protestant, back from their desire for blood. The same belief in balance which carried Erasmus could be found in the Enlightenment. Yes, these eighteenth-century thinkers spent a lot of time defining concepts. What interested them, however, was not proving they were right, but being in tune with reality.

As the eighteenth century turned into the nineteenth, it became obvious that a new wave of ideologies was going to reject doubt as a weakness, as ignorance, as irresponsibility; indeed as subversion. Perhaps this explains why the ideology of REASON and its various minor manifestations, such as Marxism and Capitalism, have so easily swept humanism off centre stage. They have all the fears of uncontrolled ideas and so use their absolutism to manipulate certainty and force with ease. Balance, on the other hand, requires care and time and, of course, the embracing of uncertainty. Humanism's seeming weakness in the face of ideology is not surprising. Narrow certainty always appears to have a short-term advantage over balance and doubt.

The curious thing about ideologies is that their promise, being eternal and all-encompassing, is therefore impossible, and therefore provokes constant short-term emergencies. In order for the day to be saved, the citizen must react with passive acceptance. Passivity is required because it is believed that the individual, left to act freely in a crisis, will do the wrong thing.

For the humanist, short-term problems are not a crisis. They simply represent reality with all its complications and contradictions. And the citizen's reaction to reality is not expected to be passive, for the simple reason that human nature is neither a problem nor something to be feared. "We're not interested in a world," as René-Daniel Dubois puts it, "in which to be human is a weakness."[3] Human nature is a positive force to the extent that it is in balance.

But a balance of what? What is this equilibrium the humanists seek?

A reasonable list of human qualities might include: ETHICS, common sense, imagination or creativity, memory or history or experience, intuition and reason. The humanist tries to use all of these. But what does it mean to be in balance?

The Athenians didn't know about the structure of the atom, in which several poles are held in a self-maintaining equilibrium, not by what we would call either a physical or a logical structure but by tension. The tension of complementary opposites. Our qualities, seen as a whole, resemble an atom. The moment one quality is cut free from the others and given precedence over them, this imbalance will bring out the winner's negative aspects.

Thus ethics in power quickly turn into a religious dictatorship. Common sense couldn't help but subside into pessimistic confusion, as if wallowing in the mud. Creativity into anarchy. Memory into the worst sort of monarchical dictatorship. Intuition into the rule of base superstition. And reason, as we have seen over the last half-century, into a directionless, amoral dictatorship of structure.

But if imbalance, which we call ideology, can so easily sweep balance aside, has humanism ever been anything more than a marginal refuge for idealism? That, of course, isn't a question. It's an answer structured as a question and it reflects the standard ideological approach towards humanism.

It is undoubtedly easier to believe in absolutes, follow blindly, mouth received wisdom. But that is self-betrayal. The question is not whether we could ever achieve a humanist equilibrium, but whether we are attempting to achieve it. Better that than to seek the imprisoning imbalance of ideology.

We've always known that it was easier to run Sparta than Athens. Sparta had all the advantages of an enormous ancillary slave population, a society based on military obedience and the absence of debate. It was harder to be Athenian and in the end they themselves failed even by their own standards. But they succeeded for a long time and those standards still mark our path. We have added to them, embroidered upon and improved them. It isn't that we have progressed. But we have progressed in our knowledge of how we ought to act. Much of the time we fail to act up to our own standards. We fail ourselves. But if we know that, then we can also find ways to save ourselves. That is the essence of humanism.

I

IDEOLOGY Tendentious arguments which advance a world view as absolute truth in order to win and hold political power.

A god who intervenes in human affairs through spokesmen who generally call themselves priests; a king who implements instructions received from God; a predestined class war which requires the representatives of a particular class to take power; a corporatist structure of experts who implement truth through fact-based conclusions; a racial unit which because of its blood-ties has a destiny as revealed by nationalist leaders; a world market which, whether anyone likes it or not, will determine the shape of every human life, as interpreted by corporate executives—all of these and many more are ideologies.

Followers are caught up in the naïve obsessions of these movements. This combination ensures failure and is prone to violence. That's why the decent intentions of the *Communist Manifesto* end up in gulags and murder. Or the market-place's promise of prosperity in the exploitation of cheap, often child, labour.

There are big ideologies and little ones. They come in international, national and local shapes. Some require skyscrapers, others circumcision. Like fiction they are dependent on the willing suspension of disbelief, because God only appears in private and before his official spokespeople, class leaders themselves decide the content and pecking order of classes, experts choose their facts judiciously, blood-ties aren't pure and the passive acceptance of a determinist market means denying 2,500 years of Western civilization from Athens and Rome through the Renaissance to the creation of middle-class democracies.

Which is ideology? Which not? You shall know them by their assertion of truth, their contempt for considered reflection and their fear of debate.

IMAGE   In a society devoted to illusion, the image assumes three more or less dangerous forms.

There is the image that the creator knows to be untrue but expects to convince the public is true. This is the straightforward lie and can be dealt with because it is precise. A pin stuck in at the right moment and it deflates or explodes.

There is the image that the creator knows to be untrue and does not expect to fool the public; just to distract or disorient them. This can be dangerous because it suggests that meaning does not matter. It is increasingly common, feeds off technology and makes mockery of the idea of civilization and language.

Finally there is the image in which the creator comes to believe. Whether the public is taken in or not, this is the most dangerous sort because it involves the denial of reality by those who have a direct impact on reality.

In all three cases the image has the advantage of appearing and therefore appearing to be true. For example, in surveys of lie-perception levels, 75 per cent of those questioned will pick out an average lie when they hear it; 65 per cent when they read it; and 50 per cent when they see it.[1]

The reason that revolutionary change is often tied to **ORAL LANGUAGE** is that this remains the most accurate means of real communication. We have great difficulty disbelieving what we see. This is one of the great risks in a society increasingly dependent on electronically manipulable images. See: **PROPAGANDA**.

INAUGURATION GALA   Religious ceremony in which each newly elected president of the United States is consecrated as the most famous person in the world. This coronation of the leader of celebrities is now more important than the formal swearing-in ceremony the next day, with its boring speeches and endless parade of nobodies.

The inauguration gala of President Clinton and his consort on January 19, 1993, was a flawless example of this ceremony. Ten thousand people paid a thousand dollars each to be there in gowns and black tie. The entire proceedings were beamed live to the nation, indeed to North America and, by the new international American networks, around the world.

Those stars laying on their hands included the actresses Goldie Hawn and Sally Field, in mini-skirts split up the side, marching out arm in arm to declare to the president-elect that they were there to speak on behalf of the mothers of America. Michael Jackson spoke for American children, with a crowd of them dancing behind him. Finally, Barbra Streisand, the high priestess of stardom, in a combination appearance as the Declaration of Independence and the Statue of Liberty, spoke and sang on behalf of America as a whole, its mythology, individualism, freedom, Los Angeles and New York. "I pray for your stamina. I pray for your health."

Attentive courtiers noted that in the course of the evening the president-elect cried seven times. They followed suit.

On June 19, 1981, Nancy Reagan had cried only once when Frank Sinatra sang lyrics in her honour during the inaugural gala. But neither of these emotional moments matched that at the end of John Kennedy's gala (also staged by Frank Sinatra) when the president-elect went on stage to declare: "I'm proud to be a Democrat, because since the time of Thomas Jefferson, the Democratic party has been identified with the pursuit of excellence and we saw excellence tonight."[2]

That Jefferson might have understood excellence to mean singers and actors glorifying a new president in the manner of a royal fête at Versailles under Louis XIV may have come as a surprise to anyone who persisted in identifying the third president with a modest, republican public demeanour. In any case, Kennedy reworked the Jefferson line a short time later when receiving Nobel prize winners at the White House. See: **LEADERSHIP**.

INDIVIDUALISM   The exercise through public participation of our obligations to the body of the citizenry.

INDOLENCE   An important newspaper **BARON** has devoted himself to exposing this word. He explains that the cause of poverty throughout the world is indolence. Ten per cent of Americans would not be on food stamps if they simply used their initiative and worked harder.

He was saying this at the **DAVOS** conference in Switzerland just the other day. People have apparently become perfectly happy to while away a comfortable existence on stamps and social-welfare frauds. If they had only followed his father's advice, they'd have "stuck it to the bastards" and become really rich. This image of hundreds and hundreds of millions of millionaires sticking it to each other, there being no longer any other category of citizen to stick it to, is so all-inclusive that there is no need for others to concern themselves with this word. See: **MYRMECOPHAGA JUBATA**.

INEFFICIENCY   The divorce of the function of an operation from its purpose.

Sometimes the standard rhetoric which equates inefficiency with government bureaucracy is perfectly accurate. Yet it would be hard to imagine operations more efficient than most state-owned utilities. They deliver water and energy, collect sewage and garbage, maintain transport infrastructures and generally make the lives of tens of millions of people possible in a relatively smooth and invisible manner.

Which is more inefficient, behind the times, conservative in its investment policies, yet wasteful in its rewarding of executives: the German State railway system or the French textile industry? The American post office or the aeronautics firms Lockheed and McDonnell Douglas? EDF (the French State electrical power corporation) or much of the West's private and deposit banking sector, which has repeatedly bankrupted itself over the last three decades through extravagant and unprofessional lending? The Canadian national medicare system or the American private system which, before attempts began to reform it, left forty million people without protection and cost a fortune to both corporations and individuals?

It cannot be argued in a non-ideological manner that inefficiency is a matter of public versus private ownership. Competition can help to discourage unnecessary bureaucratic waste, but the market-place also creates waste through its notoriously short memory, difficulty thinking more than a few months ahead and a chronic weakness for fashion, which like the shapes of shoe-heels can come and go abruptly.

The underlying cause of waste in both sectors is loss of direction. This in turn can be traced to a disconnection between the manner in which an operation functions and its purpose. The greater the disconnection, the greater the inefficiency.

The purpose of an army is to discourage wars or win them. Yet officers easily become distracted by management imperatives, internal power structures, class divisions and the prestige attached to stockpiles of armaments. As a result they tend to disfavour those officers who are competent strategists (and who favour the use of uncertainty) while promoting courtiers who delight in management, power structures, class and arms stockpiling, but cannot win wars.

Waste and confusion in the automobile industry can be traced to a similar obsession with management. Much of the instability and gross wastefulness in the financial sector over the last two decades can be traced to amnesia as to their role

in the economy—the financing of infrastructures and production.

These errors are often justified by a blunt, even barbaric,
ideology which insists that the purpose of society is the max-
imization of profit. That is to deform a narrow but useful
mechanism into an absolute yet abstract god. The obsessive
pursuit of profit is a prime example of divorcing function
from purpose and therefore an invitation to inefficiency and
waste. See: NATIONALIZATION.

INFERIORITY COMPLEX   The most dangerous characteristic
in a public figure. It feeds aggression and contempt towards
others.

Alfred Adler explained early in this century that we all suffer from a sense of inferiority.[3] The important question is
therefore to what degree is it felt? There is no particular rule
as to which child will suffer from an uncontrollable sense of
inferiority. It can just as easily be a rich kid who goes to private school, inherits seven million dollars and ends up a
press baron, as a poor child of doubtful lineage and nation-
ality born on the Austro-German border.

Individuals whose primary drive stems from their feeling
of inferiority are a threat to the public interest. Not only do
they tend to seek power in search of self-affirmation, their
insecurity actually helps them to achieve it. Once there, they
seek to demonstrate the inferiority of those under them.
Their sense that they have been wronged justifies the substi-
tution of their own emotional satisfaction for such fundamentals as the public weal and ethics.

These people fall into three broad categories. There are
those who seek to win the love of important people. They
can be found today where they have always been—clinging
to the coat-tails of those who have more power than themselves. As a result they may become known for brief periods
as the one who has the ear of the one who has power. Then
they slip away, forgotten. At a higher level, there are those
who seek to win positions where they themselves must be

loved. Both of these types are the essentially craven—the natural courtiers, courtesans and quislings. The most important love they can feel is unleashed by access to power. The effect is to confirm them in their contempt for others and themselves.

The third type seeks revenge for the humiliation of their birth and circumstances. Once in power they bluster and bully, talk about the need for toughness, show contempt for others, and consciously humiliate them. This punishment is justified by the conviction that the victims deserve to suffer because they are not strong or competitive or successful enough to resist.

The most destructive holders of power often combine these three categories.

Those who are ruled by their own sense of inferiority use their obsessional talents to manipulate the insecurity in others. That is how they come to power. This very success confirms them in their contempt for others and allows them to claim that you can always succeed by appealing to the worst in the general public.

INSTRUMENTAL REASON A clever justification for a real problem.

Philosophers from Max Weber on have gazed upon what appear to be the equally beneficial and catastrophic effects of reason when applied, and have been filled with confusion and despair. If the catastrophes outweigh the benefits and reason is thus judged a failure, the only option might well be a return to superstition and arbitrary power.

In thinking this way philosophers have turned themselves into victims of their own logic. After all, it was they who argued in the first place that the choice was between the dark ages and reason; that there were no other options.

The discomfort brought on by their artificial, stark logic seems to have provoked them to split reason into two. If reason once applied did not work, then the problem, or so the argument goes, was not reason itself but a lesser, concrete form called instrumental reason.

This amounted to an intellectual beheading. Weber led the way with two terms: *wertrational* and *zweckrational*.[4] First there was reason; pure, unsullied reason; a field-day for the positive intellect. Second there was the instrumental category; a sort of lower-case, plebeian reason which had been deformed through attempts at practical application. Interestingly enough, Weber listed the common variety ahead of the ideal sort. Being a practical man he knew which was the more important. The result in any case has been that philosophers who wish to can quite comfortably reply to any critique of rational methodology that it is merely the instrumental sort.

This is not a bad argument, but it doesn't really work. After all, the conversion of what were once marginal armaments industries into the most important industrial product of the West is the result of instrumental reason. As are the endless bureaucratic problems which plague business and government. As is the invention of a new, gigantic money market, almost entirely devoted to inflationary activity. As is the military staff methodology which has killed more people in this century than any other has put onto the battlefield.

If these systems events, which so dominate our lives and the affairs of our civilization that they may destroy it and us, are merely the result of instrumental reason, then what is there left for reason itself to be? Is reason merely a harmless ideal abstraction to be debated and dissected in universities?

The true origins of this approach are revealing. It was Aristotle who distinguished between theoretical and practical reason. This was part of the Aristotelian method upon which mediaeval SCHOLASTICISM was constructed. The enthusiasm with which contemporary philosophy has embraced instrumental reason illustrates the extent to which we have sunk into bad mediaeval habits.

The effect of this division is to let philosophy off the hook. It no longer has to deal with the relationship between ideas and reality if every idea has an independent sub-category which betrays the idea from which it emerged. Granted, the result is a pleasant illusion for philosophers. They can talk on without the disturbing interference of reality.

There is an alternative to this self-defeating argument. It would involve treating the differentiation between reason and instrumental reason as interesting semantics. It would also argue that we have more than two options—that a critique of reason does not have to be a call for the return of superstition and arbitrary power. Finally, it would suggest that our problems do not lie with reason itself but with our obsessive treatment of reason as an absolute value. Certainly it is one of our qualities, but it functions positively only when balanced and limited by the others. See: HUMANISM and REASON.

INTELLIGENCE The ruling élite's description of its own strengths. It follows that this is the primary measure of SUPERIORITY among humans.

In the late twentieth century, superior intelligence apparently resembles ascending multiples of the crossword-puzzle mind. Its strengths are mechanistic, rational and linear. It tends towards narrowness, is fearful of the uncontrolled idea, person or event, as well as of intuitive or creative characteristics, and thus of HUMANISM. The exclusive is preferred over the inclusive. Controlled mediocrity is more intelligent than either original or sensible thinking because it is responsible to existing structures.

This can be seen in the standards, exams and competitions which control entry to the various levels of power: for example, in the SAT exams which serve as the primary entrance barrier to American universities or in the *concours* which control admission to L'ENA, the school which dominates France's political, administrative and business élites.

Those who support this approach might argue that these are the inevitable deformations of the ideal by reality. After all, the origins of the word intelligence can clearly be traced to the Latin *intelligere*, "to understand," or literally, "to choose among." In other words: to understand in order to choose among the various options.

But our contemporary understanding of intelligence seems to be obsessed by choosing but terrified by understanding. We concentrate on methodology, information and control, while fleeing the entertainment of doubt, which is central to understanding.

Is this a deformation of the idea of intelligence? Language is a reality, not an abstraction. It could be that if Western civilization decides to treat a narrow range of skills as if these were intelligence, then to all intents and purposes they are, unless someone else comes along with a more accurate reading.

Can mediocrity or what amounts to functional stupidity be turned into intelligence? Why not? Societies do with themselves what they wish. In the long run, their applied definitions of intelligence constitute a will to live or a form of suicide. We seem to be increasingly interested by the second option.

IRA   The immediate image provoked by those letters is of Christmas shoppers—women and children—being bombed in central London. This pathetic scene could lead to two inaccurate conclusions. First, that the English are interested in the subject. (This definition will be the one least read in England.) Second, that blowing up women and children has harmed the IRA. Nothing in history proves that being seen as the good guy will help terrorists or militant nationalists accomplish their goal. A good image didn't help the Biafrans or the Kurds; lack of it is unlikely to hurt the IRA.

This is all the more reason for Ireland to interest the English. Yet the complex Irish questions—a Protestant-Catholic split within the North and between the North and the South; parallel class divisions in the North; the presence of the British army, to name only a few—are rarely raised in England over dinner tables or at business lunches or on country weekends. A novel written on this very rich ground is almost certain to fail. The only recent film to break through (*The Crying Game*) did so by using a black English soldier and a beautiful transvestite and setting almost all of the action in London.

Despite this general silence, there have been 3,000 murders in twenty-three years, 1,800 by the IRA. The total figure for 1992 was eighty-four.

The professional—political or administrative—interpretation of the situation turns upon specific issues such as arms shipments from Libya, ambitious Irish politicians, American funding, links with organized crime and tiny groups of fanatics. These groups believe that the desire for compromise found in all mainstream élites, who primarily want to protect their positions, can be destroyed by existential acts of violence which empty the centre of public debate. No viable ground then remains, except at the extremes. In such cases, the professionals see themselves as problem-solvers.

The professional analysis usually requires a sophisticated understanding of terrorist structures. As a result, weapon supplies may be cut off, organized crime exposed, financial sources blocked and messianic terrorist leaders eliminated. Yet somehow these clear and impressive victories almost never produce a decline in the power of the extremes. After a few months the terrorist structures mutate and a new bombing or assassination campaign begins. The authorities are momentarily discouraged, but soon factor in the new events and reanalyse the enemy.

However, the weapon supplier, whether Libya or another, was never the problem. Removing Khadaffi and his weapons from the equation was no doubt satisfying, but it was also irrelevant. There are always other arms to be had. The world is awash with them. And what terrorists need is not expensive.

Somewhat more important than terrorist structures is the weight of history. This is discounted by the professionals because neither political debate nor administrative process with its hunger for solutions has any use for the past except as a mythological dump from which fragments can be occasionally retrieved to dress up propaganda. The professionals think of society as a rational construct made up of three parts: bricks and mortar, systems or structures and individuals.

This approach eliminates the possibility that society might also be treated as a live body which has evolved out of the past. Many options for change lie ahead. The ability to respond to that future is limited, however, and often governed by what has gone before. Soldiers gassed in World War I did not enter track-and-field events after the armistice. Very few people denied education in their first twenty years go on to become intellectual leaders. Those who suffered personal tragedies in their youth are very different in later life from those who did not.

Societies are not very different from individuals. They cannot ignore or escape from their past. And if it contains great wrongs, then it may take generations and great care to escape the effects.

Even our problem-solving élites know this. Why else would they refer endlessly to the genius of Frederick the Great and Garibaldi; to the glory of France and the mission of America? If they don't believe in the relevance of the past, these positive memories are meaningless jingoism. If they do, then they must also accept that the IRA is the inevitable product of Cromwell's massacres and the virtual outlawing of an entire population's religion in the eighteenth century.

The more blindly vicious the actions of an extreme group over a sustained period, the more likely it is that they are the unconscious reverberation of some unresolved past. This does not mean that the English ought to feel sorry for the IRA or show leniency. It does mean that they will not solve the Irish problem by defeating them. Above all, it means that the English posture of boredom, contempt and lack of interest whenever the Irish question is raised reveals much more about the English than about the IRA. See SOLUTIONS.

IRONY Not long ago an American president addressing Congress equated Saddam Hussein and the Iraq war with Adolf Hitler and World War II. Yet no one applauded his deft use of irony. They didn't even laugh.

Like the subjunctive, irony has been dying a slow death. In a civilization devoted to expertise, the emotional pleasures of contradiction are impossible to sell. What people want are the facts and truth.

Serious people believe they must take everything seriously as befits professionals. The only forms of humour which work now are either heavy-handed comedy or in-jokes, as befits a civilization of inside specialists.

It may be that the single option left for serious writers is to avoid irony and the big questions altogether and concentrate instead on re-evaluating in a sober and modest manner the simple words we use every day, for example, by writing a DICTIONARY.

IRRADIATION   Done to dead chickens to prolong their lives.

Particularly popular among Americans. In other countries, vegetables are more likely to benefit. By being radiated in this way, animals and plants receive what Christianity has so far been unable to deliver to humans—an eternal shelf-life in supermarket purgatory.

Irradiation has pitted scientists, technicians and the food produce industry against most farmers and health groups. In spite of the general public's naturally positive feelings towards chickens and vegetables, they may be tempted to react in a surprised manner with such simple questions as— Why bother? What's the rush?

The answer apparently is that irradiation kills bacteria. The produce, like Sleeping Beauty, is thus frozen in time. In the process, unfortunately, the chicken becomes an eternal ghost of the free-range, grain-fed bird. This is because bacteria aren't all that bad. To remove them is to remove the temporal and interesting aspects of life. That's what undertakers do to humans. Irradiated chickens are roughly the equivalent of mummified bodies in an open casket.

But for the hungry, taste is a secondary matter. Production

levels are what count. However, Western agriculture is in a
long-term crisis caused by overproduction. This has driven
down the prices paid to producers so far as to make farming
unviable. The real question is therefore whether we actually
need more food hanging around longer.

In abstract terms it can be argued that irradiation is a
product of progress and is therefore a good thing. If the
result is that only large industrialized farms can break even,
then so be it. That is the truth of the market-place and must
be accepted as such. That is also the ideological premise of
the ongoing world-trade talks known as the GATT.

However, the more we convert to industrial farming, the
more overproduction drives down prices to uncompetitive
levels. How can low prices be uncompetitive? If they are too
low to provide a livelihood to the producer, then the industry has been rendered unviable and therefore unable to
compete in a real market. What's more, industrial farming
has major environmental side-effects which create a real cost
for society as a whole. If factored in, that cost makes this
abstract market still more unrealistic.

The real market wants less, not more. The scientific procedures used before, during and after production are all
expensive. Insecticides, herbicides, industrial fertilizers, hor-
mones, antibiotics and post-production treatment such as
irradiation raise the cost of production while ensuring the
overproduction which causes wholesale prices to plummet.
Pesticides alone represent a cost to producers of some $20
billion per year.[5]

The point is not that all of these advances should be done
away with. That would mean a return to underproduction
and highly uncertain farm seasons. But between two such
extremes there is a great deal of sensible middle ground.

By carefully and selectively reducing the use of these products, production expenses would drop, as would surplus production. The total costs might well remain the same, but
instead of being inflated by industrial overheads and subsidies, they would reflect real farming expenses. The result
could be a reasonable number of people staying on the land,

an appropriate quantity of production, a far more stable market and a shrinking need for public subsidies.

As for consumers, their choice of available produce is greater than ever before in history. We neither need nor want more. What we do want is better produce—food which instead of looking like swollen wax sculptures actually has a taste and may even be good for us. The post-modern miracle of science, the **APPLE**, is losing its appeal.

Consumers worry about the real long-term effects of industrial agriculture on their health. They don't really want to think about the 20,000 yearly "unintentional" deaths from pesticides or the 3 million cases of "acute severe" pesticide poisonings.[6] They know "agricultural run-off" is among the leading causes of water pollution. Even water tables are contaminated, thus raising doubts about drinking water. Thus to argue that industrial agriculture must be accepted because it represents progress is self-contradictory.

As for irradiation, the longer these dead chickens live, the less they taste like chicken. See: **PROGRESS**.

J

JOBS A job is a result, not a cause. It is produced by a combination of factors such as investment, research, development, markets, consumption levels, disposable currency, political stability and a positive economic climate. Jobs cannot be created. Economies are created and they in turn create jobs.

The levels of **UNEMPLOYMENT** throughout the industrial world have been at unfinanceable levels since 1973. This is endemic or structural unemployment. Officially the level in the early 1990s is some 30 million. In reality it is closer to 50 million. Authorities have disguised the full extent of the crisis by repeatedly redefining the term "unemployment" to keep the numbers down.

In Britain the rules have been changed thirty-two times since 1979. Thirty-one of these changes narrowed the definition of who is unemployed. The official figure in the early 1990s was some 3 million. Under the 1979 rules it would be 4 million.[1] A more interesting way of stating this problem of definition is that 30 per cent (some 820 million people) of the world's labour force is either unemployed or not earning a subsistence wage.[2]

Those in positions of authority know the real situation. By the early 1990s political leaders were sufficiently panicked to begin concentrating on job creation. Unfortunately these initiatives are unrelated to the basic economic policies which have been encouraged by the same leaders after being developed and put in place by the public and private technocracy. An increasingly unregulated international market-place, unmonitored technological change and an increase in unsecured part-time labour deprived of benefits combine to render the idea of job creation policies somewhat comic.

Job creation is endlessly evoked in the context of such things as retraining and worker involvement in long-term quality production. Both assume high levels of corporate loyalty.

But the global economy is defined in part as a permanent search for the cheapest production parameters. Corporations therefore increasingly see their employment obligations as short-term. Why then would they invest in long-term training? And why would executives or workers commit themselves to long-term quality production systems? And what possible role could loyalty have in an economy which encourages the employer to abandon the employee at any moment?

Most job-creation theories are either consultant-talk or wishful thinking. When employment ministers get together to discuss the crisis, as they did in Detroit early in 1994, they reappear at the end of their meetings looking bemused.

There are dozens of job strategies they can opt for. But once they are examined with any degree of disinterest, even a fool can see that they are dependent on massive changes in the economic policies recommended by the bulk of the economists, accepted by the quasi-totality of the public and private technocracies, and now finally in place in spite of their inability to produce prosperity or growth.

JOGGING An urban sport whose principal long-term effect is to cripple middle- and upper-middle-class professionals. Enthusiasts include orthopaedic surgeons and running-shoe manufacturers.

JUDGE Modern form of the word "Prince" as originally conceived by Machiavelli.

Given a choice over the final seat of authority, our public and private technocracies prefer a disinterested personage appointed for long periods of time, unattached to daily reality and limited to passive intervention triggered either by disagreement among experts or by the shortfalls in legal clarity.

The natural and continual desire of the corporatist technocracy is therefore discreetly to remove powers from elected assemblies, governments, JURIES and other public bodies in order to transfer them to legal texts dependent first on administration and second on judges, who will arbitrate when required. See: LEADERSHIP.

JURY A body which demonstrates the inherently incomplete nature of law and fact.

Law guides. Fact illustrates. The jury then considers the best possible truth. Its work is an illustration of HUMANIST balance, which explains why the profession of lawyers and judges is constantly reducing the type of cases and the conditions in which juries can be used. See: TRUTH.

K

KANT, IMMANUEL A swamp which has seeped into our minds and separated the intellect from reality.

Genius. Well-intentioned. Devoted to *the supreme principle of morality*. And yet this charming man became the Thomas Aquinas of Reason.

Kant was the first major modern philosopher to spend his life closeted in a university. With him begins the confusion between thinking and teaching. Living in isolation from the realities of his day, he knew about ideas, but knew little about the world from which they sprang or to which they would eventually be applied. Although a talented teacher, he had no sense of the philosopher's obligation to communicate with humanity and so wrote in the most obscure university language. Less than a century after others had made a concerted and partly successful effort to free philosophy from the controls of mediaeval scholasticism, he dragged it back into hermetic dialect.

Kant systematized reason. Divided it into different types. Sought to defend the independence of science and of morality. But this systematization encouraged those who followed to develop impenetrable separations between reality and the intellect which could disarm philosophy as a public weapon.

Specialists who have made a career out of teaching or examining the Kantian mysteries dare others to join them down in the morass where his essential ideas await. To those who refuse to join them they may well thumb their noses with superior contempt. That is a standard military tactic intended to draw an enemy onto unfavourable ground. When they shout out their version of the schoolboy taunt—"Kan't! Kan't!"—the public can quite sensibly stand their ground and reply, "Won't!" See: PHILOSOPHY.

KISS   One sort of kiss is private and involves lovers, babies, relations and friends. The other is public and involves a queen's hand, Christ's cheek, a potentate's toes or the conferral of an honour by someone in power.

The first is a physical emanation of emotion. The second is an expression of power and contract. It is important not to confuse the two.

When the future King of England, Scotland, Wales, Canada, Australia and New Zealand, the descendant of William the Conqueror and Elizabeth I, stood on the balcony of Buckingham Palace some years ago with his new bride and kissed her full on the lips for hundreds of millions of people watching around the world, he confused the private with the public. That is, there seemed to be some confusion between his historic constitutional role and that of a young romantic leading man—a movie star who makes his living by giving public imitations of the private kiss.

Whether kings actually kiss their wives with passion in private is their business. This particular one was the result of a clever idea to modernize the monarchy by making it more exciting. More starlike. Palace courtiers probably developed the plan.

What they missed was that you can't pick and choose among the characteristics of the star. The star is an illusion and therefore contains no separate compartments or functions. Everything being nothing, it's all one. If you act out certain scenes from your private life in public, then like a star, your whole life is dumped automatically into the public domain. There can be no invasion of privacy. Stars make their living off what spectators fantasize about them.

The prince's kiss was a banal Faustian bargain of the sort

which has destroyed dozens of politicians who try to get elected by selling their lifestyle. But a constitutional monarch's case is special. Prince Charming is a stock celluloid myth. As subsequent events demonstrated, mixing it with the myth of legitimacy, which a real king incarnates, automatically risks both. See: **HAPPY FAMILY.**

L

LAGOS A jewel in the crown of the new international economy.

Only twenty years ago this vibrant Nigerian metropolis of 9 million inhabitants was a sleepy little town of 80,000. People from rural villages all over the country expressed their belief in the future by abandoning limited agrarian lives and moving to the capital city. No sooner were they settled in Lagos than it seemed to them as if they had been kept out in the countryside by some form of hypnosis which had chained them to base sentiments disguised as stability, continuity, family life, personal security and a sheeplike desire to eat every day. Thanks to the energizing and liberating forces of competition they are now free to join the modern labour force.

By cleverly refusing to own property or become reliant on sewage systems or clean water, they have developed lean income requirements and so are able to advance themselves as internationally competitive employees. In an imaginative yet hardheaded approach to overpopulation they have managed to achieve record child mortality rates. Finally, in spite of employers' entreaties, they have brushed aside such noncompetitive crutches as job security, pensions and safe work conditions. The courageous children of Lagos, eager to improve their lot, have placed themselves in the forefront of this proud new work force.

Before the flowering of the market system, Nigerians were often limited to mediaeval barter. The world's economic experts could scarcely feel a modern industrial pulse, let alone measure it. Now the planners are able to put this country squarely on the GNP chart with other modern nations at $315 per person per annum. Soon, no doubt, their efforts will carry them even higher. The sky, as they say in Lagos, is the limit. The proof is that the Nigerian branches of international corporations are prospering and so are eager to go on paying their efficient employees.

Some Western leftists denigrate these proud people, call their prosperous capital a "squatters' slum" and their government a military dictatorship. This is the jealous babbling of the lazy. The ambition of the workers of Lagos is an example to all of us in the so-called developed world. If we wish to keep our jobs we also must become competitive. As to the claims of naïve student Marxists and overweight union bosses that the Nigerian workers are being mistreated, this simply demonstrates that we in the West have become so attached to our unearned comfort that we no longer know what competition means. Our grandparents knew. Hard work and dedication. We have become lazy, self-indulgent and dependent on support structures which in today's tough new environment are simply not realistic.

LEADERSHIP   "Why is there such a dearth of good leaders? Because we're in a leadership crisis." This is the chorus of modern lament.

The proverbial wise foreigner—Swift's giant King of Brobdingnag or Montesquieu's Persian in Paris writing home—would probably note that this is a curious obsession for democracies to harbour. Democrats are supposed to be obsessed by their own participation and that of the citizenry in general. Leadership, after all, is the cry of unevolved, craven peoples frightened by the idea of individual responsibility. The sort of people who desire nothing better than a god or a divinely inspired chief to hold them to his bosom, or better still hers, for protection and reassurance. See: **PROPA-GANDA.**

LEFT VERSUS RIGHT   The result of an unfortunate seating arrangement.

In October 1789 the Paris mob, led by women, walked to Versailles, stormed the palace and dragged the king back to town with them. The Assembly had no choice but to follow. Louis was put in his gilded cage, the Tuileries Palace. The nearest building capable of seating several hundred elected representatives in the same room was the palace stables out in what are now the Tuileries Gardens. The need to board and exercise a large number of horses had imposed a particular sort of structure. That shape in turn imposed a semi-circular seating plan on the carpenters brought in to do the emergency conversion.

It naturally followed that those who hated each other most sat as far away from each other as possible, to the extreme right and left of the podium. Thus the needs of horses helped to create our idea of irreconcilable political opposites. Had architecture permitted this semi-circle to complete itself, the reactionaries and the revolutionaries would have found themselves quite naturally sitting together. See: **NEO-CONSERVATIVE**.

LEVEL PLAYING FIELD   An ideological abstraction adopted as a universal value by the management of large corporations.

The level playing field is an idealized vision of the open market. Here the close relationship between corporate mythology and competitive sport is fully consummated. The theory is that, in a world where governments have not falsified the natural rules of the market-place, corporations will be able to go out onto the field and struggle manfully against each other. In these conditions the best "man," that is, the most efficient, will win. The result will be low prices, maximum production and varied choice for the consumer, as well as progress, continual growth and prosperity.

Curiously enough this essentially American concept has an old-fashioned British Empire etymology. But the training of élites on playing fields—Eton's or not—implied an idea of ethics. There would be competition, but it would be fair and good and among gentlemen. There was also never any suggestion that playing fields were places of open or free competition. Or that they were exempted from national regulations. Every second in sport, after all, is controlled by strictly enforced man-made rules.

The playing field is a paradigm of regulations. Its length and width are defined. It is usually marked out with lines across which a player can cross only in defined circumstances. The number of players, their roles, how long they can be on, penalties for breaking rules, regulated uniforms, pads and instruments, the length of each period, the length of the game itself—all of this is regulated and enforced. To the extent that a playing field is made level, it is by complex regulations and, as in golf and horse-racing, man-made handicaps.

Sport is a romantic metaphor for warfare. Real men fight according to strict rules and the winner takes all. The fate of the losers, whether death or humiliation, isn't of great concern. The playing field is unapologetically exclusive. It seeks to promote the winner and exclude the losers.

If the word "level" is defined as meaning unregulated and is added to the term playing field, and that phrase is applied to a whole economy, then a further step has been taken. Not only does such an economy seek to exclude all losers but it attempts to remove the normal restraining rules of sport. On this level playing field there is no room for public service, the public weal, self-restraint, responsibility or any civic virtue.

As a result, the one thing the level playing field is not is level. It is a slippery slope on which only the strongest or the biggest can grab hold. The rest slip down into a heap at the bottom and scratch each other's eyes out in an attempt to rise to the level of survival.

This idea of unregulated warfare appeals to our foolish self-pride by suggesting that only a weakling, a coward or an incompetent could be afraid to come out from behind artificial protection in order to fight like a man. Of course only a

fool rises to this kind of taunting, because an unstructured
playing field favours not only the strong but also the large
and the inefficient. Even with the fairest of rules, smaller
groups must always work twice as hard and be twice as smart.
They must use rapid action, mobility and guerrilla tactics, all
the time keeping a safe distance from the sweeping might of
the great imperial forces. If you remove the rules, you
remove the tools for survival of the small force.

History is filled with a long list of small armies and small
nations who have risen to the taunts of large neighbours.
The next recorded event is their destruction. Whatever the
explanation for these moments of confusion and error, a
fool is a fool and history buries one with little comment.

In short, the people who cry loudest for a level playing
field fall into two categories: those who own the goal-posts
and fools. See: IDEOLOGY.

LOS ANGELES   A Biblical city built, as the parable goes, on
sand, subject to earthquakes, flooding, mud slides, forest
fires, drought, race riots and gang warfare, as well as record
levels of police corruption, violence and pollution. It is
home to the film and television industry, which is devoted to
selling the American way.

LOVE   The solution to all problems in inverse ratio to
income. A state of emotion which is usually, but not always,
focused on at least one other person. A term which has no
meaning if defined. See: ORGASM.

LOYOLA, ST. IGNATIUS   Inventor of the modern rational-
education system by which our élites are trained in staff colleges, business schools and schools of public administration.
He also single-handedly stopped the Reformation by substituting for content what we would call games theory. There is
a castrating or asexual aspect to Loyola's theory of education

which appears to have come quite naturally to him. See:
GANG OF FIVE.

LUDDITES   Highly trained individuals whose careers were
destroyed by technological progress. This progress was
treated as inevitable and uncontrollable. The Luddites therefore occupied the only remaining intellectual position,
which consisted of rejecting technological progress.

This reduction of attitudes to two extreme positions was
accomplished between 1811 and 1830 when the introduction of Watt's steam-engines and water-driven wool-finishing
machines made hundreds of handicraftsmen redundant.
Industrialization was spreading from sector to sector and
quickly eliminated most crafts along with tens of thousands
of jobs.

The Luddites (named after an imaginary leader, Ned
Lud) broke up and burnt factories. Their revolt ended in a
group trial in 1813. Five were hanged. The attitude of society towards unrestrained technological progress was made
perfectly clear. The judge said the Luddites' actions were
"one of the greatest atrocities that was ever committed in a
civilized country."[1]

This was a classic case of provocation and order versus
despair and disorder. Wilfrid Laurier described the nature of
this type of conflict when he spoke in 1886 about the Riel
Rebellion. "What is hateful...is not rebellion, but the despo-
tism which induces that rebellion; not rebels but the men
who, having the enjoyment of power, do not discharge the
duties of power; the men who, when they are asked for a
loaf, give a stone."[2]

What society misunderstood early in the nineteenth century when faced by the industrial revolution was the full
nature of the change. The debate should not have been over
whether there should be technological progress or not. It
was more accurately a question of progress in what conditions: what progress, when, in what circumstances? Market
extremists would argue that what happened was inevitable

and eventually brought general prosperity. Their view ignores the social disorder, followed by suffering, followed by serious social disorder that this approach towards change brought on. Communism was the direct result. England, France, Germany and Sweden suffered recurring internal violence throughout the nineteenth and early twentieth centuries, some of it expanding into civil wars. Most of these countries passed within a shadow of revolution.

The question is therefore not whether technological progress was necessary, but whether it was necessary to go about it in a barbaric manner. It can be argued that the Luddites were wrong in 1811. But society spent the next 150 years rendering progress civilized and thereby proving that the infuriated craftsmen had been right at least in spirit. Did these decades of wasted time, effort, lives and money represent an intelligent use of human talents?

This is precisely the question which the remarkable technological change of the late twentieth century raises. As in the early nineteenth, great social disorder has been unleashed. High levels of unemployment have become so endemic that they are disguised as retirement or pre-retirement or part-time unsecured labour.

The 50 million unemployed in the West are today's Luddites. Their preliminary revulsion can be seen in the rise of destabilizing and often falsely populist movements throughout the West. The question therefore is not whether the automatization of factories, for example, is a good or a bad thing, but whether allowing undirected technology to lead society by its nose will not create far greater problems in the short, medium and even long term than it solves.

Why are we so eager to revive the crises of the industrial revolution? We have the clear memory of what it involved. We are only just beginning to come out of the profound social and political divisions it created. The naïve outsider would be surprised at our determination not to pursue a moderate, balanced approach. See: **PROGRESS**.

LUDENDORFF, ERICH   Brilliant First World War German staff officer whose abstract analyses of military problems consistently produced short-term technical gains followed by long-term real disaster.

In 1914 his revised Schlieffen Plan got the German army almost as far as Paris, but it left them short of their destination and locked into trench warfare. The party with the largest population (the Allies) stood the best chance of winning by default the slugging match which followed simply because they were better able to survive sustained bleeding.

In 1917 he approved unrestricted submarine warfare against the British in order to break their blockade of Germany. This ensured American entry into the war and guaranteed German defeat.

Again in 1917 he facilitated the return of Bolshevik emigrés (including Lenin) to destabilize the new Russian republic and force peace. The result was the Soviet regime which lasted seventy years and in 1945 decimated Germany.

The collapse of his remarkable 1918 offensive led him to believe that his skills had been betrayed by the citizenry. As so often with highly skilled technocrats, they can find no explanation for the failure of their perfect systems and so blame the imperfections of the human race.

Ludendorff was the very model of the technocrat. To the end he believed that reality could be altered by imposing perfect abstract systems. In the postwar period his desire for guaranteed absolute solutions led him to become a Nazi. See: **TECHNOCRAT.**

M

MCDONALD, RONALD   Post-modern philosopher. In somewhat the same way that Voltaire was the public intellectual face of the Enlightenment, Ronald McDonald is the face and the voice of consumer culture.

The moral underpinning of this movement is addiction. The philosophical dilemma proposed by the phrase "fast food" is: how fast can the seller make the buyer buy more? Thus the seller is a spiritual child of those religious leaders who must first incite desire in order then to channel it in a useful direction. Religious leaders can reinforce desire with fear, an advantage not shared by fast-food leaders.

The latter, on the other hand, are reinforced by **ADVERTISING** and science. Since Galileo it has increasingly been argued that scientific progress has fundamentally altered our philosophic possibilities. For example, even before modern public relations, desire was amplifiable by illusion. The desire for fast food is no different. It is based not on hunger but on the illusion of hunger. Science, however, has contributed a better understanding of three key elements capable of accentuating that illusion: salt, grease and sugar.

Salt, somewhat like monosodium glutamate, attacks the taste receptors on the tongue and excites them. If grease is combined with the salt, a chemical reaction is provoked which accentuates this excitement, which in turn translates into a meaningful simulation of hunger. The further addition of sugar will then provoke an abrupt rise in blood-sugar levels. As on a roller-coaster this can only be followed by an abrupt fall, which takes the form of a yet more extreme sensation of weakness and hunger. At this point fast food, through the ingenious use of basic science, comes close to reconstituting the old religious marriage (in fact a philosophical tension) between desire and fear. Indeed, with a new outlet opening somewhere in the world every eighteen minutes, Ronald McDonald may be the most successful scientist/philosopher since Albert Einstein. A suitable heir-apparent to Mickey Mouse. A philosopher-king. See: A BIG MAC and WHITE BREAD.

MACHIAVELLI, NICCOLO   Author of the first how-to-succeed-by-getting-power-and-keeping-it business book, which could have been the non-fiction best-seller for Christmas, 1513. See: GANG OF FIVE.

MAINSTREAM   In the humanist ideal, the mainstream is where interesting debate, the generating of new ideas and creativity take place. In rational society this mainstream is considered uncontrollable and is therefore made marginal. The centre ground is occupied instead by structures and courtiers.

The professional administrators of power—the managerial élites, the falsely Heroic leaders patterned on stars, the stars themselves and the lobbyists—appear to have gained control of the public mechanisms. In a healthy society, particularly a healthy democratic society, this would not be the case. The courtiers would be in the wings gossiping about how to get on stage.

It is easier for an intelligent divine monarch or pope to identify this sort of problem. Being the central repository of power and the sole focus of the courtier, the potentate can easily see the difference between the mainstream and the margins. Thus Pope Julius II sought out Michelangelo, not some reassuring court painter. And Louis XIV did not give power to the Duc de Saint Simon. This was the advantage of strong leadership which many Enlightenment thinkers admired. However, few monarchs or popes are intelligent. And even those who are, are quickly overwhelmed by the flood of power-seekers.

Democratic society's strength—the absence of a concentrated repository of power—is also its weakness. In the disorder of the average day, those with the skills of power can easily present themselves as indispensable, while those with something to contribute will seem insufficiently focused on immediate problem-solving. And so they will be swept aside.

The citizen's problem is how to keep the mainstream open to the needs of the public weal. This can only be done if great effort and care are expended on differentiating content and manners.

MANAGER Drawn from the French word "ménager" or one who does domestic housework, this function has gradually been elevated to the noblest of levels.

The strengths of the manager are continuity, stability and the delivery of services and products from existing structures. Unfortunately managers also discourage creativity, imagination, non-linear thinking, individualism and speaking out, an insubordinate act by which problems are identified. The manager distrusts public debate, abhors any admission of doubt and stifles unpredictable behaviour.

Management is a tertiary skill—a method, not a value. And yet we apply it to every domain as if it were the ideal of our civilization. Our confusion can be seen in the current attempts to revitalize basic school training by aligning it with the "needs" of the business community. In a time of prolonged economic crisis we have decided to concentrate on utility. But these business attitudes are themselves part of the managerial obsession. They reduce even science and mathematics to a narrow, goal-oriented management tool.

If growth and progress are what we need to get out of our crisis, then it will be found not through managerial attitudes but through the release of talents. That means teaching students to think. If mere utility is what we want, then its place is not in the schools but in a revised and modernized apprentice system.

At the level of élite education our assumptions have taken on disastrous proportions. For example, between 1975 and 1993 Canada created 3.1 million new jobs of which 2.1 million were managers or professionals. One million were low-paid and unskilled. Managers and professionals represent an important cost to the economy while producing nothing. Where then is the wealth to come from to pay for the managers? Instead of asking themselves this question, they continually look for reasons to increase the percentage of their own kind in any organization.

The more we train these people as if management were a primary skill, the more we handicap their ability to become citizens capable of providing direction. It is an understatement to say that the Western élites have increasingly failed in their obligations over the last quarter-century. They spend their time cleaning houses that are falling down. See: SAT.

MANNERS   People are always splendid when they're dead. See: POLITENESS.

MARKET-PLACE   The market-place is as amusing and charming as a risqué Peter Pan, endlessly believing in true love yet seeking the pleasure of free love, endlessly re-creating its own virginity, unequipped with memory or common sense, which is its strength and its weakness.

Left to its own devices the market is capable of the most miraculous of inventions and the silliest of self-delusions. It is an extreme romantic. It also has a real purpose—the same one it has always had. That is to organize the supply and exchange of goods or to finance the production of goods—thus facilitating and financing the economy. But the market cannot achieve in a regular and lasting manner its own purpose because it is only an unconscious and abstract mechanism. The factor which must be added in order to create the restraint, balance and consciousness necessary for long-term prosperity is human leadership. That leadership takes the form of effective **REGULATION**.

The market-place is, of course, a very good thing. Without it we are reduced to being exploited by personal or bureaucratic absolutism.

But is it a sufficient foundation upon which to build a society? Does it provide or permit a viable relationship between citizens? Does the market know so much more than we that it would be better to simply defer to it? Must we pray before its opaque inevitability?

In all earlier civilizations, it should be remembered, commerce was treated as a narrow activity and by no means the senior sector in society.

In our current faith built on competition, efficiency and the market-place, the technocrats' role as religious facilitators has been expanded to one of paramount importance. However, the message coming out of this priesthood is sometimes difficult to grasp, with its meaning buried inside the impenetrable dialect of post-modern economics. But if all of that is simply stripped away, what remains is a simple message: our repeated attempts since the eighteenth century to regulate economies have apparently failed. By extension this priesthood is saying that, from classical Greece on, all of our attempts to control the savage economic elements which surround us in order to bring about reasonable stability have been pointless.

It appears that we should have been passive all along. Had we relaxed and let the market decide, this abstract economic force would have found its own natural balance. In other words, what at first glance appears to be a practical, down-to-earth approach to doing business turns out to be a straightforward rejection of the idea of civilization. Part of the explanation is that our contemporary priests are better at **ECONOMETRICS** than they are at general social analysis. Most of them don't really seem to know much about how civilizations function or how humans have dealt with similar problems in the past.

After all, past civilizations have successfully regulated their economic lives over long periods of time. And they have done this to the general advantage of society. Collapse, when it comes, more often has to do with social change than with the forces of the market-place. Societies rise, grow old and die; we all know that. In the meantime centuries of successful economic regulation have made social structures work in places as varied as Athens, Rome, mediaeval Europe and in much of the modern West.

Our priests have reduced past history to its short and sharp failures, instead of concentrating on the long periods of success. Market economists are little more than naïve nihilists. If we were to apply their approach to other areas, painting for example, we would reduce the history of art to chocolate-box pictures and conclude that the human race should stop painting and merely receive images from the landscape which surrounds us. See: HOLY TRINITY–TWENTIETH CENTURY.

MARXIST   The only serious functioning Marxists left in the West are the senior management of large, usually transnational corporations. The only serious Marxist thinkers are NEO-CONSERVATIVE.

Marxism is primarily an analysis of how society works—or rather, how it must work. This dialectic is based upon the struggle of the classes and the battle of the unregulated market-place in which the strongest win. It is a market-place which cannot be tempered, according to Marx. It must and will run free and so function as a battleground between those who have power and those who don't. The market-place will seek to maximize profits even if this is to the disadvantage of most. Profits and power are the truth of the economic struggle and economic determinism will decide the social structure.

Most functioning Marxists had stopped believing this sort of stuff by the end of the Second World War. They had come around to the ideology of stable bureaucratic management. In that they resembled the technocrats of Western governmental and corporate bureaucracies.

But these Western corporate managers and their academic acolytes were in fact thrown into a state of confusion by the collapse of 1929. It seemed as if the pure capitalist analysis, of which they were the official inheritors, had failed. An unrestricted market-place had led not to ongoing growth and prosperity, but to total economic collapse. The ideology of a natural and general equilibrium produced by competition had been given its chance and had self-destructed for all to see and suffer the consequences.

A good thirty-five years passed before the corporate leaders were able to erase from their own memory and from that of the public this failure. They then rediscovered with a virginal ideologic enthusiasm the virtues of the unregulated market.

This time they were supported by an intellectually sophisticated explanation for the dialectic provided by a group of economists centred at the **CHICAGO SCHOOL**. They were able to dispense with the idea that public institutions could achieve social stability, protect the weak or encourage a wider distribution of wealth. Their new argument would have made Marx proud. It was not that they did not wish to help the weak or promote fairness. It was the natural rules of the market-place—the dialectic—which made the class struggle inevitable.

The only disagreement between the Neo-conservatives and Marx is over who wins the battle in the end. This is a small detail. Far more important is their agreement that society must function as a wide-open struggle.

Some people are surprised that Marxism should have re-emerged on the Right. However, ideas, once launched, become public property. And they often reappear in several disguises before discovering their true form.

MELON, THE See: STRAWBERRY.

MEMORY A practical quality which allows us to weigh what has already been done against what might be done now. Memory is therefore a key to responsible action.

The rational method has slowly reduced memory to romanticism. "This power of retaining," as Samuel Johnson put it, "is particularly useful for identifying old actions which have simply been dressed up in new clothes for reapplication by a new generation."[1] In the contemporary Oxford definition, the solid operative words Johnson used are gone. In their place are "recollection, remembrance, remember."[2]

Romanticism is a fantasized version of the past. Unpleasant events and personal or national failures are erased, while comforts and successes are exaggerated. Or wrongs may be exaggerated and comforts and successes erased. On either side romanticism is intended to energize false hopes. In its most exaggerated form it denies the relevance of memory and constructs free-standing abstract ideologies.

Memory—that is, the real power to retain—is central to the idea of a **HUMANIST** equilibrium. It is despised by the sophisticated structures of management, which delight in romanticism as a useful plaything.

MONARCHS, IN PARTICULAR, ROYAL ALLIANCES Essential to the development and spread of rich desserts.

Catherine de Medici arrived in France with macaroons. Marie de Medici was energized by the sugar injections of her Neapolitan pastry chef, who brought such hometown specialties to Paris as the *millefeuille*. The absorption of Normandy by the French kings helped to popularize the northern habit of combining vast quantities of butter and cream with something sweet. King Stanislaus Leszinski of Poland poured rum on his *baba* for the first time in 1736. The Hapsburgs sponsored endless variations on the trinity of bitter chocolate, cream and cake throughout their vast empire. Emperor Franz Josef's favourite was the Ischler Törtchen from Zauner. It has the deceptive appearance of a large double cookie, but the butter-crumbly cake is filled with a chocolate-and-vanilla cream, apricot marmalade on top, bitter chocolate covering that, and sprinkled with crushed pistachios.

That the utility of royal families was coming to an end could be seen in late nineteenth-century Vienna, where so much good work had been done, when Franz Josef's wife, the Empress Elizabeth, had a personal gymnasium installed in her royal apartments and began to watch her figure as if she were an actress. From there to a commoner-become-Princess of Wales who suffered from bulimia has been an unfortunate direct line. See: **WHITE BREAD**.

MONEY MARKETS, INTERNATIONAL   An imaginary market in which a multiple illusion of currencies is speculated upon without reference to the normal agreements on value.

The quantities of money traded bear no relationship to growth or production. They are manifestations of pure inflation. The international money markets represent the regularization, through a specialist technocracy and a revolution in technological communications, of the speculative economy. The South Sea Bubble, John Law and all the other great financial manipulations of the last three centuries have finally been normalized as standard business practice.

Simpler people may be confused. They may feel that the economic instability which has persisted for two decades will not recede until some order and control has been brought to this inflationary speculation. The more sophisticated among us know that times have changed and that markets no longer need to be related to reality. These international money markets are a new truth. Of what and for what is irrelevant. Only the naïve would concern themselves with those questions. There is a market. There is competition. All the rest is idle chatter.

MONEY, THE VOLATILIZATION OF   The act of causing
wealth to disappear from an economy. This is most effectively done through speculation in areas unrelated to
growth.

Societies get into trouble when they begin to believe that
money is real, which it isn't. Those foolish enough to forget
that money is in the nature of a working illusion based on a
tacit agreement about value also tend to mistreat their currency. For example, they may shove it out onto an unregulated market-place where every punter can give it a kick.
They may endlessly print it, which produces classic inflation.
Or they may use it for speculation in an uncontrolled manner, which will cause the money to evaporate. All of this constitutes volatilization and causes poverty.

Money comes closest to respecting the agreement on
value when it is earned and multiplied through investment,
labour and purchasing. Investment and labour produce real
goods which can be bought. The money lent for investment
earns interest for the banks. The wages earned by labour are
deposited in those same institutions. If the banks in turn
lend a reasonable multiple of this money out to people
investing in real growth or in the sort of property which
practical needs make necessary, there is a potential for real
growth in value.

But if banks use this value to speculate or lend to those
who speculate, they risk volatilization. For example, if they
speculate unnecessarily in the international currency markets and lose, then the real wealth created by investment,
production and labour simply evaporates with that lost
money. If they lend it to those who speculate in property, as
has increasingly happened over the last thirty years, then the
day the property boom collapses, the real value which the
speculators had borrowed also evaporates. The same is true
of the large merger and take-over speculations of the last
three decades. And of the international money-market
binges.

Speculators and corporate managers berate us for not
working hard enough to create sufficient wealth to fuel

growth. But a more reasonable explanation for the lack of solid money in our society is that repeatedly over the last thirty years the citizenry have deposited the real wealth they created by investing, working and producing. And repeatedly their élites have borrowed that money and volatilized it. See: **DEPRESSION.**

MORAL CRUSADE Public activity undertaken by middle-aged men who are cheating on their wives or diddling little boys.

Moral crusades are particularly popular among those seeking power for their own personal pleasure, politicians who can't think of anything useful to do with their mandates and religious professionals suffering from a personal inability to communicate with their god. In military terms, a diversionary tactic.

MORO, ALDO A leading Christian Democrat and former Italian Prime Minister. Moro was kidnapped on March 17, 1988, by as yet unidentified terrorists. After a two-month drama in which the police had no success, his body was found in the trunk of a car in the centre of Rome outside 9 via Michelangelo Caetani.

This is a short block away from—in fact equidistant between—the headquarters of the Christian Democrat party and the Communist party, which are just down the street from the Gesù, the Jesuit headquarters which, curiously enough, is across the little piazza del Gesù from the Italian headquarters of the Masonic Order. Only the mafia are missing from this intimate neighbourhood, but then they rarely advertise their office locations and often prefer to work indirectly through the good offices of political, social and religious organizations.

The killers' choice of a drop-off location indicates a sense of humour. Either that or they didn't have far to drive.

There is now a fine life-size medallion of the slain leader's head beside a very large, elegant bronze plaque high on the wall at number 9. The plaque contains several extensive explanatory paragraphs written in a handsome raised lettering, also bronze. Unfortunately the script size is so small that no one can read the message.

MUSEUMS Safe storage for stolen objects.

There are those who bridle at the idea of this thievery. On the other hand, spreading the creativity of the past around the world has protected it against war and disaster. Museums seem particularly concerned by the safety factor since they keep most of their objects in basement vaults. There curators can keep them catalogued and invisible while they go out to complete their collections by buying more or soliciting from COLLECTORS.

MUSSOLINI, BENITO Much more than Hitler, he was the nascent modern Heroic leader. Mussolini combined the interests of corporatism with public relations and sport, while replacing public debate and citizen participation with false populism and the illusion of direct democracy.

His uniforms and strutting manners at first glance date him. But these were only a particularity of the time. His approach may have left an improvised rough-around-the-edges impression, but he was inventing a genre. And it wasn't as rough as all that. He declared himself for and against policies without relationship to his real intentions, rather in the way consumer goods are now test-marketed in search of public desires which can then be exploited. He turned himself into a figure as imaginary as the Marlborough Man, by inventing his own past and arranging for biographies to be written which were pure fiction. Already in 1927 he was saying that "invention is more useful than truth."[3]

Mussolini returned to power in Italy in 1994 in a composite of three leaders. The head of the contemporary fascist party, Gianfranco Fini, had brought his party to its true home by adopting an anonymous technocratic image. Umberto Bossi's Northern League took on all the characteristics of rough-and-tumble false populism to disguise self-interest.

But the most wide-ranging refinement of the Mussolinian principles can be found in Silvio Berlusconi. His control of all private television and use of it for propaganda is flawless. He has adopted the early Fascist policy of advancing behind a major football team. This divisionary "populist" method was laid out in detail in 1939 by Mussolini's son-in-law, Count Ciano.[4] Berlusconi stated after buying U.C. Milan that in the future his empire would be like an iceberg, with the football team being the visible part. The name of his political party is a football chant—Go Italy! As for his rhetoric about free markets, it contradicts his use of monopolies, oligopolies and the technocracy. His rise to riches through close association with the most corrupt of politicians makes a mockery of his promise to clean things up.

None of this is secret. It is all widely and publicly discussed. Yet knowing does not seem to help.

The rise of the new Mussolinians demonstrates the failure of our hope that knowledge could defeat wrong. Knowledge unattached to a sensible balance of human qualities—such as ethics, memory, common sense and reason—is powerless. Knowledge unattached to humanism merely encourages the passive acceptance of what we know to be wrong.

Berlusconi is the modern face of corporatism. But he represents a general, not an Italian phenomenon. Similar false populist movements and individuals are springing up throughout the West. In the United States, English and French Canada, France and Germany they are capitalizing on the anger and confusion in the citizenry. The interests they represent are in large part responsible for the problems they denounce, but their appearances deny the relationship.

The depths of this illusion-versus-reality problem can be seen in the reaction to events in Italy of the weekly magazine **THE ECONOMIST**, the technocrat's Bible. A few days after the election, their lead editorial was devoted to a respectful and ethically neutral analysis of the Berlusconi-Neo-Fascist-Northern League success. What mattered, they concluded, in a tone reminiscent of similar interests faced by, the first rise of corporatism in the 1920s and 1930s, was that the new government "safeguard the economic legacy" of their predecessors.[5] In the next issue, the same page was devoted to railing against the hypocrisy of those who protested the rise of child labour in the GLOBAL ECONOMY. See: CORPORATISM and DIRECT DEMOCRACY.

MUZAK A public noise neither requested nor listened to by individuals. It is the descendant of a school of public relations invented by the Nazis.

The underlying premise of Muzak is that individuals can be reduced to categories. If you can identify which category each individual belongs to, you can make them do what you want by providing the appropriate emotive surroundings and stimuli. The idea is to identify the few standard characteristics which link all individuals or satisfy them in particular circumstances. The Nuremberg Rally was an early attempt at creating this kind of total motivational atmosphere.

Born in elevators and supermarkets, Muzak has spread to restaurants, hotels, airplanes, telephone hold services and waiting rooms.

The public-relations experts believe that human beings fear silence—that is, the absence of constantly imposed direction. It is further believed that if we can be relieved of our fears, we will gain enough self-confidence to buy, eat, vote, fly, or simply go on living.

This approach, with its contempt for individuals, is the product of a false sense of superiority inside the world of public relations. "False" because their superiority takes the form of CYNICISM which is itself a sign of insecurity.

It isn't surprising, therefore, that Muzak often does not produce the intended results. Many people become annoyed when their hearing is invaded, particularly when the sound is persistent. Others fall silent and feel constrained, because they are part of a tradition that believes music should be listened to.

Designed to ease light talk in restaurants, background music more often reduces people to silence or to whispers. Intended to relax passengers as airplanes taxi down runways, it tends to enervate the majority who, had they wanted to listen to music at that moment, would have chosen other music. Places of entertainment or escape have come to resemble miniature brave new worlds where it has been calculated that the individual will disappear into a category. For example, restaurants which are not as good as they think tend to play baroque music. Expensive hotels, which seek to express quality but do not trust the taste of the rich, will mix Mozart and Sinatra together, as if they were one.

When employees are asked to turn it off or down, they reply:

1. The system is beyond their competence.
2. Other people would complain.

When asked whether anyone has ever complained about its absence on a day when it was inadvertently not turned on or, indeed, whether anyone has ever actually requested this sound or asked that a particular section be repeated, the employee will move away from the questioner.

MYRMECOPHAGA JUBATA Ant-eater. The existence of this predator demonstrates that thinking 71 per cent of the time, as ants do, won't prevent you from being eaten. Thinking less than that, as humans do, will almost guarantee it. See: **ANTS.**

MYTHOLOGY Having killed God and replaced him with ourselves, we are dissatisfied with the results. How else can the rise of mythology be explained?

The man-god we opted for was a very narrow being whose powers were dependent on reason. We've now tried him in several costumes—above all, that of the superman and the systems-man. The result has been the reinstallation of a multiplying horde of mythological gods that have been tailored to leave us officially on our throne.

Nietzsche was only the most famous to lay out this pattern. Wagner projected the gods back onto the world stage with heavenly music. Jung gave them the authority of medical science by laying them out as archetypes from which none of us can escape. "Called or not," he had carved over his door, "the gods will come." Hitler and Mussolini combined in a single personage the Greek/Roman gods, those of the woods and rational man. This was so successful that public relations and modern politics still feed off their basic model. Comic-books and films delivered human gods who were somehow the result of an intervention by a deity, based on the model of Zeus sleeping with a mortal or God with Mary. Superman evolved into *Mad Max* and *The Terminator*. Mysterious and powerful aliens began to fill our lives, at first via science fiction, then in films and television series such as *Star Trek* and *Star Wars*.

It was inevitable that false popularizers would roll the Jungian myths together with the all-powerful wood gods and so encourage the idea that if man could not be the only god, then he must be a passive victim of destiny.

But we need not be passive victims. This is the product of the options we have laid out for ourselves. By refusing the larger **HUMANIST** vision, we have left ourselves an unsatisfactory choice between arid reason and the false comfort of mythology. See: **UNCONSCIOUS**.

N

NAFTA Not a free trade agreement.

Signed by Canada, Mexico and the United States in 1994, the North American Free Trade Agreement replaced the 1988 Free Trade Agreement (FTA), between Canada and the United States. It wasn't a free trade agreement either. Long before either treaty was signed all three countries were approaching virtual free trade.

Why then such insistence on the term? This is a classic example of the **DICTATORSHIP OF VOCABULARY.** "Free" carries positive baggage. Who can be against freedom? "Free trade" promises prosperity. Only romantic dreamers can be against it.

NAFTA, like FTA, is an economic integration agreement. It respects the corporatist model in which an unregulated market is given primacy over all other aspects of society by the simple act of excluding those other aspects from the treaty. It places the cheap, unsecured labour of Mexico and the southern United States in opposition to the middle-class labour of Canada and much of the northern United States. The effect on the cheap labour can be seen in Mexico's Maquiladora Zone. The effect on the more expensive can be seen in endemic high unemployment rates.

NAFTA creates the mechanism for a social *fait accompli* without the social issues being discussed. It frees the transnational corporation and its managers from geographical realities and obligations.

This approach is the exact opposite of that used in the European Community, which is attempting to balance political and social realities with market forces. See: FREE TRADE and LEVEL PLAYING FIELD.

NANNYISM   Nannies are foreigners, except in England. The standard English nanny is strong on received wisdom and weak on thinking, more opinionated than bright, self-assured well beyond any understanding of the real world. What nannies do understand is the nature of their power over children, who must be broken to the potty, accustomed to basic prejudices and prepared for life as members of a group, not as individuals.

The average English male Conservative Party voter, member of parliament or government minister either has had a nanny or belongs to a class (the middle or lower-middle) which subscribes to the values of nannyism. No ideological system could be better suited to subduing, using or humiliating the average male. With these individuals in hand, Mrs. Thatcher controlled the mechanism necessary to control the country as a whole.

That some cabinet ministers spoke warmly of her sex appeal says a great deal about their childhoods. Nannies manage children by controlling their bowels and creating a titillation/punishment tension around their genitals.

That Mrs. Thatcher eliminated every other woman in sight should not be attributed to traditional jealousy. Nannies rule alone. Their chief enemy is not wet* dreams or dirty hands, but the only other viable female figure—the Mother—who is an amateur, given to romanticism and liable to use natural rather than meritorious authority over a child.

Nannies impose rich and powerful life-models (dukes, for example, or the United States) on their children because they themselves are insecure snobs and must appeal to ideals above and beyond both themselves and those who employ them.

Nannies never change their mind. That would involve

thinking and doubt. They walk stiffly, briskly and talk energetically to deny the existence of doubt.

Nannies teach their children that strangers and foreigners are dirty, untrustworthy and lazy.

A nanny does not know how to talk to strangers and foreigners. What she does know is that the world contains three categories: the ideal rich and powerful life-model, the parents and the child. Foreigners are neither of the first two. They must therefore be an inferior sort of child and she treats them as such. To the English-speaking foreigner this will appear to be crude but comic behaviour. For those born to other tongues, her bullying approach will sometimes seem inappropriate, but most often inexplicable.

* Mrs. Thatcher insulted the more intelligent sort of Conservative for being weak and "wet." Good boys do what they're told. They control their genitals. What isn't clear is why those who are obedient to their nanny are considered manly, while the others, the bad boys with their wet dreams (a sign, after all, of potency) are treated as if their manhood were in doubt. See: **SPECIAL RELATIONSHIPS**.

NATIONALISM   See: **TRANSNATIONAL CORPORATIONS**.

NATIONALIZATION
1. Ideology.
2. A way to finance political parties.

Nationalization enriches friendly lawyers, accountants, bankers and investors. They then make contributions to their benefactor's party, give jobs to defeated or retiring candidates, enrich the private lives of politicians with travel and entertainment and, in certain cases, fill their on- or off-shore bank accounts.
3. Sometimes a sensible thing to do.

Utilities and essential services are usually created by the state. Sometimes they are created by private investment

and it later becomes clear that the interests of private profit are not the same as those of general public interest.
4. Sometimes made necessary by a change in economic factor.

Private industry may have been interested in the development stage of an essential industry because it offered large profits. But in the long term it will revolve around providing services, not maximizing profits. The market will therefore seek larger profits by increasing the cost to the public, which weighs down the basic social and economic structures. Or it may cannibalize the sector to gain short-term profits by selling off capital goods and property. The job of the government is to maintain the services which the citizenry require.
5. A basic requirement of national defence.

ARMAMENTS production was once largely publicly owned. Now it is largely private. Yet it is an artificial industry entirely dependent upon government money. And its only purpose is to provide for the protection of the citizen through the state. By allowing it to become a private business, we have reduced its primary role of security to a tertiary element. Instead, its new primary aims are to enrich a small number of people, to provide sophisticated make-work projects and to be manipulated as the leading tool of governmental economic management.
6. An area of gratuitous self-gratification when applied as an abstract social theory.

Government ownership may or may not change the effectiveness of these sectors. Only in rhetoric can a clear argument be made one way or the other. Both the private and the public versions of these sectors are run by technocrats. Whether the ownership is a joint stock structure or a governmental structure, there will be little difference in the way they do their jobs.

Governments, like any organization, have the energy to do a good job only in a limited number of areas. A sensible approach is to establish that level and then move sectors in and out of public ownership as required.

7. A way to undermine economic growth.

Unnecessary nationalization impoverishes the national wealth by paying large sums of money to a small number of owners. This could encourage growth by removing large non-growth areas from the market-place while compensating risk-oriented businessmen with money they could then invest in new growth areas. However, the business community reacts to nationalization with fear and anger. They therefore take the cash and invest it overseas. See: PRIVATIZATION.

NATURAL DEATH An odd concept which begs the meaning of the unnatural. It can arrive in four ways, three of which are pleasant:

1. Evacuating your bowels immediately after waking up (described in polite conversation as found dead in the bathroom).
2. During orgasm (died peacefully in bed).
3. While playing tennis or jogging.
4. In old age.
See: DEATH.

NEGATIVE WEALTH A quality proper to business leaders whose debt load is out of control. Less important people and governments do not have negative wealth. They have DEBT.

NEO-CONSERVATIVE The exact opposite of a conservative.

Neo-conservatives are the Bolsheviks of the Right. Like the Bolsheviks, they appear in restrained groups driven by a simple ideology. They seek practical ways to achieve real power in order to make revolutionary changes. These "practical ways" usually involve creating a misunderstanding over the "revolutionary changes" to follow.

The first step in the advancement of a Bolshevik movement

is the establishment of intellectual respectability. This was achieved by hiring bevies of **ACADEMIC CONSULTANTS** to lay out a marginal idea—that the West should revert to the rough capitalism of the nineteenth century—as if it were not only an historic necessity but a natural inevitability. Their determinism literally mimicked the Marxists. What a few years before had been seen as marginal nonsense was now driven home as received wisdom by right wing newspaper columnists.

The second stage involved a series of *coups d'état* within established conservative parties, beginning with those of Britain, the United States and Canada. The movement was then able to enter elections disguised as a conservative renewal. They won power with the support of an electorate which would be among the first to suffer from their policies—the middle and lower-middle classes.

The third step again mimicked the Bolsheviks. This was the key to destabilizing the opposition—including the now-captive and confused conservatives—in order to win re-election. They redefined the political spectrum so that their marginal ideas occupied all of the territory from the extreme right to the centre. This left many conservatives redefined as dangerous liberals (the Wets, moderate Republicans and radical Tories). The liberals suddenly resembled socialists and the socialists, communists. In other words, the great mainstream which had presided over the remarkable rise of the West was squeezed over to the marginal edge of public debate.

Since the essential characteristics of Neo-conservativism are revolutionary, it was perfectly natural for them to begin by disguising their actions behind reassuring phrases. What they believe is that wholesale change in structures is the only way to change society. Continuity, careful progress and memory are their enemy. However, to admit this in the early stages of holding power is to risk losing it. Eventually they felt free to turn on those who rejected their ideas of change and tar them as cowards.

With hindsight it can be seen that the movement was and remains a paradoxical mixture of silly abstract ideology and crude self-interest. The Neo-conservative recipe for public action seemed to have been drawn directly from that of MUS-SOLINI, which turned on praise of free enterprise, insistence on the need to reduce bureaucracy, suggestions that unemployment relief was part of the economic problem, *sotto voce* hints that social inequalities should be increased not removed, and an aggressive foreign policy.[1]

By the early 1990s they had so successfully redrawn the intellectual map that whenever liberals returned to power they spent their time mouthing Neo-conservative formulae. At the same time, a growing number of political parties appeared who were openly corporatist or Mussolinian. Thanks to the respectability given their ideology by the Neo-conservatives they could present themselves as moderate conservative reformers. They began to make serious political inroads in Canada, the United States, Germany and, of course, Italy. There, three parties drawn from the Mussolini mould triumphed in the 1994 general election. No Neo-conservative movements elsewhere in the West expressed despair or concern.

All of this explained why the Neo-conservatives treat CYNI-CISM as a sign of wisdom. It is not unreasonable to place them among the last true MARXISTS, since they believe in the inevitability of class warfare, which they are certain they can win by provoking it while they have power.

NEW WORLD ORDER A sweeping vision of a changed world in which life will be both different and better. This concept projects the assured resonance of ideology although devoid of ideological content, as well as of sweep, as well as of content. In the past the word "new" has usually been inserted into political programs when the intent is to erase all memory of past experience. The use of the word "world" betrays a certain megalomania. And "order" resonates with a long history of para-military projects.

The reaction of many sensible people to the New World Order was that we might do better to be kind to ourselves.

After half a century of putting up with two rival—and once new—world orders, it might be nice to relax into the luxurious sloth of not trying to build a new New World Order right away. Something more modest might be appropriate.

These concerns were not fully expressed before fashion changed and this new dream was abandoned and forgotten.

NIETZSCHE, FRIEDRICH Mussolini's favourite writer—filled him with "spiritual eroticism."[2] See: MUSSOLINI.

NIHILISM The only socially acceptable attitude for those who reject Western society's evolution into a civilization of structure which has a place in the grid for each individual.

In the words of Cioran, the most eloquent and bitter of contemporary nihilists, "If you try to be free, you die of hunger. They will not tolerate you unless you are successively servile and despotic."[3] Nihilism is acceptable because its refusal provides breathing space for discontent without creating the threat of an alternative. Nihilistic rock or rap, nihilistic movie heroes, nihilistic lost-generation novels. These attitudes of despair provide a steam-release valve for social pressures. Nihilism is preferred over ideological refusals, even though those are dependent on wholesale change and therefore, in practical terms, also provide harmless breathing space.

The one truly unacceptable social attitude is to refuse refusal while limiting acquiescence to conscious cooperation. This means constantly judging a society which insists upon being taken for granted.

O

OIL

1. Illustrates that price is rarely related to cost in a free-market system.

   In this case cost is rarely more than a few pennies, the price rarely less than double-digit dollars. The differential can be glimpsed in the ease with which the oil states (and indirectly the oil companies) financed the entire Gulf War; $626 billion in 1990–91 alone.

2. Illustrates that "strategic" commodities cannot be priced by buyer-seller competition.

   Oil acquired this status the moment it was widely used. In fact the status was actually declared by the First Lord of the Admiralty, Winston Churchill, before the First World War, when the decision was made to rebuild the British navy, then the largest in the world. The non-competitive nature of strategic goods is usually forgotten by those who want to use the market-place to reduce the cost of **ARMAMENTS**.

3. Illustrates that if a strategic commodity is strategic, people will go to war over it.

   Once Saddam Hussein had been thrown out of Kuwait, none of the Allies worried very long about whether he stayed in power or what he did to his minorities. Nor did they worry about whether the returning Kuwait regime would rule in a less mediaeval manner. The oil delivery system had been restored and that was the cause of the war.

4. Illustrates that the Holy Trinity is still a viable concept.

After all, oil is a commodity we consume on our way to buy more while driving on a petroleum-based surface.

OLYMPIC IDEAL   The Greek games began in 776 BC as a competition among amateur athletes from the different city-states. The purpose was to bring the citizens of the rival cities together in an apolitical gathering, which would reduce squabbling and develop a larger sense of community.

The rising merchant class in those cities subsequently inverted their purpose by introducing the idea of city rivalry into the games. The city-states then began subsidizing their athletes indirectly and often invisibly. The amateur athletes were soon living a parody of amateurism. They had careers and future income riding on the competition. Winners became heroes, that is to say political heroes. They were fed at the cost of the state for the rest of their lives.

Subtle corruption gradually turned into rank dishonesty. Athletes were eventually bribed to lose. In AD 394 the games were abolished because they had become a parody of the amateur idea, a focus of corruption and a source of political rivalry.

The Olympic Games were re-established in 1896 as a competition among amateur athletes. One of the purposes was to bring citizens of rival countries together in an apolitical gathering. What the Greeks managed to do in 1,170 years, we have done in less than 100. See: **XENOPHOBIA.**

ONE   One should never say "one." It is a neutered pronoun which suggests that one is too proper to have a sex. A term once popular in Victorian parlours, it is now most at home in committee meetings where everyone wants to have one's way, but no one wants to take responsibility.

OPTIMISM   When applied by ourselves to ourselves, a pleasant and sometimes useful distraction from the oppressiveness of a day and the certainty of death.

When encouraged as a social attitude it is an infantalizing force which removes the individual's conscious power to criticize, refuse and **DOUBT**. Optimism, like patriotism, is the public tool of scoundrels and ideologues. See: **PESSIMISM**.

ORAL LANGUAGE   From Draco and Solon in early Athens onward our oral talents have gradually been displaced and eventually diminished by our talent for writing. That this progress from the oral was indeed an improvement doesn't need to be argued. Cultures entirely dependent on the spoken word become its prisoner. The story of our progress in writing materials has run parallel with an explosion in the human imagination.

Yet even though the oral no longer had any quantifiable utility beyond common daily intercourse, it never lost its energy. This was because, as Harold Innis demonstrated in *The Bias of Communication*, those who have power always attempt to control language and knowledge.[1] They have found it possible to control the written language for lengthy periods of time. Then there is an explosion that has invariably been ignited by the force of the uncontrollable oral.

Among these moments of piercing directness there is, of course, Socrates, with his refusal to write anything down. Christ's preaching, St. Francis's disarmingly innocent verbal rebellion. Dante, although writing, was consciously attempting "to be of service to the speech of the common people."[2] The simple elegant prose of Erasmus was after the same thing. Written. But written in such a way that the oral process was freed from the prison of theology—that is, ideology— and scholasticism. The plays of the Renaissance now seem to us very written, but then they were a response to censorship and largely unpublished, with a last minute ad libbed quality. Pamphlets and the novel, as Swift and Voltaire demonstrated, were developed not for study, but to be read as if they were spoken and, indeed to be read out loud so that those who didn't or couldn't read could participate. Newspapers were invented as an answer to suffocating scholasticism. They arrived with an urgent, last-minute thrown-together sense of information and opinion so recent that it was hardly written. And the whole phenomenon of parliaments, assemblies, public rallies and public debates represented a great oral swelling which brought us democracy and citizens' rights.

The twentieth century has produced a qualitative change in this written-oral tension. There is now more free-floating knowledge, information and opinion than we could ever know what to do with. We are drowning in information which, being unlimited, without shape and rarely of applicable relevance, has itself become a form of control.

For the first time knowledge is not power. Instead public language has become a disordered distraction. The centre of power has moved to a second language which is made up of a myriad specialist dialects. It is not powerful because it is functioning language—it isn't—but because each dialect is attached to a mechanism of practical power.

This scholastic language doesn't mind being obscure, ineffectual, meaningless or boring. It has none of the pretensions of real language. It is simply the instruction manual of the corporatist system. Irrelevance as a language of general communication is what gives it power.

Meanwhile the first level of language floods out through satellites beaming five hundred television channels and information highways delivering endless quantities of information. The effect is to solidify the division between language and power. The very quantity of what is being delivered reduces the citizen to the role of passive receiver and so makes language unusable as an effective weapon against power.

This is one of the explanations for the return of inevitability in public affairs on a scale unseen since Solon and Socrates began to break down the passivity imposed by the gods and destiny of Homeric myth.

It seems now as if the progress in writing materials has bypassed linguistic utility, at least for the moment. For the first time, not controlled but an uncontrolled written language has become a force for human passivity.

Many of us feel a certain innocent pleasure when we are absorbed in this maze. Millions more every year dive into their personal electronic screens and swim like eager minnows through the shapeless sea of information as if the ability to swim were in itself a victory or a power.

The very idea of power prospering from uncontrolled instead of controlled passivity is truly something new. The traditional idea that some sort of freedom and control over those in power can be achieved by reverting to a simple oral language simply doesn't work when modern communications systems are drowning us in an oral language which has no practical relationship to power.

But true oral language is not simply spoken. It is also tied to a certain use. For a start it is aggressive and inquisitive. This Socratic model has perhaps finally come of age.

The point is not to plunge into quantities of information or to be absorbed into majestic highways of information. To the extent that the information and activities involved are facilitated then so much the better. But this is the illusion of language. It is little more than information gathering, like a municipal employee picking up litter with a pointed stick.

Oral language is more properly an individual expressing concern. It can be practically applied by emulating that annoying old man who arrived early every morning in the market-place in order to begin upsetting as many people as he could by asking endless blunt questions. See: SOCRATES.

ORGASM The most common emotive experience, sometimes shared, sometimes not.

Although the orgasm is technically a muscle spasm related to the reproductive process, human imagination relies upon its status as a conscious emotional act. According to the World Health Organization there are 100 million of these every day, making it thousands of times more common than birth and death.[3] For those who do not see themselves as having replaced **GOD**, it is a workmanlike replacement for a religious experience. Samuel Johnson defined it as a "sudden vehemence,"[4] which may be why the orgasm has become the last refuge of twentieth-century individualism. See: **PENIS**.

P

PANIC   A highly underrated capacity thanks to which individuals are able to indicate clearly that they believe something is wrong.

The managerial approach, so dominant in our society, does not include the possibility of error. It depends on sequential expert solutions. If there is a problem, the relevant expert will suggest an adjustment. Panic here can only mean that a situation is out of control; that is, the individuals who are meant to be managed are individually out of control.

Given their head, most humans panic with great dignity and imagination. This can be called democratic expression or practical common sense. Managed control, on the other hand, can be termed structural ideology; that is, an ideology not of content but of form. See: **CONTROL**.

PARTICIPATION   Democracy is built and maintained through individual participation, yet society is structured to discourage it.

And ours is the most structured of civilizations. Forty-hour work weeks. Work breaks calculated to a minute. Weekends measured for recuperation. Various specific leaves for sickness and giving birth. Set holiday periods. Official days of celebration or mourning. When it's all added up and the time to eat, copulate, sleep and see families is included, twenty-four hours have been accounted for.

The only built-in space of time for individual participation is a fixed period for voting, which probably averages out to an hour a year. The only time society formally organizes extended participation is over matters of violence. (Military service or when a judge orders convicted criminals to do public service.)

Why is the function which makes democracy viable treated as if it were expendable? Or rather, why is it excluded by being reduced to a minor activity requiring the sacrifice of time formally allotted to other things?

Nothing prevents us from revising the schedule to build in four or five hours per week for public participation. Our failure to do something like this is a statement either about the state of the democratic ethic or about the real nature of power in our society. See: **CORPORATISM**.

PEACE DIVIDEND   One of those amusing little phrases used for about twelve months by people in the know.

Like "the **WAR ON DRUGS**," "the recession is over" and "peace in our time," this term belongs in the short-term Utopia category.

What with disorder in the former Soviet Bloc and fear that a major cut-back in **ARMAMENTS** production might cause more economic problems, it has since been decided that there will not be a peace dividend after all. No one has actually announced this change in plans. To do so would suggest that the citizenry remember what they have been told. The peace dividend has simply disappeared from the lips of everyone in the know. Better not to tax the populace at large with the complexities of continuity, and just get on with the next amusing phrase. See: **DUAL USE**.

PECTORAL MUSCLES   Every young man should have two large ones. The question is what to do with them thirty years later when they transmogrify into breasts.

PENIS All organized societies are dedicated to controlling the use of this remarkable instrument. Yet the cultures of these same societies, whether through fiction, film, advertising, social mythology, even jokes, are devoted to praising the penis as innately uncontrollable.

This contradiction can be seen most clearly among elected officials, in particular presidents and prime ministers, who are far more potent than the average citizen. Careful calculation of the time spent by Presidents Kennedy and Mitterrand in corporeal activity will confirm that, once meals and sleep are deducted, little more than an hour and a half per week remained for the governing of their respective countries. In spite of the republican and democratic revolutions of the eighteenth and nineteenth centuries, the modern leader has inherited the all-powerful penis of the old divine monarchs, itself inherited from such interfering gods as Apollo and Zeus.

Elected leaders are so potent, in fact, that we feel obliged to insist upon their remaining semi-chaste—that they limit themselves to monogamous sex, preferably with the bride of their youth, particularly if she resembles their mother. It is a proof of our progress that the Greeks never gained such control over their gods. This is a modern adaptation of the old Egyptian rule that the only safe way to produce an heir was to marry the Pharaoh to his sister.

The practical philosophical point seems to be that semen expended in other than a legally sanctioned vagina bleeds public policy to death. See: **SEX**.

PESSIMISM A valuable protection against quackery.

Of greater use to the individual than scepticism, which slips easily into cynicism and so becomes a self-defeating negative force. Pessimism is a conscious filter which disarms ideologues and frees us to act in a practical manner.

The only dangerous pessimist is the one who has power, is optimistic about himself and pessimistic about those he governs. Imprisoned as our society is by rhetoric, these public pessimists are increasingly hard to identify. They can be identified by their tendency to go on constantly about solving problems, finding solutions, creating prosperity, winning wars and ending crime; yet the more optimistic their rhetoric, the more pessimistic their real actions.

The healthy pessimist moderates his public actions with self-doubt and listens carefully for the reverberations in society which can be translated into sensible opportunities. Élites who are optimistic about themselves and pessimistic about the governed are ready to be changed.

PHILOSOPHY Is either about language or thought. Or both. But language is about public communication and it has been some time since the philosophers communicated with a quantity of people large enough to be called the public. Language is either public or it is an expert's dialect, which is a far lesser thing. Philosophy cannot be a lesser thing since it leads the way in examining and encouraging thought. What value could thought have if no one but a few professionals could think it? It would be little better than an instruction manual for a VCR.

Surely language and thought are about reality. And so are humans. How then could philosophy be about language and thought if its obscurities cut it off from reality and so from the people it is meant to serve?

Philosophy has not been so locked into the padded cell of internal references for internal reference's sake since the era of the mediaeval scholastic strait-jacket. Yet it remains central to understanding the strengths inherent in Western civilization. Amplified by history and literature, philosophy must be a tool of realism which repeatedly permits us to rediscover ourselves and shed the linguistic obscurantism of whatever power structure is in place. In doing so, we alter or shed the structure itself.

Philosophy's flight from reality has paralleled the rise of expertise and professionalism. This began seriously at the very moment that the ideas of the eighteenth-century

Enlightenment philosophers—who had spent much of their lives fuelling public debate by striving after clarity and communication—were becoming a central part of political experiment. In Germany, in their shadow, a more private and obscure philosophical approach was emerging. IMMANUEL KANT was more than a genius. He was the first great modern SCHOLASTIC. The liberating philosophers of the seventeenth and eighteenth centuries had struggled with ideas outside of the universities. With Kant philosophy was dragged back inside where the scholastic tradition could reassert itself.

Two centuries later it can reasonably be asked whether philosophy is any more than one more among thousands of professions. At its worst it resembles accountancy, with professors of the history of philosophy mistaken for philosophers and busy limiting their profession to the arranging of ideas in plus and minus columns.

Language depends on the use of mutually agreed-upon terms—not because they represent truth, but because they provide a medium for communication. However if the terms and phrases have been so elaborated by specialists that they are mutually agreed upon only by the experts, then they are no longer a medium for communication but a dialect for exclusion.

In some areas—the sciences, for example—the maintenance of a truly common language is more difficult than others. There is a strong temptation in philosophy to invoke this clause of unavoidable complexity. But the counter-argument is that philosophy must be what it has always been; that is, central to the reality of our civilization. That means it must remain within the terms of real communication.

For example, the return in force during the 1980s of the discredited nineteenth-century *laissez-faire* approach to society happened as if its disciples were presenting a new truth. The philosophers were under an obligation to help everyone understand that what was being proposed was a return to a specific past which included a well-documented philosophical

history. The installation in the late twentieth century of a
CORPORATIST structure within the democratic states has come
without any public debate, thanks in part to being disguised
in a new vocabulary. Why were the philosophers unable to
explain this? The memory of corporatism as a tool of fascism
is, after all, only fifty years old. And why have they been
absent from the debate which has transformed so much of
popular democracy into a system eager for anti-democratic
Heroic leadership disguised as false populism?

These three examples are not minor political incidents.
They are no less important than the Lisbon earthquake or a
profusion of corrupt courtiers or the laws restricting religious belief which brought the philosophers of the seventeenth and eighteenth centuries out into the public place.
These are some of the major events which make our time
what it is and yet philosophy remains virtually absent from
the scene.

PLATO   Brilliant novelist. Accomplished humourist. In spite
of which he wasn't as much the author of Socrates as he
would have wished.

Socrates and Aristotle remain the martyr and the genius
of the Western intellectual tradition. However, it was Plato
who—like St. Paul and Thomas Aquinas for Christianity—
acted as the general manager charged with shaping our
understanding of the past and therefore our expectation of
what we might be able to do in the future.

The democratic citizenry in Plato's model could only be a
childlike mass incapable of evolved—that is, disinterested—
thought. And thus incapable of looking after the public
good, because dominated by superstition, prejudice and
fear. The enlightened aristocracy of Knowers that Plato prescribed as the solution to the citizenry's flaws is the élite
which our rational corporate society has persisted in producing.

Given Plato's success in locking his argument into place, it
isn't surprising that today, as in Athens, democracy works to

educate and create the sort of élites who do not believe in democracy.[1] In fact, the Platonists have always taken themselves so seriously that they miss Plato's fictional and ironic talents. They have interpreted him as being more severe about the weaknesses of the populace than he actually was.

As for Plato's intellectual position, it did not spring entirely out of cool philosophical musing. It was partly the product of his reaction to the Athenian treatment of Socrates. What Plato retained from his master's tragedy was that Athens' greatest thinker had been unjustly accused under a democratic system and had responded with a defence speech which Plato interpreted as showing contempt for the 501 jurors who represented the citizenry. They in turn convicted him. This was the searing emotional drama which determined the slant of Plato's theories.

Bitterness. Contempt. A desire for revenge. These are tricky components in the construction of a philosophy—particularly if the writer is a genius with an important contribution to make. The greater the genius, the more likely it is that he will be able to redefine these destabilizing factors as if they were disinterested theory.

The result of Plato's successful absorption of his master's ideas is that there are a lot of Platonists around who think of themselves as having a Socratic approach to life. The key to this may be that the former is presented as a state of being and the latter as an attitude or a method. To the extent that Plato invented Socrates, this confusion is perhaps not surprising.

But the messages are quite different, even opposite. We can only imagine that Plato worked hard to make his master's mind appear to be one with his own. He must have been restrained by some combination of Socrates' penetrating genius, which could control a posthumous scribe; Plato's own genius which, however bitter, held him to a reasonably faithful reconstruction; and perhaps most important, the presence in Athens of an audience which also remembered what Socrates had said and done.

In spite of the obvious and profound differences, our own

civilization seems unable or unwilling to see these two men as separate entities. Yet it is the Platonic tradition which has fed the corporatist, technocratic, anti-democratic ideology. The humanist, citizen-based, democratic movement has been nourished by SOCRATES.

PLATOON A film which confirmed its director, Oliver Stone, as the legitimate heir to Leni Riefenstahl. As in *TRI-UMPH OF THE WILL,* false mythology is created making nonsense of reality without seeming to use manipulation or propaganda.

Platoon presented itself as the first attempt to reconcile Americans with what had happened in Vietnam by telling the everyday truth of how soldiers experienced the war. It was indeed constructed to heal the still-suppurating wound inflicted on the greatest nation in the world by its defeat in open combat at the hands of a small, poor, Third World country.

Stone's method was built upon a deceptively simple dramatic conflict. His platoon was made up of a young, naïve and well-intentioned officer who commanded young, well-intentioned soldiers, including the naïve hero, Chris. The source of power in the group was a blondish, pale, beautiful, gentle yet strong and wise sergeant. These people all believed in the American dream and saw themselves as victims of injustice. The source of power in their company was also a sergeant—a senior staff sergeant. However, he was dark-skinned, cynical, scarred and cunning. The first represented the American ideal; the second was the devil. To be more exact, the second represented a constant in American history—the traitor, Benedict Arnold in modern dress, the man who believes that men of principle are weak, the force of evil within each person and therefore within the nation. His cynicism and crude interpretation of reality enable him to trick others into temporarily betraying the American dream.

The film rises through two successive apocalypses. The first ends with the Christ sergeant being abandoned to a swarm of Viet Cong while the company rises above him in helicopters in the care of the devil sergeant. It is a false resurrection. A betrayal. We last see the good man who died for them on his knees with his arms out as if on a cross.

In its final culmination of apocalyptic violence—a confused night of smoke, explosion, light and sound—the platoon is defeated without the Viet Cong becoming visible. They remain vague shadows in the trees. They can not appear. In Stone's mythology America is neither fighting Vietnam nor defeated by it. America is struggling to defeat the enemy within itself. The great and good people are attempting to cast out the devil. The early morning reveals a wasteland of bodies, some half-alive. One is the devil sergeant, another the naïve hero. He executes the devil, thus freeing America.

The film ends with his rising from the disaster, again in a helicopter. In voice-over, Chris reflects as he is evacuated:

> Looking back, we did not fight the enemy, we fought ourselves—and the enemy was within us.... The war is over for me now, but it will always be there—the rest of my days.... Be that as it may, those of us who did make it have an obligation to build again, to teach to others what we know and to try with what's left of our lives to find a goodness and meaning to this life.

This is the true resurrection.

Stone has vaporized the defeat by converting it into the caricature of a morality play about a civil war. The wound of defeat was converted into a cathartic experience in which the American dream persisted.

Art heightens **MEMORY**. As Riefenstahl demonstrated, propaganda can erase it, as well as any sense of ethical reality. Stone's visual manipulation literally exorcised the public's memory of failure and of responsibility. In the aftermath of *Platoon*, other films, such as *The Hill*, were made, reflecting this new perception, and slowly the general manner in which the whole war was treated softened and became positive.

POLITENESS   A mechanism of control distinguished by urbane, smooth, courteous, refined and other agreeable mannerisms of social intercourse. We are conditioned to think of this control in classic Marxist terms as a phenomenon of vertical class structure. Those divisions still exist with their paraphernalia of the said and the unsaid—the said being about control, the unsaid about power.

But in a **CORPORATIST** society the real class divisions are horizontal. Thousands of specialist groups—public, private, interested, even disinterested—are spread throughout society like inaccessible volcanoes sending up little puffs of smoke as their official communication with the outside world. This is corporatist politeness: the solutions, the answers, the truths all swathed in the expert **DIALECT** of the particular class. A second, more complex level of dialect is used inside the volcano as the equivalent of the old social "unsaid" with all its assumptions of rightfully held power.

An obsession with polite or correct public language is a sign that communication is in decline. It means that the process and exercise of power have replaced debate as a public value.

The citizen's job is to be rude—to pierce the comfort of professional intercourse by boorish expressions of **DOUBT**. Politics, philosophy, writing, the arts—none of these, and certainly not science and economics, can serve the common weal if they are swathed in politeness. In everything which affects public affairs, breeding is for fools. See: **PUNCTUALITY** and **VOLTAIRE**.

POWER, PUBLIC   The single purpose of power is to serve the public weal.

There's nothing new about this. The Encyclopaedists said it clearly in the eighteenth century:

> The aim of all government is the well-being of the society governed. In order to prevent anarchy, to enforce the laws, to protect the citizens, to support the weak

against the ambitions of the strong, it was necessary that
each society establish authorities with sufficient power
to fulfil these aims.[2]

Do those who gain power, administrative or political,
understand this? Is the system in which they labour designed
in order to make this possible? Does the "sophistication"
required to succeed in contemporary technocratic systems
turn power into the sort of self-justifying goal which rewards
courtesanage rather than the service of the public weal?

These are simple questions which have been asked many
times over the centuries. Each time the reply is of vital
importance to the lives of those whose society is at stake.

PRAETORIAN GUARD   See: WHITE HOUSE STAFF.

PRIVATE LIVES   The private lives of public people may be
considered private only so long as they don't trade on them
to advance their public careers.

If an individual presents himself to the public for election
as a happily married father of three, then he has made his
weekend with a secretary or his visit to a prostitute of either
sex a matter of public interest. If he makes a point of drinking milk in public, then the public will want to know whenever he gets drunk. If he buys his suits at Wal-Mart for the
cameras, then proceeds to holiday on rich men's yachts, he
will be photographed with telephoto lenses. But if he were to
present himself to the public for election as a believer in specific policies, he might well be judged on those while his
genitals, interesting though he himself might consider them,
would be forgotten by those not directly concerned as being
of little relevance to the public good. He would probably
even be able to fall down drunk in public from time to time
without anyone much caring so long as the interests of the
citizenry were being looked after. See: *AD HOMINEM.*

PRIVATIZATION

1. Ideology.
2. A way to finance political parties.

Privatization makes friendly lawyers, accountants, stock-brokers, bankers and investors rich. They then make contributions to their benefactor's party, give jobs to defeated or retiring candidates, enrich the private lives of politicians with travel and entertainment and, in certain cases, fill their on- or off-shore bank accounts.

3. Sometimes a sensible thing to do.

There are new areas of development in which the public interest is served by public involvement. When that area is well established it may be a good idea to transfer it to the private sector so that the public can concentrate on new areas of development. This suggests that capitalism is not very good at substantial risk when it involves long-term investment. It also suggests that the private sector owes a debt of gratitude to the citizenry who have been willing to risk their painfully accumulated shared wealth in order to encourage innovation.

4. A backward step if utilities or essential services are involved.

Privatization means a return to the sort of private monopolies which two centuries of experience taught us were politically and socially dangerous. The basic needs of the populace cannot be entrusted to the linear and short-term needs of private investors.

5. A way to undermine growth.

Privatization encourages private investors to lock up their capital in utilities or well-established sectors which are dependent on stability and rarely at the centre of innovation. This money is no longer available to be invested in those risk areas which encourage new ideas and create GROWTH. See: INEFFICIENCY and NATIONALIZATION.

PROGRESS   Often presented as the central moral tenet to succeed Christianity, progress is a complex and ambiguous mixture of technique and ideology.

This ambiguity is erased in our society by reducing the subject to a simple question: Are you for or against progress? thus denying any middle ground. The imposition of a false question to create an equally false moral quandary is a strategy often used by ideologies to ensure the desired answer To be for is to seek the salvation of mankind (and more recently of women). To be against is to join the LUDDITES and other pessimistic sentimentalists in their dark corners of refusal, destruction and disorder.

Like most ideological terms, the actual meaning of progress is vague. Historically it has meant not improvement but movement—that of a king, for example, making his progress across the kingdom. We, of course, have the right to change the meaning of words. Indeed political movements and *académie* fix definitions which suit their interests. But language will end up meaning whatever a civilization wants it to mean.

But precisely what progress are we referring to when it is evoked as a moral necessity? The progress of the species mankind itself? In which domains? Physical? Mental? Ethical?

Does our health-obsessed population on average run faster farther longer than the average Athenian or Spartan citizen? Is the Western individual as capable of hard physical labour as the eighteenth-century European peasant or the settler in the new world? We are taller than they were, but is that progress or simply a matter of protein? We live longer, but that is not a change in the species itself.

Our civilization knows more than mankind has ever known. Yet it would be difficult to argue that the brain itself has progressed. We still function on a series of basic principles laid down between 500 BC and AD 300. There have been some serious amendments, for example in the sixteenth through eighteenth centuries, but nothing radical since then.

As for ethical progress, it would take a remarkable imagination to prove the case, living as we do at the end of the most violent century in history, with Western middle-class governments eliminating essential support systems for the poor and children constituting some half the clients of food banks.

Where we have made progress is in what we can do or construct. The progress of knowledge. Technical progress. Social progress.

But can a specific example of progress be counted as an improvement if it is not part of an integrated change? In other words, does not each specific progress carry within it the power to destabilize other elements if there is no integration? An unintegrated improvement may actually provoke an equal regression. Or an improvement may prosper beside an equal regression which will negate it.

Human life itself is a good example of this. Remarkable scientific breakthroughs over the last century have permitted us to live longer and longer. However, parallel and often related scientific breakthroughs enable us to kill each other with increasing efficiency and in ever larger numbers. Medical science has progressed, been converted into drugs and equipment and applied to large national and international structures thanks to precisely the same methods which have permitted the invention, production, sale and use of arms with which we have maintained record levels of violent death throughout the twentieth century. Perhaps most interesting has been the parallel regression in ethical standards among our highly trained élites who manage this creativity, sale and violence. They are the result of the same education system which produces doctors and medical scientists and manufacturers of medical drugs and equipment.

The standard explanations for these contradictory activities are professionalism, the technological imperative and practical reality. What is forgotten is that applied ethics are always central to an integrated view of the human experience. Whatever the political fashions and obsessions of the moment, history eventually judges progress by that standard. Progress as we have chosen to define it today admires and rewards disintegration.

Beyond needing integration to be effective is the even more basic idea that, without applied memory, progress is merely spasmodic—a sort of uncontrolled muscle spasm which may do as much harm as good. This idea of applied memory isn't very popular in scientific, corporate or even managerial circles. They are more interested in the momentary excitement of discovery, of isolated competitive combat and of pure power.

One of the accurate truisms of history is that a civilization which allows the quality of its water and of its water distribution system to decline is on the way out. Over the last 2,000 years we have had clean running water in our cities three times.

The Romans installed complex engineering systems to gather water from distant sources and deliver it via aqueducts to their cities. Once there it was distributed through an intricate underground grid, often from house to house. Remains of these systems can be seen even in the foreign provinces of the Roman Empire.

For half a millennium these systems seemed to disappear. Then with a sophistication greater than the Romans, the Arabs reintroduced them. After conquering Egypt in 803 they built Al Fustat, the original Cairo, with the equivalent of a septic tank under each house.[3] In Morocco, in Fez, part of the twelfth-century system still operates, delivering water to each house via ceramic pipes. The river from which it has always collected its water is now badly polluted. However, the delivery pipes still work, each of them graded in size according to a taxation schedule. Larger house, larger pipes, higher taxes. Thanks to these widespread and varied systems the Islamic world was able to develop some cities of 400,000 to one million inhabitants (Baghdad, Cordoba, Al Fustat) and many of 100,000. At that time—the glorious era of Charlemagne—Christian Europe couldn't manage more than 10,000.

We in the West began slowly to install complex urban grids 150 years ago. At first we simply delivered dirty water. Then we discovered the advantages of clean water, which the Romans and the Muslims seem to have grasped without any scientific understanding of germs. From what we know about the past, the water delivered today is dirtier than that of the other two civilizations at their prime. Thanks to the same technical progress which has polluted the water, we are also able to treat it, which makes it clean to the extent that it removes the traditional short-term risks of disease. This liquid usually smells and tastes of the cleansing agents which make it theoretically safe to drink.

By the standards of the Roman and Islamic empires we are now well advanced in our own decline since we have fouled most of our surface sources and are doing the same to our water tables. The question which this poses is whether our ability to treat the water we pollute can be identified as progress.

To be well advanced on our third time through the sophisticated use of water distribution suggests that even in the most basic and important areas we easily forget our own progress, and for centuries at a time. In the early stages of this amnesia, "to forget" actually means we pollute our water sources as if we do not know about our dependence on clean water. Our sophisticated explanations, justifications and bandaging, filled as they are with the laws of the marketplace and the industrialization of agriculture, are irrelevant. History is indifferent to SOPHISM. The sight of millions of Westerners drinking bottled water is a reminder of our disconnection from reality.

If we are unable to act in a consistently integrated manner in such an obvious and essential area, then it isn't surprising that our remarkable improvements in thousands of other areas should leave us confused as to the true meaning of the word progress. Most of us are now willing to admit, at least to ourselves, that we are confused.

But we don't know what this confusion means. Clearly our technical progress over the last two centuries has been miraculous. Clearly we also know less and less whether this continuing progress will produce improvements or regressions or both. And if so, in what dosage.

Three things, however, have become clear: progress may or may not be inevitable as part of a society's evolution, but according to our contemporary assumptions it is not a moral tenet of civilization; progress will turn upon itself and seek negation unless it is part of a larger integrated view of society: progress as we have defined it rewards basic competition and management based upon the pursuit of power for power's sake. Under this same definition what progress denigrates and if necessary punishes are any serious attempts to focus on an integrated view of human actions.

PROPAGANDA The means by which the thousands of organizations in a **CORPORATIST** society communicate with each other and with the general public.

From its origins in the Vatican Congregation for the Propagation of the Faith (*Congregati de propaganda fide*), a body devoted to spreading the Christian doctrine in foreign lands, the idea of substituting propagation for explanation was seized upon by the Heroic national leaders of the late eighteenth, nineteenth and early twentieth centuries. Propaganda married romanticism with facts, which seemed to replace any need for understanding. With the invention of marketing tools such as the press release, advertisements, sound bites, PR firms and press officers, this rather exclusive way of influencing people was quickly available to anyone with a budget.

Where once a government minister had a press officer, now every section in a ministry has one. Private corporations have whole communications departments. The American army alone has a corps of some 5,000 Press Officers.

The purpose of these several hundred thousand communications experts is to prevent communication or any generalized grasp of reality. Their job is to propagate the faith. See: *TRIUMPH OF THE WILL.*

PROPERTY One of the two definitions of marriage.

PROPERTY DEVELOPMENT   One of the causes of our continuing economic crisis:

1. A society obsessed by property sucks essential capital out of growth areas and sinks it into the passive domain of land, bricks and mortar.
2. While property development can create both infrastructure and short-term jobs, it is of limited use in feeding growth. Once built, a building has two economic functions: to justify the collection of rents or interest (passive); or to become a focus for financial speculation over the value of already existing goods (deceptively active).
3. Speculation unrelated to growth has become a central value of Western economies. Property is an important part of that speculation, as is the **MONEY MARKET** and the **ARMAMENTS** industry. All are forms of pure inflation and drain capital from areas of real investment and growth.
4. Since the 1960s Western economies have been repeatedly seduced by binges of property speculation. Each time, short-term massive profits wipe out all memory of the preceding disaster. Never before in history have there been so many South Sea Bubble catastrophes in such a short period of time.
5. The banks and big pension funds are central to this amnesia because they are the two principal sources of capital: the first through debt financing, the second through recirculation of the largest available deposits of money. If there is to be new growth in our economies it must be financed from these two sectors. But they prefer to buy property.

   What attracts them is the illusion of concrete collateralization. When a developer goes bankrupt, the lender gets the property. On paper the lender can't lose. Curiously, however, these institutions have repeatedly lost money in property over the last several decades. The reason is simple. The property may be real but the value is not. It is a product of speculation.
6. The managers who run the large deposit banks have a taste for big buildings. They have wasted large amounts of

capital by constructing remarkable headquarters buildings and imitative towers in every financial centre around the world. The only function of these palaces is to warehouse a non-productive managerial class.
7. Every society needs housing and work space. A civilization mindful of its future makes sure that everyone has a bit of property. An evolved civilization attempts to ensure that both private and public buildings are of the highest possible quality. Architecture at this level is an ethical expression of society at large. The sign today we are merely involved in speculation is that our buildings relate less and less to any primary use or need. See: **DEPRESSION.**

PROPRIETY   A strong indication that the period of revolutionary change initiated with the Renaissance, the Reformation and the reintroduction of reason has ended is the return of public farting. The new middle classes which began their rise in the sixteenth century identified themselves in part by their sense of group decorum. They, unlike the peasants and aristocrats, did not make sounds or smells in public. In the late twentieth century their self-control has weakened.

The catalyst may have been the linkage of middle-class urban eating habits with cancer of the colon. The direct result has been the rise of healthy food, which is prettified peasant food, including large quantities of reconstituted dried beans.

Hundreds of millions of people living in simpler communities around the world have never stopped eating beans and they are not noted for their farting. However, they drain off several times the water in which dry beans soak before cooking them in a last change of fresh liquid. They do this because the fart-producing enzymes gradually slip from the beans into the water.

If hundreds of millions of non-specialist, non-intellectual individuals know this, why has the information not spread? Is it because our modern élites are educated and work in isolation from society as a whole? Are technocrats as cut off from reality as eighteenth-century aristocrats once were? Is their compulsive exercising and eating of fibre a paradoxical simulation of normal life not unlike Marie Antoinette's desire to play with the sheep on her miniature farm just a few yards away from the palace at Versailles?

Or are these newly healthy individuals merely the victims of their own past? After all, cookbooks are as much symbols of the middle-class structure as is public propriety. It isn't surprising that these manuals in their modernized forms don't take the possibility of farting into account and therefore rarely mention the fact that peasants repeatedly change the water in which they soak beans.

There has never been so much information available, particularly about food. If the middle classes have taken to farting, the most probable explanation is that they have decided, consciously or unconsciously, that they want to. See: **RATIONALIZE** and **WIND**.

PUBLIC RELATIONS A negative form of imagination. In Mussolini's phrase, "invention is more useful than truth."[4] See: *TRIUMPH OF THE WILL.*

PUBLIC TRUST The ease with which the governed and the governors slip into a state of mutual contempt demonstrates how delicate a flower this trust is.

The contempt felt by the governors is an unfortunate strand of the Platonic inheritance. For those who cling to power without modesty, contempt for the populace provides a sense of superiority as well as a group to blame for their own failures.

The public can't be blamed for responding with similar emotions. They are encouraged in this by false populists, corporatists and other enemies of democracy because the destruction of public trust is the first step towards destroying a political system.

PUNCTUALITY A characteristic of executions, religious sacrifices and bullfights.

Humans deal best with the premeditated taking of life if it is made to seem inevitable. This sort of willed inevitability quite naturally must start on time, which restores to the victim their dignity. They die with the knowledge that they have not suffered a haphazard alleyway mugging.

Devotion to punctuality in any other area suggests an obsessive, directionless or insecure personality. See: **MANNERS**.

R

RATIONALIZE A transitive verb meaning to close, to shut down, to make redundant, to go bankrupt, to fire.

Administrative dialects seem to have been inspired by the baroque politeness of the Victorian middle-class tea-party. Reality is described through allusion and indirection. Technocrats speak as if they can only dignify their lives through verbal **PROPRIETY**.

Rationalization is to economics what bleeding was to eighteenth-century medicine. The underlying idea is that those who rationalize their activities will improve themselves through self-imposed suffering. It is particularly interesting that the élite most inspired by **REASON** should have chosen a derivative of that word in order to indicate failure. A Jungian might argue that this is an unconscious cry of despair or, more optimistically, for help. Until recently rationalization meant lying to yourself about what you are doing.

Metaphors of To Rationalize include To Restructure, To Downsize.

REALITY You should not, as the Washington hostess Alice Roosevelt Longworth pointed out, trust any balding man who combs his hair up from his armpit over the top of his head. Or rather, it is the considered opinion of most members of our rational élites that, in any given difference of opinion with reality, reality is wrong. See: **IMAGE**.

REASON Whatever anyone says it means, someone will argue that it means something else. The one thing they will agree on is that reason is both central and essential to our civilization, which is curious since they don't know what it is.

One of the peculiar characteristics of key terms is that the more we apply them to the real world, the more we claim that we are not experiencing the real thing. A dictatorship of the proletariat, once installed, will never be the promised dictatorship of the proletariat. A true self-regulating market will somehow never be true or self-regulating enough. These arguments resemble the rhetoric of mediaeval scholastics. Those who use them seem to be on a mission to rescue their favourite abstract theory from its latest catastrophic defeat at the hands of reality.

With half a millennium of conscientious application under its belt, reason is regularly declared to be farther than ever from the revelation of its true meaning. But an annoying sort of commonsensical citizen might stick to her guns and repeat, whenever faced by this interminable kant, that reason is what reason does.

As the religious debates which preceded the rational debates demonstrated, if you treat all questioning of what is declared to be the central principle of society as a rejection of it, you leave no room for reasonable re-evaluation. Thus it is invariably suggested that those who question the way in which we use reason are actually calling for a return to superstition and arbitrary power. The unspoken basis of this argument is that there are no other important human qualities or that these other pretended qualities are not qualities at all. In this way we are denied access to what we know to be our own reality.

The hypothetical **DOUBT**ing citizen could suggest that reason might make more sense if it were relieved of its monotheistic aura and reintegrated into the broader humanist concept from which it escaped in search of greater glory in the sixteenth century. In this larger view it would be balanced and restrained and given direction by other useful and perhaps also essential human characteristics such as common sense, intuition, memory, creativity and ethics. In such a generous context it would be easy to see that reason on its own is little more than a mechanism devoid of meaning, purpose or direction.

The rhetorical defender of the rationalist faith will immediately question whether these other characteristics are indeed independent qualities or whether they are merely lower-case concepts which can be dangerous if let loose. But why must we reduce our options to a choice between the true God and a golden calf?

Between our periods of purist folly, we keep coming back to the idea that we are balanced creatures. That is, we can be if we try. It may be impossible for each individual to achieve equilibrium. But when the varying strengths and weaknesses of the citizenry are combined, the idea of a balanced society becomes reasonable.

Reason detached from the balancing qualities of **HUMANISM** is irrational. The promise of a sensible society lies in the potential reality of a wider balance. And in that equilibrium reason has an essential place. See: **INSTRUMENTAL REASON.**

RECESSION "The recession is over."

This phrase has been used twice a year since 1973 by government leaders throughout the West. Its meaning is unclear. See: **DEPRESSION.**

REFERENDUM or PLEBISCITE Most commonly used to deform or destroy democracy, referenda casually offer a false choice—to accept a change proposed by those who have power or to refuse it. In other words, there is a single option, which is not a choice.

They are often presented as a populist tool of **DIRECT DEMOCRACY** which translates into undermining representative democracy.

They can indeed be tools of democracy, for example, if the citizens of a territory want to choose between belonging to one of two countries.

Referenda were introduced as a political tool under the French Revolution, but they came into their own under Napoleon. He used them to create something new—a populist dictatorship. Referenda resembled a democratic appeal to the people, without requiring the long-term complexities of elected representatives, daily politics and regular elections. Instead he combined his personal popularity with a highly focused appeal on a single subject. The result was that he could later claim the general support of the populace on any subject for undefined periods of time. In 1804, Napoleon used a referendum to become emperor, thus destroying democracy. Hitler did virtually the same thing in 1933 and again in 1934. In two referenda he got more power than an absolute monarch.

Those who propose the question invariably argue that a yes vote will solve problems; a no vote will bring on the apocalypse. This was as true of Napoleon as it was of the Canadian government's constitutional referendum in 1992.

All the efforts of those with the power to pose questions are concentrated on making the populace understand that they "need" to vote yes. "Necessity," William Pitt once said, "is the plea for infringement of human freedom. It is the argument of tyrants; it is the creed of slaves." And as André Malraux noted, "the slave always says yes."

Even at its best, democracy is a cumbersome and often tiresome business. Nor is it surprising that the gradual conversion of political propaganda into an important profession—public relations—which runs together social, economic and political questions, should favour the Heroic referendum approach over the complex multi-faceted and slow process of electoral democracy. The result is that we are increasingly subjected to the Heroic view of government. Even legislative elections are being turned away from their normal mix of issues and personalities to the illusion that a single candidate's position on a single issue or a personality flaw is all important. Single-issue lobbyists are as devoted to converting elections into referenda as public-relations firms.

And the press quite easily fall into the plebiscite game-plan, because they find it easier to harp on about the same subject, dramatizing, hyping it in fact, than to deal with a mix of complex issues.

A new face. The reduction of debt. Immigration. Nationalization. Privatization. Free Trade. One of these is the answer to our problems. It will allow us to avoid the apocalypse. The choosing of hundreds of representatives in the context of hundreds of issues, big and small, is in this way reduced to a plebiscite. Referenda are thus anti-democratic because they lend themselves so easily to the politics of IDEOLOGY.

REGULATION   Economic regulation protects the MARKET-PLACE from itself by introducing common sense. In the process it protects society.

This was how we avoided the cruel and destabilizing effects of the 1973 Depression. Unfortunately, those regulations also became an excuse for treating the crisis as less than it was. In an astonishing intellectual somersault, our élites seemed to be reassured and took to blaming the crisis on the costs of the stabilizing rules which had saved them.

This required extreme self-delusion. In any of the earlier depressions, the hurricane of social and economic disorder would have swept them out of power. As for the business leaders, and the middle class in general, most of their money and property would have disappeared in the storm. This is not to deny that over-regulation is a problem. It is. But regulations neither created nor maintained this crisis. And they are not THE problem. Among the unfortunate by-products of an ironic situation has been the encouragement of the worst characteristics in our élites. Increasingly they believe that because they still have power they must be right.

The challenge of the last twenty years—one to which we have not risen—has been to find a new way to think about economic crises. We had the right to congratulate ourselves on our success in regulating the current disaster, providing we then admitted that the disaster was real. In other words, regulation is at best a temporary harness on a force which can outlast and eventually outmanoeuvre any civilization. Regulation buys time. The question is, how should that time be used? We have wasted the last twenty years by denying reality and engaging in ideological arguments. There isn't much to be gained by assigning blame now. Even so, the Neo-conservative academics could easily be put at the top of a shame-ridden list.

Part of our problem is that the inventiveness of the marketplace quickly makes regulations irrelevant or counter-productive. The business community, their academic lobbyists and political agents react by crying out for deregulation. But then the market tends quite naturally towards a blunt and negative manner of expressing its dissatisfaction. It is not a mechanism of finely balanced human relationships. It cannot be expected to understand or to propose civilized human arrangements.

To the extent that deregulation has been conceded over the last few years, it has been disastrous for sectors as varied as banking, transportation and much of heavy industry. A more sensible approach might have been to re-examine the underlying mechanisms of regulation in order to bring them into the late twentieth century.

Duplication, unnecessary complications, administrative delay, barrier after barrier of detailed rules—all of these added up to a self-defeating maze constructed over the years, but not a force of evil. To re-establish society's real intent we needed simply to digest this accumulation of detail into new, lean and straightforward regulations.

While the ideological debate between regulation and deregulation has stretched on, our economic systems have been undermined by revolutionary changes in the marketplace. There have been endless inventions in the area of international financial speculation. And the transnational corporations have become increasingly sophisticated. Most postwar economic regulations, although complex and heavy-handed, have become marginal. With the end of the centrally administered European-based colonial empires in the early 1960s and the end of the **BRETTON WOODS** financial agreement in 1973, our systems of economic regulation became irrelevant.

The transnational corporations and the money markets have declared the era of human-designed regulations over. Now the market must reign. Because few people in the business community are paid to think about phrases such as "Western civilization," they don't seem to realize that they are proposing the arbitrary denial of 2,500 years of human experience.

The only way to stabilize the markets in order to protect them from themselves, and in the process to protect ourselves, is to rethink how to regulate them. This means neither fortress nationalism nor anarchical internationalism. A very careful balance can exist between the two. Bilateral or trilateral economic integration pacts such as the FTA and NAFTA are not the solution. They are regional victories for partial market deregulation at the expense of social balance. International trade negotiations such as GATT probably aren't much more useful. These arrangements are part of the old-style regulations. They cannot deal with either the transnational corporations or the money markets. The European Community is a serious attempt at rethinking and reregulating a large area of human society. But it remains a regional arrangement, and so will be unable to maintain its very real standards against the attacks of the transnational corporations and the money markets.

If what we want is stability and prosperity, then we have little choice but to concentrate our imaginations and our efforts on a new and far broader version of Bretton Woods. Given the developments in technology and the disorder in international trade, this is the only sensible way to release the market-place from its own self-destructive instructs. See also: **DEPRESSION, HOLY TRINITY–LATE TWENTIETH CENTURY** and **SEVENTY-THREE.**

RESPONSIBILITY   Nobody is responsible in a corporatist society. That's because the real citizens are corporations. Individuals only work for them and follow orders. It follows that individuals see themselves as chosen for victimization.

RICHELIEU, CARDINAL   Father of the modern nation state, modern centralized power, the modern secret service and a major civil building boom brought on by a glut in the dressed stone market following Richelieu's forced dismantling of defensive city walls. See: **GANG OF FIVE.**

RIGHT   See: **LEFT.**

RIGHT VERSUS WRONG   Sooner or later societies solidify to a point where the justification of existing structures becomes a social duty and public discourse is reduced to an absolutist formula which depends on the concept of right versus wrong.

The very idea of the middle ground then becomes an enemy of public order. Yet the middle ground is where change may be constructively considered. Only there can individuals embrace doubt in order to reconsider society without rejecting it.

At some level—conscious or subconscious—those who feel driven to defend right versus wrong know this does not mean that they are necessarily right. They know they are confusing the ethical concepts of right and wrong with an absolutist approach towards the practicalities of everyday life. But on their practical level of day-to-day life, in which careers, reputations and incomes are made and lost they understand that error is punished and certainty rewarded.

Ours is a society in awe of false stability and which functions by admiring power and denying reality. Even the careful legal codification of the late twentieth century—designed to protect the citizen against various forms of malpractice—

can encourage the professional denial of the middle ground. If those who are expert and those who have power know that being wrong means they must be punished, then public debate is impossible. The result is an unrealistic status quo. The denial of problems becomes a duty. This illusion will hold like a well-built dam until the waters of reality rise high enough to rush over the top.

But if reality can only be applied in unexpected floods, the question of right and wrong or being right versus being wrong will always be swept away precisely when it is needed. Only a society which admires, even rewards, the admission of error can avoid this weakness by concentrating upon the middle ground.

ROTTEN BOROUGH   An electoral area in which the representative is chosen by financial interests. A "Rotten Borough system" suggests the sytematic corruption of electoral democracy.

This initially English phenomenon involved a lord who owned all the local votes. As balloting was done in public, he could verify the way each was cast. The 1832 Reform Bill eliminated the Rotten Boroughs. During the second half of the twentieth century they re-emerged in a more sophisticated form and quickly spread throughout the West.

The 1992 American election produced a Congress which had been shaped by more than one billion dollars in funding from private interests.[1] To suggest that corporations made these investments in order to serve the public interest would be to assume that they are run by incompetents.

The unabashedly crude way in which money shapes the legislatures of Britain, France, Canada, Italy and so on throughout the West is made doubly surprising by our determination in most cases to continue on as if this were not happening. The single example of the pharmaceutical industry, their political investments and the resulting legislation on drug patents and pricing is a blatant case of old-fashioned rotten-borough politics. The lord pays out money and then monitors how the beneficiaries vote. The borough is replaced by the legislature. Silvio Berlusconi's use of corporate money, public relations in place of policy and his own television stations and newspapers in the 1994 Italian election shows how far democracy's suicidal tendencies can carry it. And still we go on acting as people did in the eighteenth century—as if such corruption of the public weal were simply the way things always work in the real world.

That this system often manages to choose good representatives reassures us that the problem is secondary. But in the eighteenth century good people were also chosen through the Rotten Boroughs. Some of the greatest parliamentarians in the history of modern democracy sat for areas controlled by a single lord.

The problem with Rotten Boroughs is not that they eliminate personalities or LEADERSHIP. After all, any system can promote competent and even remarkable people. Dictatorships can do this more easily than democracies. Any absolute monarch or Führer can pick out the smartest available people and appoint them to office. The problem with Rotten Boroughs is that legislatures shaped by corruption are unable to do the job expected of them—that is, to serve the public interest. Behind a great deal of artifice and some useful policies, their principal activity is to be of service to their financial masters.

Much of our hesitation in controlling special interests comes from a sense that even if they are misusing the democratic mechanisms, to control them would put limitations on all honest citizens. But democracy was never intended to guarantee unlimited individual rights.

There has always been a division between those rights which either contribute to the public weal or at least do not harm it versus those which are negative, vicious or destructive. The line between these two categories may not be perfectly clear, but in general it can be seen.

The destructive freedoms are easily identified. We are not allowed to kill, rob, enslave or beat each other. That is, we are not allowed to infringe on the individual rights of others. Corruption of the legislature falls into the same category because the corrupter mistakes the removal of someone else's freedom for an expression of their own.

What's more, our legal system gives the corrupter comfort in his view. It ties the privilege of the corrupter to the citizen's right to freedom of speech, even though the actual effect is to limit the freedom of speech of most citizens. Thus our basic democratic rights can be deformed into a negative force. That is why democratic societies have so much difficulty dealing with those who do not respect fair freedom of speech. The Brownshirts, Blackshirts and Bolsheviks were able to use their own freedom of speech to remove that of others, at first by simply shouting them down.

The use of money—as with Berlusconi—to fund floods of advertising and television commercials is a new and more sophisticated way to shout people down. It is neither free speech nor communication. Rather it deforms public debate into **CORPORATIST** rivalry. Some of these corporatist groups may have ethical messages—human rights or ecological groups, for example. But they will always be outnumbered by self-serving special interests. In either case, what they obscure is the democratic process itself, which is not intended to be a competition between corporatist groups for control of the elected representatives.

The problem in controlling corruption is not therefore whether to put limits on freedom of speech, but how to organize society so that everyone has real access to their freedom of speech. For example, to limit the size of corporate contributions during elections, while leaving the real cost of running for office unlimited, is to put a severe limitation on free speech.

But if the electoral process were removed from the market-place entirely, then this single, across-the-board limitation would guarantee maximum freedom to all citizens and opinions. Modern communications are not necessarily the enemy of fair debate. They also make it possible for legislatures to fund all election expenses for all groups. The removal of all private funding could accomplish more than just cutting out the corporatist groups who attempt to dominate the citizenry. It could also reduce the overall cost of politics and focus public debate more on issues than on flimflam.

No doubt the special interests would respond by running their own candidates, but this would have a number of advantages. They would be identified as special interests, which is not the case today. They would be running without financial advantage, which is also not the case today. The special interests would be free to try their luck at the bar of public judgement instead of attempting to buy candidates. Finally, the common sense of the citizenry would be able to judge in a relatively clear situation which parties, policies and candidates were aimed at serving the public weal, which is not the case today.

ROUND TABLE An organized group of managers from leading American companies. The Round Table designs policies favourable to the corporations for which its members work, then sells them to the various levels of government.

This is not a lobby group but a corporatist organization; one of the most important in the developed world. At first glance the name of the group seems inappropriate. What possible link could there be between Arthur, Lancelot and the quest for the Holy Grail and a group of anonymous technocrats looking out for themselves and their systems? The answer is that they see themselves as the knighthood of technocracy and they claim the legitimacy of their corporatist power. See: CORPORATISM.

S

SAT   A system of standardized American college entry exams designed to nurture and reward functional illiteracy.

Originally used only inside North America, the Scholastic Aptitude Tests and their equivalents are spreading around the world in response to a corporatist desire for global fixed standards in specialized education. Consisting mainly of multiple choice and fill-in-the-blanks questions, the SATs are the archetypal product of a society which believes above all in the possession of facts and the rule of expertise. In spite of "substantial revisions" in 1994,[1] the underlying premise of these tests is that to each question there is a single correct answer.

The skills they seek to measure are short-term memory and the ability to reduce knowledge to structures not unlike those of basic accountancy. They discourage thought, consideration, doubt, imagination and creativity. In sum, they reward mechanistic skills and punish intelligence. Exams of this sort are the first great barrier which students must clear in order to enter the functioning élite. Who they eliminate, who they encourage, the signals they send as to which skills society will reward, which not, have an important impact on the shape of our élites and what they think their role is.

The SATs are not simply illustrations of a crisis in our civilization. They are an active agent, thanks to their deformation of successive generations of the élites. The cry throughout a troubled West is that we need standards. Perhaps. But we don't need destructive standards. See: **WISDOM**.

SCHOLASTICISM The dominant mediaeval school of teaching, inquiry, knowledge and argument. One of the Enlightenment's main enemies. Scholasticism was duly defeated and destroyed. It mysteriously re-emerged at the centre of power in the second half of this century.

The key to the mediaeval movement was its ability to tie up intellectual inquiry and language in an endless maze of high-quality irrelevance. In this way it protected established authority from serious examination.

The *Encyclopédie* described Scholasticism this way:

It substituted words for things; and frivolous or ridiculous questions for the great questions of real philosophy; it explained unintelligible things via barbarous terms.... This philosophy was born of the spirit of ignorance.... It reasoned from a basis of abstraction rather than of reality; it created for this new sort of study a new language. And disciples believed themselves wise because they had learnt this language. We can only regret that most scholastic authors made such a miserable use of their intelligence and that they limited their writing to such an extreme subtlety.[2]

Scholasticism was launched in the thirteenth century by Thomas of Aquinas who applied Aristotelian logic to Christian purposes. In this way he managed to smother most relevant debate for a good three centuries.

The similarity of mediaeval and modern scholasticism can be seen in this statement by Frederick Copleston, a great historian of philosophy as well as of Aquinas: "The practice of starting from a revealed premise...and arguing rationally to a conclusion, leads to the development of Scholastic theology..."[3] This is precisely the method used to train contemporary technocrats in most fields. It is also the phenomenon identified by Harold Innis in the social sciences where, "...confident predictions, irritating and incapable of refutation, replaced discussion of right and wrong."[4]

In contemporary terms, Scholasticism creates impenetrable dialects, uses obscure language to prevent communication and separates intellectual inquiry from reality by adopting a relentlessly abstract approach. It continues to serve established power. See: ANTI-INTELLECTUALISM and DECONSTRUCTIONISM.

SCHOPENHAUER, ARTHUR   Hitler's favourite writer.

"My teacher," the Führer said.[5] This appears a curious choice given that Schopenhauer avoided military service at a moment of crisis for Germany in its battle against Napoleon. He wasn't even a German nationalist. He did see himself as a follower of Plato and Kant, which indicates a taste for authoritarianism and for obscurantism, although he criticized the lack of clarity in others. There was a certain pessimistic idealism about him which is often a romantic basis for tyrannical action.

When asked why Nietzsche wasn't his favourite writer, Hitler is said to have replied, "I couldn't do anything with him." Perhaps what he meant was that being himself as unbalanced as Nietzsche, they made an ill-suited couple for public mythology.

HEROES rely heavily on philosophers who express romantic pessimism. Schopenhauer's attraction for Hitler may have been his overwhelming sense that evil was overwhelming the world and that the "root of all evil...is the slavery of the will." The only solution was to turn "away from life to aesthetic contemplation and asceticism."[6] Men like Hitler and Napoleon can be counted on to claim that if destiny had not forced them to become tyrants, they would have withdrawn into solitary contemplation.

Schopenhauer also detested women which, in the Saint Jerome—"Women are bags of dung"—tradition, is a sentiment closely related to the uncontrollable feeling that evil is inundating us. It is a little simplistic but not untrue to say that men who hate women will take out their sexual problems on the world if given a chance. Romantic pessimists like

Schopenhauer are thus very helpful in providing respectability for criminal acts. See: **KANT, NIETZSCHE** and **PLATO.**

SECOND-GENERATION FERTILIZERS, HERBICIDES and **INSECTICIDES** Rhetoric over reality.

For half a century the chemical industry has insisted that their agricultural aids had no side effects, indeed were harmless and simply brought prosperity. Gradually, as the result of determined campaigns funded mainly by volunteer citizens' groups, governments began to ban certain chemicals. The public began to realize they had been lied to. At no time did the chemical industry change its tobacco-industry-style defence. But growing public concern indicated that they were no longer believed.

In the early 1990s, a soothing phrase began to circulate: "The first generation of products were flawed, but, thanks to new research and industry initiatives, a second generation of products has been so perfected that they have no side effects and are harmless." The originators of this sentence have not been identified. However, those not employed by the industry note that there has been a great deal of renaming and repackaging of chemical products for agriculture. Environmentally friendly words are all over the packages. The actual contents are marginally different. See: **SOPHISTS.**

SERIOUS Proper to ideology, conformism, expertise, political correctness of all sorts. A form of social control. See: **COMEDY.**

SEVENTY-THREE In spite of the word-games preferred by our leadership, the Western economies have been in crisis since 1973.

Like a juggler with too many balls, we have been attempting to handle an apparently contradictory combination of slow growth, unemployment, inflation and debt. Whenever we manage to get one or two into the air, the others fall to the ground. We bend over but by the time we get one of them back in the air, another lies at our feet. After a few years of this, the sensible conclusion might have been that we were doing something fundamentally wrong. Instead we have gone on trying to pick up the fallen balls.

The explosive incidents of 1973 now seem little more than distant anecdotes. The oil-producing states organized themselves into an effective cartel. The price of a barrel of oil soared while supply dropped. By the early nineties, after two decades of inflation, the price of oil was more or less back where it started. The crisis of '73 therefore ought to have been over. But depressions are usually unleashed by specific events which, although relevant to the crisis, are not the cause. They are catalysts which unite all the economic imbalances from which society doesn't really know it suffers. That negative formula, once achieved, turns into a profound economic collapse.

Conventional economic wisdom tracks its way out of the seventies on a curve of financial recovery into the eighties. The problems of the late eighties and the early nineties are thus disassociated from those of the seventies. But the prosperity of the eighties was neither generalized nor integrated in the social structure. It was based largely on growth in artificial or inflationary areas such as paper speculation and property speculation. Arms manufacturing was the closest we came to industrial growth. By the early nineties, it was received wisdom to think of the eighties as an unhealthy anomaly. Yet there was no tendency to draw the logical conclusion. If the eighties did not constitute a recovery, then we are still in the crisis of the seventies. See: **DEPRESSION**.

SEX Despite being a common activity, demand always runs ahead of supply. This has made sex the market-driven aspect of personal relationships, running somewhere behind property in the schema of economics.

Demand, in sex as in commerce, is an irrational mystery.

The long-term contractual approach requires property arrangements such as marriage. In the speculative pay-as-you-go market, it is often linked to meals and entertainment. In either case sex has become the most successful bull market of the last three decades. Theoretical demand stretches so far ahead of real supply that sex has become the opiate of the people.[7]

In 1992, a French court established the per-session value of sex between a husband and wife. The man had been denied intercourse for two and a half months after a doctor mistakenly daubed his penis with acid during a treatment. Damages were awarded on the basis of FF300 per missed coupling. The court was not suggesting that this was the absolute value of sex or the value of sex between that particular couple. Rather, they were ruling that, since money is our society's only regulated reward system, sex must have an equivalent monetary value and in that particular market—a small provincial town—it was worth FF300 per session. The couple might have received ten or twenty times more had they lived in an expensive district in a major city. See: MARKET-PLACE.

SOCRATES Deliberately misunderstood.

Deliberately misunderstood, and yet. And yet he somehow manages to pierce these barriers of misunderstanding in order to assert his DOUBT and therefore his humanism.

The PLATOnists continue to use him as a justification for the central contradiction in our society. They continue to argue that the higher or philosophic life must include a contempt for democracy because the citizenry are worse tyrants than a tyrant. This conviction remains at the heart of our élite education. It has been the foundation of a great variety of dictatorships over the centuries, ranging from well-intentioned left-wing reformers to ambitious right-wing colonels. And yet, there is enough force in the Socratic approach to resist these deformations of meaning, enough spirit to inspire repeatedly the idea of the citizen and of democracy.

In this century we have seen power swing repeatedly back and forth between democracy and the tyrants while élites have served one or the other, but always with a sense of their own superiority towards and even contempt for the democratic system. This is the internal drama from which the West seems unable to free itself.

Embittered disciples are rarely the right people to portray their master's ideas. Plato nevertheless gives us enough information that we can draw conclusions opposed to his own. The explanation for his frankness may be that he was far from being the only living witness of the trial. If he wanted his point of view to be taken seriously, he had to provide a description of what Socrates had said and done which would ring true in Athens. As a result, from Plato's own text it can reasonably be argued that his emotions caused him to minimize, misrepresent or ignore four key points.

First, whatever the flaws of a democracy, Socrates would not have been permitted to teach anyone in a dictatorship. Had Socrates been a Spartan he would have been executed at the beginning of his career.

Second, Socrates wasn't rude to the jury or to the citizenry. He was rude to everyone. That was his method. It did not mean he considered himself of a superiority which justified contempt for lesser intellects. He simply had a foul character. He did not withdraw into intellectual isolation as to an ivory tower. He spent his life wandering around Athens annoying everyone in the city. He must have thought they were worth annoying. And yet Plato's Socratic conclusion, accentuated by the Platonists into an ideal, turns on the need for superior and therefore isolated élites. The rational idea of the technocratic élites is a product of that deformed interpretation.

Third, even though his conviction was a virtual certainty, Socrates stayed around for his trial in order to address the jury. He was encouraged and expected by both his friends and the authorities simply to go into exile for a while. He refused. The only sensible conclusion we can draw is that he believed in the democratic system enough to risk his life for it. Plato somehow managed to conclude that democracy should be condemned.

Fourth, Socrates stayed around for his execution. Again, he could have easily escaped into exile after his conviction. Again, this is what most people expected, indeed hoped he would do. The Athenian legal system, unlike that of many dictatorships, was not hungry for blood. It was a flawed control mechanism which acted as a warning signal. When people crossed the line of what was considered to be bearable public decorum they were driven by the system to leave the city for a time. Socrates however chose to respect the system to the extent of letting it kill him.

To suggest that Socrates would have participated fully for seventy years in a system that he had contempt for and rejected, and that in a final gesture of masochism he would invite the system to kill him is to suggest that he was not an intellectual master worth following. To suggest—as the Platonists do— that being old, Socrates felt like dying and therefore tricked the Athenian legal system into murdering him, not only insults his honesty, but his intellectual integrity and indeed his intelligence.

That he had constantly cajoled the system to do better is quite another matter. Plato's bitterness can be understood. But that should have been a matter of personal grief, not the foundation for a philosophy which betrays Socrates by favouring dictatorship. See: **FREE SPEECH** and **ORAL LANGUAGE**.

SOCRATIC INHERITANCE, THE   Our advanced education systems continue to insist that technocrats, whether for the private or the public sector, are products of the Socratic method, which they claim for themselves. But in the Athenian's case, every answer raised a question. In our society, every question produces an answer. See: **ÉLITE EDUCATION**.

SOLUTIONS   An absolutist abstraction which may make more sense in chemistry or mathematics than it does in everyday life.

The assertion that problems are terminated by being solved suggests that problems actually are solved, which can only mean that they are free-standing obstacles to a better world. Thus in medicine the illusion of a **CURE** obscures the reality that we are merely being treated. A more modest view might be that problems are reduced or limited or made more bearable if they are seen and treated as part of a larger phenomenon which has slipped out of balance.

Thus inflation is never eliminated. It is reduced and controlled by being treated as an integral part of a larger phenomenon which includes such things as production, innovation, employment, stability and growth. Those who believe that solutions eliminate problems talk of strangling inflation and put their efforts into linear mechanisms such as money supply and interest rates. Each time they reduce inflation there is a negative repercussion for production or employment or growth.

Neither peace nor war eliminates the other. A healthy balance minimizes war by paying attention to related factors such as prosperity and stability.

Like most absolute abstractions, the conviction that problems can be solved has a religious reverberation. It is as if solution has been mistaken for salvation.

SOPHISTS   The original model for the twentieth-century **TECHNOCRAT**; more precisely for the **BUSINESS SCHOOL** graduate and the **ACADEMIC CONSULTANT**.

These fifth-century BC teachers wandered around Greece selling their talents to whomever would hire them. Their primary talent was rhetoric. They were not concerned by ethics or the search for truth. Long-term consequences, indeed reality in most forms, did not interest them. What mattered was their ability to create illusions of reality which would permit people to get what they wanted.

SPECIAL RELATIONSHIPS Great powers rarely think of themselves as having special relationships.

What they do have are either allies or client states. Allies are countries which think as much of themselves as the great powers do. They must therefore be dealt with as equals, no matter how small or weak they may actually be. The client states think less of themselves and thus talk a great deal of their special relationship, the way courtiers once boasted of their access to the king.

The Calvary of kings is that they must humour this flattering fiction, at the very least by saying nothing. Periodically, they will have to build up the courtier's flagging ego by bestowing signs of personal concern upon him.

In the case of client states this may take the form of a sumptuous state visit. Under General de Gaulle's presidency, these events were referred to as *les visites des rois nègres*. Better still, the great king may ask the head of a client government to advise him on a matter of particular importance. This sort of consultation ideally takes place not in the office of the king but in the house, in order to personalize the relationship. There are other more banal and therefore less valued ways to confer a special relationship. The most common is to stand in front of cameras with the client head of government in order to say how much he or she is appreciated.

For a full decade Washington felt obliged to maintain the fiction of Mrs. Thatcher's special relationship with the president. In a more ingratiating style, Brian Mulroney based his entire national strategy on the fiction of his special influence over Canada's neighbours. The word fiction is important in these cases because the great power does not, over the course of a pleasant dinner, forget its interests or alter its policies.

The term special relationship is also common among middle-level politicians who fear defeat in an upcoming election and so invoke their president or prime minister. Also among innocent young girls when talking about the ideal liaisons they will have when they grow up. See: **BANALITY** and **NANNY-ISM**.

SPEECH-WRITERS   People complain that our leaders no longer read, which is an insult to their speech-writers.

It is equally fatuous to complain that we don't know what our leaders stand for. Their speeches are perfectly clear. The only unknown is what they actually stand for.

We have no right to complain about this. We have insisted that we need leadership and so have reverted to the divine monarchy in which, whatever else he may be, the leader is presented in public as a symbol. Like his clothes, his words are chosen for him. Language is treated as performance, not communication. That he has not read the books his speeches quote or initiated the thoughts his speeches think is neither here nor there. Either we wish discussion and doubt or rhetoric and reassurance.

We have chosen the latter. A leader who read and thought and spoke in more than sound bites would disturb us because he would sound undecided. He would be forcing us to listen and respond to the authentic noises of a human brain functioning in a position of responsibility.

In order to avoid being exposed to even a hint of this through private contact with their leader, a growing number of speech-writers go on to become columnists, authors and even political candidates of a forthright type. They are then paid to think in public. Places such as the opinion pages of newspapers have become a substitute for the leader's mind. The columnists tell us what the leaders must be thinking. This is more than a reversion to the reading of entrails. It is a further development of the courtier-based society. The leader needn't worry about thought. Other people will pay professionals to tell the public everything that is in his mind.

STANDARDS OF PRODUCTION   The social and economic equivalent of criminal law. A counterbalance to the barbaric tendencies of blind self-interest and abstract market forces.

Above all, standards of production are the practical expression of ethics; that is, of a civilization's inherent right to regulate subsidiary activities.

The purpose of these standards is to establish socially acceptable relationships between citizens. Slavery, for example, was once acceptable in most societies. In most it is now forbidden. Workplace safety, employment guarantees, pensions and so on are modern refinements on the rejection of slavery.

An unfair advantage goes to those who refuse standards. A civilization that has established middle-class standards of production cannot compete against one that has not, just as an army that forbids the use of poisonous gas cannot fight one which uses it. A society which permits those individuals who wish to murder to do so has slipped into anarchy. As Afghanistan or Sicily or Yugoslavia have demonstrated, the absence of standards puts those who are not murderers at a disadvantage. The only difference between these murderers and those who propose a market-place deprived of standards is that one believes in corporal violence and the other in economic violence. These are intimately related forms of barbarism. They assume an elimination of practical ETHICS.

STRAWBERRY, THE   Interchangeable with the melon, this object, tasting vaguely of plastic or acidic cardboard, is offered in every hotel, restaurant and supermarket in the world every day of the year under the heading fresh fruit.

Its qualities include:

1. Modernity: it is principally the product of irrigation, chemical fertilizers and pesticides.
2. Modesty: it is quite happy to live its growing life under plastic.
3. Adaptibility: pick it green, send it on a plane around the world, it remains as unperturbed as if it were a plaster copy.
4. Patient: it will sit eternally on a shelf and not rot.
5. Mythological: it evokes happy songs, picnics, shortcake and cream, white wine and a hot summer sun.

Some will argue that a real strawberry still exists, growing somewhere, full of flavour and scent and waiting to be picked. But what value has the vague romanticism of the real thing when measured against the transcendant strawberry, the platonic strawberry, which the genius of rational organization can place on every plate on request? See: WHITE BREAD.

SUBJUNCTIVE That mood which most clearly admits to the existence of doubt.

The importance of grammar as a reflection of civilization's true condition can be seen in the gradual disappearance of the subjunctive from Western languages.

What does it mean when a society eliminates the threshold of the possible en route to what is probable? Self-confidence? This must be a society which doesn't evolve through questioning. It simply finds the right answers and acts upon them. But to believe only in the present and the future without any intervening and unruly process could also be taken for a naïvety so extreme as to constitute stupidity. Such a desire for certainty also suggests a willingness to be manipulated.

Every tense and mood of a language has its enemies. Those of the subjunctive are public relations, propaganda, opinion polls and the religion of expertise. A civilization which rewards so generously the ability to sell illusion as if it were reality is unlikely to reward grammar which examines the uncertain ground between the two. See: DOUBT.

SUPER BOWL In the United States more women are battered on the day of the American football championship than on any other day of the year. This should not be taken as a characteristic of football itself, which has been an important and agreeable factor in stabilizing the gonadal energy of young men for more than a century.

The Super Bowl is relatively typical of competition used as a social value. Everyone, except the few who are best at the game, is reduced to the disembodied role of a spectator.

Spectators do participate through some of their senses. Eyes, ears, mouths and emotions can be used to worship their substitutes. But in this process the seated are deprived of their existence as individuals capable of action. Instead, they become passive participants in the mythology of gladiatorial Heroism.

The aim in football is to move the pigskin across the goal-line. This positive skill is unfortunately little more than the exotic spice of the game. The central characteristic, involving most of the players on the field, is that the movement of the football is halted in each play by a physical assault on its carrier. Spectators may well get excited about these repeated demonstrations of basic masculinity. The more excited they become through passive participation, the more their own active manhood may be put into doubt. In the final analysis, a guy's got to prove his own worth by hitting someone himself. Or it may simply be that American women are unbearably slow fetchers of beer.

SUPERIORITY Most superior people suffer from an INFERI- ORITY COMPLEX. With nations—groups abstracted to resemble a person—this paradox can easily become pathological. After a few generations of defiant assertions, everyone forgets that their sentiment of superiority is based upon their fear of inferiority.

The confusion then produced by reality's failure to live up to mythology often brings on racism and violence. These are classic tools for those in despair who wish to banish doubt. Low levels of racism and violence may mean that an individual or a nation no longer feels the need to feel superior. They may then actually be superior. See: WESTERN CIVILIZATION.

T

TALENT Sylvester Stallone has stated, "I could play Hamlet if I wanted to. I just don't want to."[1] Mr. Stallone may be understating his case. He may be able to play Lear.

Society increasingly encourages individuals to make great claims for themselves as an act of self-affirmation. But this is to apply the ethos of the sandbox to social organization. It also suggests that the individual is being encouraged to exchange self-respect for the dream world of public relations.

A sensible person accepts the positive things others say about him, whoever and whatever they are. However, history will make up its mind about each of us, after we're dead. See: **HEROES**.

TASTE There is no such thing as good or bad taste. As Coco Chanel pointed out, there is only taste. This suggests that moral judgements such as good and bad may have no relevance to fashion. Perhaps fashion is just fashion. To be enjoyed or ignored or, for that matter, deplored.

In late imperial Rome, the great aristocratic pagan families were horrified by the rise to power of the lower-middle-class Christians whose churches were so plain and ugly that they were scarcely more than hovels. These rustic believers knew nothing about architectural principles and, we can surmise, had heavy accents and dressed without style. No doubt they were what those with taste would call common. Gradually, however, the aristocrats themselves followed the odour of shifting power and began to convert. Eventually the law left them no choice. It was probably a few generations before they actually thought of themselves as Christians, but in the meantime they brought taste to the church: architecture, decoration, mosaics, painting, liturgy, music. At last the bishops began to wear chasubles as magnificent as their positions. At last the language of prayer and song began to sound elegant and powerful. The beauty that resulted from the participation of the great old imperial families became an integral part of our pleasure in ourselves as civilized people. The new pagan Christian taste was quickly confused with the original Christian message of moral clarity. But those links were and remain purely imaginary.

As Queen Elizabeth II replied, when asked how she felt about taste, "Well, I don't think it helps."[2] True and untrue. It does not, in any ethical sense, help. It may even confuse and weaken ethical standards. On the other hand it does help us to get through the day. "For the pleasure of your eyes," the classic Arab souk merchant will incant to draw you into his stall. And why not. We do have eyes. But not, as Ovid pointed out, for debating taste. *"De gustibus non disputendum est,"* which simply indicates that Coco Chanel knew her Roman poetry.

TAXATION   The only purpose of this unpleasant business is to pay for the services the citizenry require, which means taxing a sufficient percentage of the total wealth found in the state.

Modern taxation is often described as a revolutionary change which permitted the financing of widespread public programs by limiting the rights of private property. This isn't so. The modern tax is merely the latest administrative form of an age-old procedure. And it limits the rights of private property far less than any earlier system did.

For most of history the collecting of taxes involved brute

force. Monarchs spent the income on themselves, their aristocracy and their armies. They often rented out the tax-collecting privilege to individuals who became spectacularly rich in the process. In the seventeenth and eighteenth centuries those whom we would now describe as irresponsible speculators were often private-sector tax collectors.

The taxpayer has always complained about extravagant governments, often with reason. What has changed is the definition of the citizen upon whom the money is to be spent. For the first time, most of the population qualifies as a citizen.

It can reasonably be argued that governments, like all large corporations, waste some money. However, this only accounts for a small part of the shortfall in public funds over the last quarter of the twentieth century. Most of it can be traced to the state's inability to tax the wealth on its territory.

In the late 1950s, early 1960s, the large joint-stock companies carried between 30 per cent and 40 per cent of the tax burden in most Western countries. This was an effective way to raise funds and finance the state because it taxed the national wealth at a point when it could be measured as a factor of production and was gathered together in large sums. This period of theoretically high taxation did not dampen what was a time of great corporate prosperity.

Nevertheless the managers of these corporations set about lobbying for a reduction in tax rates. Within a short time the corporations were carrying only 10 to 15 per cent of the tax burden.

This new financial liberty did not bring new investment, growth or prosperity. Nor did the money go to the shareholders. What these funds did bring was an explosion in the quantity of managers. Pointless mergers, takeovers, splendid new office headquarters and other inflationary activities proliferated. The joint-stock companies more or less wasted the billions which tax reform had won them and thus played a role in provoking and prolonging the economic troubles of 1973.

As the corporate contribution shrank, the burden of financing the state fell upon the rich and near-rich, which included some of the senior managers. In fact, there could never be enough money in these pockets to compensate for the lost corporate contribution.

The rich protested loudly at the right doors, threatening to take their money elsewhere. So the burden kept on shifting. It settled increasingly on the middle classes, who, had they been willing to pay 100 per cent of their income in taxes, could still not have come up with enough to balance the public budget.

In desperation, governments turned to various indirect sources of revenue. They started lotteries and went seriously into the **GAMBLING** business. They also created and increased sales taxes.

Managers and economists said that sales taxes were a good idea because consumption was an efficient point at which to tax the national wealth. This is false for three reasons: only a small part of the national wealth passes through consumption patterns; financing trillion- and billion-dollar public operations by taxing a few cents at a time is so inefficient as to be silly; for individuals and small businesses the administration of sales taxes is time-consuming. It represents time wasted on a non-productive activity; thus the administration of sales taxes is inflationary.

But there was nowhere else for the burden to shift because the corporate managers had carried their organizations still farther away from taxability by embracing globalization. To any attempts at serious taxation they began invoking the demands of international competition. Tax them and they'll be gone to some land of lower taxes and cheap labour.

What is now called the debt crisis is in good part the taxation crisis. The managers and the academic consultants endlessly repeat, sometimes accurately, that the state must cut back to deal with the debt. But the shrinkage is never enough. Besides, most cuts are not to the state but to the citizens' services.

That the ability to tax fairly and effectively the full national wealth has now escaped the nation state is not so serious as it at first appears. After all, the problem is fundamentally that of the individual citizen who, throughout the West, continues to believe in a basic social contract.

Received wisdom has it that nothing can be done because globalization and **TECHNOLOGY** dominate. In fact a simple decision by the Group of Seven that they want their taxes and intend to collect them would be enough to force a change of direction. After all, the billion-odd citizens of the Group of Seven represent the bulk of the consumer market for the products of the large corporations.

Ensuring that they carry their fair tax load is a simple matter of cooperation among those who have a right to a percentage of the national wealth.

TAYLOR, FREDERICK   Founder of the Harvard Business School, management consultancy and the modern technocratic manager-led concept of capitalism. Lenin's favourite economist, after Marx.

TAYLORISM   A management system in which workers are viewed as additional pieces of machinery.

Invented by Frederick Taylor in 1895, Taylorism or Scientific Management was a precursor of automatized production. Ironically, it also improved the treatment of workers. They could no longer be exploited in the traditional sense because machinery must be looked after or it will break down. Taylorism also brought increased general prosperity and the workers benefited from this.

However, their status had been fundamentally altered. The system no longer saw them as human individuals, but as elements in a system to be managed by experts.

Taylorism was central in the rise of the United States to world power. When democracy and capitalism are cited as an explanation for America's success, it is more accurately a reference to democracy and scientific management.

Taylorism was also a great hit in Nazi Germany. Albert Speer, Hitler's economics minister, was a disciple of the movement and this is one of the explanations for Germany's success in holding out against superior Allied forces later in the war.

Taylorism is the ultimate abstract structure. Not only can it impose itself on reality for limited periods, it is more effective in a crisis than in normal times. Speer's approach was like a gigantic Harvard Business School case study (both the school and the case study are a Taylorist invention).

Curiouser than Speer's admiration was that of Lenin. He had been seduced by Taylorism while still in exile and carried its message back to Russia. Lenin spoke repeatedly of the necessity to Communize Taylorism. The first Five Year Plan was written largely by American Taylorists and directly or indirectly they built some two-thirds of Soviet industry. The collapse of the Soviet Union was thus in many ways the collapse of Scientific Management.

Yet the Russian government immediately hired a Harvard professor of economics, Dr. Jeffrey Sachs, to help them out of the crisis. His methods—filled with complete abstract systems—were strangely reminiscent of Taylor's. Underlying his proposals was the need for an absolute break with the past. These brilliant financial and structural reforms lacked only one element: a recognition that several hundred million people live in Russia, that they must eat every day. Or at least every second day. And that if they did not, they would reject the new regime and return to the old patterns of bureaucratic communism.

The various attempted coups and electoral reversals suffered by the forces of reform are in part the responsibility of this Harvard economist. When in 1994 his policies were finally rejected by a frustrated electorate, who opted for a return to the old ways under the old technocrats, Sachs resigned in protest, claiming that the crisis had been caused by an insufficiently absolute application of his policies.

Note: In his defence it should be said that he had also called for a halt to Russian debt payments. The finance officials of the G7 countries, whose leaders enjoy making speeches about the victory of democratic capitalism, continued to insist on regular payments. This helped to sabotage the Russian reform movement. See: DEBT.

TECHNOCRAT A word which means what it says, but perhaps not as we normally understand it.

The roots appear to be describing someone who has power (*crat*) thanks to their specialized knowledge or skills (*techne*). Observation of the technocrat at work is enough to tell us that the roots have been inversed. This is someone whose skill is the exercise of power. It follows quite naturally that there is no suggestion of purpose, direction, responsibility or ethics. Just power. John Ruskin described this function as "intricate bestiality."[3] See: TECHNOLOGY.

TECHNOLOGY Inanimate, passive material which is not science.

In any civilization, technology is shaped, directed and controlled by the conscious effort of society. Individuals who treat technology as an animated force capable of deciding the direction of society are engaged in the destruction of civilization.

Science is not technology. Science, as Samuel Johnson pointed out in his dictionary, is knowledge.[4] And knowledge is understanding. It is easy to argue that science is animate and inevitable. But once it is applied it is no longer science.

The application of science—that is, technology—is a matter of options, matching chosen means to chosen ends. Societies have often decided not to use technological breakthroughs made possible by science. After several experiments with gas warfare, most societies decided to abandon it. After dropping two atomic bombs, society dropped no more. Although capable of altering the disposition of habitual criminals through surgical and technical intervention (lobotomy, shock treatment, castration), few societies do this. Although DDT was an effective insecticide, most societies have decided to stop using it.

With the explosion in activities known as the industrial revolution, a growing number of people began to believe that technology was inevitable. This created a conflict within society which first crystallized in the LUDDITE rebellion of 1811. The new rational technocracy—itself devoid of social direction—tended to accept the idea that technological development would provide not simply economic but social and political direction. This pushed those who disagreed into the realms of romanticism and idealism—that is, into a rejection of reality. They mistook the destruction of rural society and of nature itself by the industrial revolution for a fatal opposition between progress and preservation.

This was a false opposition. Civilization implies integration. Both progress and preservation, if they are seen as self-contained truths, imply exclusion. Civilization desires progress through science as actively as it desires a healthy society and a natural environment. Integration or BALANCE makes both possible, providing neither is allowed to run wild.

It is often forgotten that World War II was seen on the Allied side as a battle against the dictatorship of technology in a corporatist world indifferent to the individual. Charles de Gaulle, speaking at Oxford in 1941, examined the threat of technology to the individual. What makes de Gaulle's attitude particularly interesting is that he had devoted his career, before and after the war, to the advancement of technology and professionalism. The only way out, he said, was for "society to preserve liberty, security and the dignity of man. There is no other way to assure the victory of spirit over matter."[5] The message we repeatedly receive from the postwar technocracy is that the Axis was right after all.

One of the few things expected of our technocracy by the citizenry is that they will use their administrative skills to manage the integration of technology with the interests of society as a whole. Unsuited as they are to this simple task, the technocracy have responded that they would rather manage the citizen.

TENNIS A middle-class version of professional wrestling.

These gladiator sports provide easily identifiable stereotypes of mythological Heroes. Team sports soften and confuse the spectators' topology. Two-on-two or, better still, one-on-one leaves no room for doubt as to who is the prince or princess, who the beautiful but spoiled Achilles, who the strong but dull Hector, who the Menelaus moaner always betrayed by fate.

The secret to the success of tennis may be that the racquet is an ambiguous, blunted weapon suitable to the business class, but nevertheless with the feel of having descended from the more aristocratic rapier of the duellist. After all, the game originated with the French nobility, a fact which has always endeared it to the *nouveau riche*. And the word itself comes from "Tenez!"—which was shouted out by the person hitting the ball. At first glance this means, "Look out! Here it comes." But the aggressivity of the stroke suggests that it really means "Take that!"

TENURE A system of academic job security which has the effect of rating intellectual leadership on the basis of seniority. This may explain why universities are rarely centres of original thought or creativity.

The initial justification for tenure was the need to protect freedom of speech, due to the justifiable fear that controversial professors might suffer at the hands of disapproving financial or governmental interests. The continued development of law now means that this essential freedom could be protected in far simpler ways.

A subsequent justification for tenure turned on the idea that stability and peace are necessary for thought and creativity. Unfortunately, there is no reason to believe that academics are or have been for some time at the centre of original thought or creativity in Western civilization. There are happy exceptions, particularly in the sciences. But it could far more easily be argued that the stultifying isolation and stability of a university career has discouraged originality.

This is certainly one of the explanations for the return of **SCHOLASTICISM**, with its highly sophisticated *a priori* approach to learning. The scholastic uses the tyranny of expert rhetoric to suck the life out of free speech; and the tyranny made possible by their position of authority to force this rhetorical approach on their students.

THE   A very definite beginning to an assertion.

The truth. The answer. The solution. The true god. The dialectic. The rules of the market. The right thing to do. The only thing to do. The leader.

But how do they know? It might be possible to assert, for example, that in so far as pastry goes, the best *opéra* can be found at Auer in the old city in Nice. Some people may disagree. They may assert that another *opéra* in another *pâtisserie*—Dalloyau in Paris, for example—is the best. However I am prepared to demonstrate that they are wrong; that they are giving in to habit, personal interest or romanticism. The fundamental questions are the quality of the chocolate, the restraint in using sugar and the resulting variety of separate tastes.

Auer makes the best *opéra*. This is the most definite assertion I would be willing to make. See: **A**.

THINK TANK   An organization which invents disinterested intellectual justifications for the policies of the corporate groups that fund it. The result is an unfortunate confusing of knowledge and power. This growth industry now involves 226 important think tanks in the United States, sixty-seven in the United Kingdom, forty-six in Germany, forty-two in France and forty-two in Japan.[6] Thinking for money is a venerable **SOPHIST** tradition which has found its place again in the late twentieth century. See: **ACADEMIC CONSULTANTS.**

THIRD WORLD   More a social than an economic model.

It can be opposed to the balanced, integrated model of middle-class compromise which is generally sought after in the West. The Third World is characterized by civilized, rich, highly trained, multilingual élites who govern a weak middle class and, further down, the vast majority of the population. What we call Third World is, in reality, a reconstitution of the eighteenth- and nineteenth-century Western model.

The European and North American technocratic élites, who are generally unilingual, provincial and relatively illiterate except in their particular area of specialization, are often confused by the remarkable sophistication of élites such as the Mexican, who are clearly superior to those of the middle-class model. Our élites conclude that they cannot be the products of a Third World country, but of a more natural, open system better able to respond to the needs of the **GLOBAL** economy.

TOUGH   A characteristic claimed by presidents and prime ministers as the most important quality for a leader. Their most onerous responsibility.

This suggests a real or false naïveté about the position they occupy. Anyone can be tough once they have the levers of power in their hands. It is the easiest possible attitude, requiring neither courage nor reflection—and least of all intelligence.

Compassion is far more difficult. Effective and fair compassion—not the paternalistic or opportunistic sort—is even more so. Resisting the myriad corruptions of office is hard. Actually creating the best policies and turning them into effective actions requires hard work and intuition. Balancing the long term with the short requires remarkable common sense and intelligence. But being tough is leadership as defined by a sergeant-major.

The leader who vaunts her toughness is actually saying that she has contempt for the citizen and—since she is speaking directly to us—that we have contempt for ourselves. See: LEADERSHIP.

TRADE   A miracle drug which used to be a practical commercial activity.

It is now believed by (almost) all respectable economists, politicians, businessmen and bureaucrats that more trade is the best way to get out of our depression because it creates jobs and wealth.

Curiously enough we have traded more in the last twenty years than ever before in history. Each year there have been remarkable net increases, yet we have continued to sink deeper and deeper into depression. Could this possibly mean that not all trade creates jobs and wealth? Or that trade does not always create jobs and wealth, but can also destroy them?

Would it be more accurate to say that some trade creates and other trade destroys? Which it does appears to depend on where we are in history, on economic circumstances and on geographical positioning. If so, then trade is a potentially valuable mechanism with no inherent value.

This isn't what Adam Smith and David Hume thought. But then their idea of commerce revolved around much smaller companies run by merchants and manufacturers who had the direct involvement of ownership. Without entering into the endless debate over whether commerce produces rationality and temperance, it can be argued that—with the rise of a governing technocracy which does not own, of shapeless transnational corporations and of corporatist values—the role of trade has been radically changed.

Jobs and wealth are created by imagination converted into creativity, as well as a willingness to take risks on creativity and to think in the long term. There must also be enough economic stability to make a long-term risk and creativity profitable. To the extent that trade encourages these factors, it is a positive mechanism. To the extent that it discourages them, it is negative.

Why then are we blindly obsessed by the idea that ever more trade must produce prosperity? Our experts keep telling us that just a little bit more will do the trick. Yet in separate conversations the same experts tell us that industrial production in developed countries is a doubtful prospect and that chronic unemployment may be here to stay. Increased trade seems to accentuate not discourage these problems.

The explanation may be that ours is a society which punishes creativity and rewards conventional thinking. And the most conventional idea of the last quarter-century has been that only through trade can we prosper. As this linear conviction presses on through continuing failure, the fear grows that a mistake is being made and so we press on ever more desperately, trading the way some people believe they are dieting when they have anorexia.

A more sensible approach might be to treat trade not as a religion but as a commercial activity. This might free us to think about the practical implications of today's trade mechanisms. What are we trading and to what purpose? If the effect of something is not positive, then only ideological blindness or masochism can make us insist that salvation lies in doing more of it. See: HARD WORK.

TRADING WITH THE ENEMY ACT   The ultimate American military weapon.

After the defeat of conventional forces in Vietnam and Cuba, this act, which prevents all commerce between the United States and its enemies, was meticulously enforced. Given the intricacies of international investment and trade, not a great deal can be done by anyone else with a country which the United States has blacklisted.

Thus the government in Hanoi survived for a dozen years on straight cash inputs from Moscow. Once the Soviet Union began to collapse and their aid with it, Vietnam had little choice but to surrender and convert to the market system. The same act remains in force against Cuba and will eventually prevail.

Two small details are perhaps worth mentioning. This act seems to win very precise victories for the free market. It has no effect on political or social systems. For example, the political prisoners remain in Vietnam's jails, including harmless Buddhist monks.

Second, the act is not enforced against all of America's enemies. Take the case of the **WAR ON DRUGS** which presidents regularly declare. More than half of the heroin sold in the United States comes from Burma, with the connivance of the Burmese government, one of the two or three most unpleasant dictatorships in the world. The death, violence and disorder in American cities brought on by the drug culture certainly justifies the use of the word "war." Yet Washington doesn't even discourage U.S. companies from investing in Burma, let alone forbid them by applying the act.

What exactly must an enemy do to be treated as one? It might be useful if the State Department were to issue an instruction booklet for confused revolutionaries, dictators and other foreign types.

TRANSNATIONAL CORPORATIONS   The seat of contemporary feudalism.

Received wisdom has it that the new feudalism is nationalist and was brought on by the collapse of the Soviet Bloc. The transnationals, given their support of the global economy, are seen as internationalist. This is a comic misrepresentation of feudalism, which had only an incidental relationship to geography and race. In no way does the nationalist phenomenon resemble the feudal system.

Feudalism was a highly abstract international order. It was the opposite of the Roman Empire, which remained in

Western memory as the model of a concrete international system. The death of Charlemagne in 814 ended the dream that Rome's administrative, military and economic order could be re-created under a Christian barbarian king, crowned for that purpose as Holy Roman Emperor.

Power quickly slipped into the hands of thousands of barons, princes and minor kings, each with power over their various estates, duchies, provinces and kingdoms. But these bits of land and the people attached to them were merely pawns in the ongoing struggle between noble families for power in the great feudal order. The principal interest of the aristocracy reflected their central loyalty, which was not to their land but to their class, with its religious structure, rules of conduct, honours and privileges.

Lands and populations endlessly changed hands. They were traded in negotiations, joined arbitrarily by marriage, bequeathed by death, transferred or confiscated with each loss of a noble's title. Feudalism consisted of endless manoeuvres to change the balances of power within the social order.

Wars were surprisingly inconclusive. Protocol determined who could fight whom, given their respective social standings, and under what conditions. The purpose of this incessant but apparently aimless fighting was to force minor adjustments not to a concrete system but to an abstract social order.

There is nothing new or feudal about the recent explosion in nationalism. This slow and continual drive went into its modern phase in 1919. We are now witnesses to the playing out of various local or racial obsessions in the West, but these bear no relationship to real, that is useful, power.

Where the nationalist forces win, the local élites can hope for a few privileges to pump themselves up, along with a decorative façade which asserts that they have control over events within their geographical area. In reality they are limited to secondary and passive activities—principally the definition of who is to be included in their "race" or group, along with formal responsibility for their welfare. However, the economic factors which will decide that welfare are defined and adjusted on a different plane—that of abstract feudalism—which escapes their control.

The more the local élites apply political control over their concrete area, the more real economic power slips away from their group out onto the abstract international plane of the transnationals, for whom these local bits of land called countries, and the populations attached to them, are mere pawns in the ongoing struggle of individual corporations for more power in the great global economy. And so the rise to "power" of nationalist groups actually decreases national power. The smaller the group, the more extreme and disastrous this paradox. Nationalism is the consolation prize for the losers in the battle for power at the end of the twentieth century.

Theoretically the counterweight to the abstract power of the transnationals should be a large national group. This may help, but not if used in isolation. International economic feudalism is based on the constant ability to shift investments or production from one national area to another in an ongoing auction for more favourable conditions. The ultimate weapon is the threat to decamp each time there is discussion of wage levels, job security, health standards, environmental standards or any standards at all relating to place and people.

The feudal economy's power lies, therefore, in the patterns of production. The power of the concrete national groups lies in the patterns of consumption.

In other words, the only realistic counterweight to economic feudalism is an agreement on common standards among a group of national areas sufficiently large to control the patterns of consumption. Consumption, after all, is the transnational's source of income. The key to a corporation's success in the feudal order is not its ability to produce (however low the cost) but its ability to sell.

The European community is an attempt to create international standards through control over consumption patterns.

But so long as the United States and Japan follow different rules, their group is not large enough. The Free Trade Agreement between Canada and the United States and NAFTA (Canada, Mexico and the United States) were both sold to the public with emphasis on the advantages to consumption. These treaties were really about patterns of production. They restructure large geographical areas to suit the methods of abstract economic feudalism.

Transnational systems revolve around goods, not individuals. In a citizen-based civilization the purpose of goods is to satisfy the needs of the citizenry. In an abstract market-based civilization of the transnational sort, the purpose of the citizen is to serve the logic of a supply-and-demand system.

This inversion couldn't help but have an effect on the rational élites. For much of the nineteenth and early twentieth centuries the technocracy attached itself to the nation state. Gradually, in the second half of the twentieth, the leading edge of the technocracy has attached itself to the transnationals.

The technocrats' devotion to structures and pure power led them quite naturally away from the logic of geography and onto the more abstract plane. That this international system cannot satisfy the economic and therefore the social needs of the particular area from which a technocrat comes is beside the point. As in the Middle Ages, local personal distress is an unfortunate inevitability in the search for larger, more important truths, such as the ideal structure of production.

The citizen remains confused by this switch in loyalties. For example, the taxpayer funds the training of technocratic business élites in the hope that they will attack economic problems. In reality their very training leads them to aggravate the situation by serving on another plane.

The rational, corporatist assumption of Western education makes it difficult for us to face up to the return of feudalism. The technocrats, with their mechanistic ways, see all structural movements as inevitable. Structural inevitability is their replacement for the concept of the public weal.

Most of those who reject this mechanistic determinism see the transnationals as villains in an international plot.

If only it were that simple.

These complex structures resemble centipedes, with sections spread around the world. They have an internal logic tied to lower costs and higher sales. Their sections die, prosper, move or divide according to that logic. Local populations are of no concern. Nor are the local chapters of the serving technocracy. As with the mediaeval social order, it is the order which matters, not any particular holders of specific titles.

The transnational has no direction or purpose. That's why it can benefit or destroy individual societies with equal disinterest. The whole system is a negation of the idea of civilization. Humanism and a citizen-based equilibrium are impossible in such circumstances.

In the late twentieth century we have reached the culminating moment in a movement first identified a half-century earlier by thinkers such as Harold Innis and Fernand Braudel. Technological change or a mercantilist movement can do more than change society. It can reduce everyone, even kings, to bit players.

As the transnationals have gained power, so the frustrated citizenry have been tempted to fall back on the nationalist myth for defence. But just as economic feudalism destroys a citizen-based society by operating on a separate abstract plane, so nationalism does the same by operating on yet another abstract plane—that of racial determinism. What's more, nationalism is powerless against the transnationals and simply accentuates economic problems.

The citizen's problem over the next few decades will be to control feudalism without denying the possibility of humanism. This means making use of the nation state—because that is the practical, concrete shape of our existence as citizens. But using it in a cooperative manner to establish international agreements on standards which spread far enough to make them enforceable. If we fail, we'll soon find our-selves trying to rebuild society from scratch, having disman-tled it in the name of abstract determinism. See: CORPORATISM, REASON and STANDARDS OF PRODUCTION.

TRICKLE-DOWN ECONOMICS The silliest economic theory of the twentieth century.

A government invests $100 billion in fighter airplanes. With a bit of luck, some of the R and D will trickle down into civil aeronautics, for example, giving a billion-dollar boost to a passenger airplane project.

But if what the government wanted was to give civil aero-nautics a billion-dollar boost, they have just overspent by $99 billion. What's more, they have done it in a slow, awkward and uncertain way. On the other hand, if what they needed were new fighter airplanes, they shouldn't have been dis-tracted from their duty by some unessential passenger planes.

Trickle-down economics was introduced in the early 1960s by men like Robert McNamara. For thirty years it caused delay and waste and justified overspending. By the late 1980s its credibility had worn out. It was then rebaptized as **DUAL USE** economics.

TRIUMPH OF THE WILL The inspirational and technical source of modern advertising, public relations, political packaging, feature film mythologizing and most television documentaries.

It was Hitler himself who in 1934 insisted that Leni Riefenstahl make a feature film in the guise of a documen-tary about the Nazi party's annual Nuremburg rally. Hitler's genius for this new art of propaganda had led him to choose a young dramatic film-maker who was also a professional dancer and actress. What he wanted, as Robert Dassanowsky-Harris has pointed out, was far more than propaganda.[7]

Riefenstahl immediately understood that this film could have no plot. Its place would have to be filled by an intense use of the effects normally used to illustrate the story. This dazzling use of form would replace content. The result was a dramatic tension which had little or nothing to do with the banal events of the rally. Indeed, there was no need for anything to happen at the rally. And so, thanks to the use of modern equipment, dramatics could replace drama. Indeed the most remarkable characteristic of *Triumph of the Will* is that it is devoid of content.

Many of Riefenstahl's methods had been used before. Some by other ideologies, some by commercial film-makers. As for the formal realization that "content" was an obstacle to the exercise of power, Mussolini had worked his way through that problem in the 1920s. Riefenstahl, like Hitler, could take advantage of Mussolini's and Stalin's experiments in public relations. What was new was her understanding of talking movies, which were only five years old, as a tool of public discourse.

She drew together all the known techniques of cinema-graphic public relations and used them to package the most important raw political force of the time. The result demonstrated that the techniques of cinema allowed not simply separation of verbal, historical and contemporary meaning from the image which theoretically represented them, but the domination of language and real events by the dramatic use of images.

Her primary technique was that the camera never stopped moving and so the viewer was caught up in the drama of motion as if on a roller-coaster. Much of the time her cameras were following banal objects like the back of Hitler's hand. Marching legs. Shovels. Flags. The sun rises to a swell of rising music and we see in the beautiful Gothic windows of Nuremburg houses that Nazi flags are swaying gently like the lace curtains favoured by little old ladies. Legs goose-stepping aggressively to soft music are alternated with small babies playing to booming martial music.

Most shots last no longer than five seconds. Close-ups constantly alternate with mass movement. The Brownshirts—whose élite had been massacred by Hitler a short time before—are shown having romantic, boyish fun as if at a scout camp while the speeches go on about fraternity and loyalty. A speech by Hitler to a national work brigade insists that Germany must be classless and that all Germans must engage in manual labour. It is succeeded a few minutes later by another speech in which Hitler says to senior party members that they are the élite—the ruling class which will reap the benefits of power and run everything. The words have been so subsumed in the visual drama that there is no real sense of contradiction.

Indeed, as the portrait of a real event the film makes no sense at all. Yet the viewer is constantly breathless. This divorce of image from reality, precisely in order to suggest meanings for which no argument is offered, has remained the central theme of propaganda.

Calvin Klein sells underwear with muscular young people who aren't wearing any. Like Hitler, they are presented as totems. Diet Coke shows their bottle against the photo of a crowd of intense marathon swimmers about to race away. The only words are "TASTE IT." As with the Brownshirts having boyish fun, the product, the images and the words have no relationship. The non-linear suggestion, which avoids all the burdens of proof and argument, is that wearing Calvin Klein underwear will make you beautiful and muscular. Drinking Diet Coke will have the same effect, except that you must wear goggles and a bathing suit. To note that Calvin Klein actually produces a cheap and banal product or that soft drinks make you fat and rot your teeth would be a cynical reference to an irrelevant reality.

In any case, it isn't about selling underwear. In a 1992 examination of television advertising during American presidential elections, the most obvious characteristic in every election and relating to every candidate was that these ads were "not communicating information but eliciting emotion."[8]

Whenever a party leader speaks in *Triumph of the Will*, the viewer can make a concerted effort to shut out the moving image, the mesmerizing light, the emotive music and coldly isolate the individual. Most of them turn out to be middle-aged portly men with strangled little voices. They look comic in their uniforms. They contradict their own heroic images. But the film techniques sweep all of that away and they become like gods bathed in heavenly light on deific podiums. These techniques are habitually used nowadays at political meetings from the local level to the nomination of leaders.

Goebbels later explained what was being invented under Hitler's guidance. "This is the really great art—to educate without revealing the purpose of the education." The Nazis saw this as "apolitical" education or, as Anton Kaes puts it, politicizing through entertainment.[9] Part of the secret to the success of this technique is the transformation of the documentary into dramatic art or, as Oliver Stone has demonstrated, of dramatic art into the documentary.

The point is not that the moving picture is essentially dishonest, but that its techniques permit a separation of the image from reality and the creation of an alternate reality which may be an absolute lie. See: *PLATOON.*

TRUTH   A reassuring notion which, in practice, is difficult to identify. The determination to establish truth often means that violence must be done to other people.

"Truth is life," Frank Lloyd Wright said,[10] which inevitably includes death and suggests that while a reasoned answer is useful, it will not be true—unless life (or reality) is denied. For those who are afraid of reality—that is, of life—it is important to find a naïve construct which can be identified as truth.

One explanation for the popularity of courtroom dramas is that they turn endlessly around the problem of truth. The specialists battle over details in a complex procedure involving policemen, lawyers, expert witnesses and judges, while the JURY watches, listens and waits. The professionals struggle with structure while the citizen strives to retain a clear sense of the spirit of the law.

Each knows that a trial is not primarily about guilt or innocence, but about realizable truth. What can we know? Can we really know it? What can we understand it to mean?

That is why the reduction of law to technical judgements produces public anger. The area of criminal justice is only a lightning rod for general frustration. The frustration with the bureaucratic process is not one reducible to sentiments of right or left. It is an anger that the search for truth has been reduced to regulations which are only peripherally concerned with reality. To reduce law to the letter, in opposition to the spirit, is perceived by the citizenry, whose law it is, to be the ultimate betrayal. See: WISDOM.

U

UNCONSCIOUS The introduction of the unconscious and the collective unconscious by **FREUD** and Jung permitted the reinstatement of the gods and destiny in modern society.

REASON had been used to tie down every conscious human act and thus formally eliminated from our lives the rule of superstition and ignorance. The *discovery* of the unconscious opened wide a back door and created a new irrational power called **MYTHOLOGY**.

UNEMPLOYMENT An expensive luxury.

So expensive that industrialized societies cannot afford more than a certain percentage of the adult population unemployed for more than a few years. This seems to be less than a decade and somewhere between 5 and 7 per cent.

Unfortunately there is no practical relationship between this little funding problem and the economic policies which have held sway in the West throughout the last quarter of the twentieth century. To all intents and purposes they exist on separate planets.

It is therefore entirely possible to follow faithfully all of the recommended policies relating to growth, competitiveness, efficiency, trade and retraining, only to find that the economy is being bankrupted by the level of unemployment. What this suggests is that our economic policies are abstract ideologies unrelated to the real societies they are invented to serve.

UNITED STATES

1. Centre of the greatest empire in the history of the world.
2. The first great empire since Rome not to see itself as the official reincarnation of Rome, which may mean that, unlike the others, it is Rome.
3. The constant recipient from Britain, the immediately preceding empire, of courtierlike attentions in the degenerate, late-Athenian style, which may confirm 2.

   The Roman élites looked to Athens for their reassuring cultural background. As the size and imperial nature of the empire grew, so the insecurity of the honest Roman soldier-farmers came to the fore and they turned increasingly to the slick Athenian men of culture. Roman architecture became more and more derivative of Greece. And Rome itself was permanently swarming with Athenian gentlemen who had fled their ever-more provincial homeland to advise the new rich on decor, grammar and the proper form of public debate.

   In much the same way New York, Washington and Los Angeles swarm with ever-larger numbers of British actors capable of the grand style, journalists, editors and antique dealers. The élites remain addicted to English furniture and fussy patterns, to the English country-house style and (like the Romans trooping off for a bit of culture in Athens) troop off regularly to London.
4. A nation given either to unjustified over-enthusiasms or infantile furies.

   Such theatrical extremes are often the privilege of the truly powerful. What distinguishes the American versions is the carpet upon which they are played out—an admirable **MYTHOLOGY** of individual freedom which real life converts into a short-term view of the best chance for personal gain.
5. A degenerate civilization. A nation in decline.

   These are broad themes which are hard to quantify when the history of the empire is still in progress. In any case, what do "degenerate" and "decline" mean? Rome was degenerate in AD 100 and in serious decline. The borders were undulating with barbarians. The empire itself was slipping into revolt. Then Hadrian came to the throne. Between AD 117 and 138 he motivated everyone capable of motivation. The empire recovered. As a result, the fall of the Roman Empire took about 350 years.

6. A highly sophisticated **THIRD WORLD** country.

The three-way contrast between the complex, civilized, rich and highly trained élites, the weak middle class and the vast majority of the population who are excluded from the benefits of the empire and so participate mainly through the great American mythology is what first strikes those who come from more middle-class societies. The nation whose mythology is devoted to equality is increasingly a society of class divisions in the style of the Third World.

7. A late-nineteenth-century state.

There are certain truths about each country having to do with geography and history that can't really be changed, even by Herculean will-power. When revolutionary attempts are made to change a nation's "circumstances," the result is usually confusion and disorder. The United States seems to be largely a product of high capitalism. The nation became a great empire thanks to a system of unregulated capitalism which first involved slaves, then semi-slaves and powerless immigrants. There have been recurring attempts to bring the nineteenth-century system into check, but these have never lasted more than four or eight years. As a result, the natural state of the empire has been and continues to be unregulated capitalism.

8. A profoundly divided nation destined for permanent civil war.

This is the inescapable result of building a nation on the enslavement of one part by another. Those who think of society as a living organism cannot help seeing organized mass slavery as a self-inflicted wound which can never heal. The larger and stronger the body grows, the more it will feel pain and bleed. Humans learn to live with agony and violence. We are a species as adaptable as rats. But the violence of America must be in some way the inheritance of its economic creation.

9. A nation from which the second-largest commercial export is cultural products and which, as a direct consequence, treats free access everywhere for these products as the primary characteristic of a free country.

The domination of smaller local cultures by that of America is seen as the inevitable result of the irresistible attraction of American culture. If the result is that these smaller societies lose their cultures, this is seen as the intelligent expression of their freedom. American culture, like that of Japan, is structured to eliminate or to assimilate all but token foreign penetration.

10. Several completely separate countries unified only by two mechanisms: an internal market, gigantic, rich and varied enough to make foreign markets of little importance; and a mythology so brilliant and pure that it can never interfere with real life.

11. Home of Thomas Jefferson, the most remarkable public figure yet produced by the modern West.

12. Centre of the greatest empire in the history of the world.

UNIVERSITY   A place in which a civilization's knowledge is divided up into exclusive territories.

The principal occupation of the academic community is to invent dialects sufficiently hermetic to prevent knowledge from passing between territories. By maintaining a constant flow of written material among the specialists of each group they are able to assert the acceptable technique of communication intended to prevent communications. This in turn establishes a standard which allows them to dismiss those who seek to communicate through generally accessible language as dilettantes, deformers or popularizers. See: ACADEMIC CONSULTANTS and SCHOLASTICISM.

URBAN RICH   People for whom society means dressing up to go to balls for fatal diseases.

URBANE WEATHER PATTERNS
RAIN IN JUNE.
   Terrible for June brides.

RAIN IN JULY, AUGUST.
   Terrible for summer holidays.

RAIN IN SEPTEMBER, OCTOBER.
   Terrible for the *vendange*.

RAIN IN NOVEMBER.
   It rains everywhere in November, except South Africa, where the climate was perfect before the political problems began.

RAIN IN DECEMBER THROUGH APRIL.
   Terrible for skiing.

RAIN IN MAY.
   Makes the mosquitoes impossible during the summer.

RAIN AND LACK OF RAIN IN AGRICULTURE.
   Farmers complain about everything. Besides, they're subsidized.

SNOW
   Terrible except in ski resorts.

SUN
   Causes skin cancer on beaches.

WIND
   Causes headaches and sometimes suicide unless you own a sailboat.

V

VENEREAL   From Venus, the goddess of love, this word refers to the reality of desire. With the rise of Protestantism and science the word "disease" was tacked on in a revealing combination of categorization and moralizing.

"Which disease?" "The disease of love."

VENICE   The original model of modern dictatorship, in which commercial power finds its cultural expression in painting, architecture and music. Anything, that is, except language.

The merchant princes of the Venetian Republic feared that debate, whether in the cultural or the political form, would undermine the state's commercial imperative. They used their power and money to build palaces and churches. To decorate them with painting and statuary. To fill them with the most glorious music. The lists of great Venetian artists and composers are endless. So long as the Republic remained an aggressive economic power, the list of writers was an empty page. The power of language was limited to commercial paper or gossip so that it could not interfere with the corporatist dictatorship.

Words didn't gain a larger, more important role in Venice until the plays of Carlo Goldoni began to examine and mock society's structures in the eighteenth century. By then the Republic's power had slipped away and the hard-edged, *nouveau riche* forms of the city were mutating into a harmless romantic shell. See: **CAPITALISM.**

VICO, GIAMBATTISTA   Neapolitan philosopher of the early eighteenth century. Perhaps the first modern humanist thinker to be buried alive beneath the propaganda of the rational absolutists.

Vico criticized the vaunting of judgement without context; that is, of rational abstractions applied piecemeal without reference to reality or history. His was an inclusive approach opposed to what he saw as rational exclusion or exclusivity. Above all, he reintroduced the role of time and space, which humanists regularly return to, in order to argue that problems cannot simply be isolated and solved. They belong to civilization in all its senses. Whether "solved" or left alone, they will reverberate well beyond their small space. Vico's was an argument of equilibrium or **BALANCE.**

VIRGINITY   Our tendency to confuse chastity with goodness has been replaced by other confusions. But the equation of personal physical purity and public ethical virtue remains.

This is a long-standing *non sequitur* in Western civilization, predating even Christianity. It is an area in which we could learn a great deal from the clarity of the Buddhist tradition. There virginity and general physical virtue has a role. It indicates that the individual is withdrawing from any contact with the day-to-day activities of the world in order to concentrate on his own salvation. Monks don't fornicate, but neither do they garden.

The rest of the populace, who are unwilling to make this great effort, must live as best they can knowing they run the long-term risks of reincarnation. There is lots of room for them to do good, either through practical actions or by feeding the helpless monks. Virginity and physical puritanism are there if they want to embrace them, but this is unlikely to affect whether they are reborn as a slug or a king.

VISION   A state of honesty which is often misrepresented as a divine purpose.

At the end of Euripides' *The Bacchae*, Agavë holds the dripping, lacerated head of her son, whom she has herself killed and ripped to pieces while caught up in a vision. Her father, Cadmus, says: "And whose head is that you are holding in your arms?"

Agavë: A lion's—so the women said who hunted it.

Cadmus: Then look straight at it. Come, to look is no great task.

Agavë looks; and suddenly screams.

Agavë: What am I looking at? What is this?

Cadmus: Look at it steadily; come closer to the truth.

Agavë: I see—O gods, what horror! Oh, what misery![1]

Visions of redemption or infinite wealth or superior destinies for a particular racial group are among the thousands of false visions in whose face we fear to look, and so believe that we are hunting lions.

Yet Shiva Naipaul has quite rightly pointed out that: "a people without a vision must inevitably perish."[2] People who are panicked by the temporary nature of their own lives, insist that vision involves subservience to structure. They reassure themselves by believing that humans can have no purpose unless it is grand enough to make the individual a servant of some rational or universal system. In such a case, a flawed methodology such as the market-place or centralized management or free trade—each of which can be useful if treated as a practical method and balanced with others—is happily mistaken for a vision.

But an honest vision is a matter of seeing; at best of seeing ourselves. When we cannot, we slip into a life of pretence where our existence is dependent on those who can see on our behalf. These religious or political or economic visionaries encourage us to wallow in comforts which we shall know only by reflection and promise.

To see is to come to terms with ourselves. For a community or a nation, an honest vision is a shared internal agreement on the nature of the relationship between the individuals. Although this is a practical rather than an abstract relationship, it is not principally one of self-interest or of contract. It is a matter of seeing the shared interest.

VOLTAIRE
"That nasty man who did so much good."

Paul Valéry

Is it because Voltaire wasn't afraid to be nasty that he did so much good? Almost certainly. There is no convincing evidence that writers can do their job by being nice.

And why should they be nice? To be asked to dinner? To be part of a corporation of writers, which like all corporate groups rewards discretion? To be rewarded with money, prizes and titles?

Nice writers are usually working for someone or senile or in the wrong business. Those who have done the most good, as Voltaire pointed out, have "mostly been persecuted."[3] The nasty sort continue to be persecuted in most countries. In the West they have to deal with more sophisticated assaults such as bankrupting lawsuits and job loss. Worst of all—in this society of expensive communication systems—they are threatened by irrelevance.

What about their messy personal lives, their greed, their jealousies, their hypocrisy? Who cares? Voltaire himself had a more than average number of flaws and contradictions. He still created the language which ended a regime.

Writers aren't supposed to be life models or religious prophets, clean of mind, clean of body. Nor are they supposed to be loved.

Their only job is to make language work for the reader. That is the basis of free speech. Whatever the vested interests of the day may be, they invariably favour an obscure language of insider's dialects and received wisdom. So the writer turns nasty. It's a public service.

W

WAR Children love war, especially civil war.

In peacetime parents think children can be told what to do. Civil wars are wonderful because suddenly children can be grown-ups. It's an opportunity to get rid of their parents, sometimes permanently. Instead of being bribed with toy guns and games, they can shoot real people. They can shoot each other.

WAR ON DRUGS A type of war which is redeclared every few months by Western government leaders without intervening victories or defeats.

Hundreds of millions of dollars are spent on police work, sophisticated anti-drug technology, special helicopters, detection equipment, border controls, spraying jungle areas from the air and undercover campaigns, both local and international. The result is periodic drug busts which are publicized as big or enormous or horrifying or exciting. These are accompanied by celebratory photo sessions for the press, involving bags of drugs and piles of captured weapons.

However, the authorities have never managed to intercept more than 10 per cent of the drugs sold each year.

These powders are virtually undetectable. They flow like water across all governmental barriers seeking out the inevitable openings the way floods flow to the lowest ground.

There are thousands of smuggling networks at any one time. Yet the police may spend years uncovering a small group. Within a few weeks a new network will have replaced the one which was "smashed," as the headlines announced. The reality is that drugs can only be dealt with at the stage of production or that of consumption. Everything in between—which is where we put all our efforts—is a waste of time.

The causes of production and consumption are the same. They involve some combination of poverty, despair, social instability, lack of education and lack of economic alternatives. If governments were serious about drugs they would spend their money not on combative reactive technology but on removing the causes.

This would mean integrating the problem of heroin and cocaine production into the forefront of foreign policy, which is never done. Although drugs represent the single largest nefarious influence in international finance, they are not considered a sufficiently dignified matter to balance against strategic concerns or trade competition.

As for consumption, Western countries continue to find themselves too short of cash to do other than let the social infrastructures of the poor stagnate. Even a reform-minded American government finds itself scrambling to find funds for education and health care. In the United States alone, two billion dollars a year could be recuperated from the government's subsidies of drug wars lost, in advance.

WEATHER FORECASTERS Experts who never apologize for being wrong.

The concept of expertise seems to negate that of accountability. Thus, while there is nothing remarkable about being wrong, it is astonishing to speak to the same audience the next day without either an apology or some sort of explanation. Since for the purposes of argument it must be assumed that neither speaker nor listener has received a blow to the head during the intervening hours, there is a suggestion that either the expert or the expert-worshipper cannot bear the admission of error and therefore of a flawed past and therefore of memory. Like sunshine and rain, expertise always resides in the future.

WESTERN CIVILIZATION This phenomenon is particularly aggressive about its superiority. Even among themselves Westerners are constantly asserting that they have the best religion, language, method of government or production. They can't wait to tell people everywhere in the world how to dress, pray, raise their children and organize their cities.

Non-Westerners are at first charmed, then paralyzed by our insistent self-assurance. And when, a decade later, our reorganization of cities such as Bangkok has led to disaster or of most African economies to famine and urban poverty, they find themselves pressured to take Western advice on how to get out of their mess.

What makes us such know-it-all busybodies? Christianity? The deformation of Christianity? The Reformation? The fall of Christianity? These are just four among the dozens of standard and contradictory explanations.

It may simply be that we have not got over being the Barbarians. Indeed our problem has never been the fall of the Roman Empire but, with a few Italian exceptions, that we are not the Romans, who felt the same way about not being the Greeks.

Western history harps on about the growing reliance of the degenerate Romans upon the virile Barbarians to man their armies. So virile that we eventually sacked Rome and took it over. This interpretation leaves the impression that Rome was filled with overweight people lying about in a drunken stupor or fornicating. We tend to skip over the high and, from a Christian point of view, positive civilization into which Rome had evolved. Even a glance at the fifth-century mosaics of Ravenna shows a level of artistic skill which we, the Barbarians, saw, admired, but were unable to absorb. And so it was lost for a thousand years. We may have conquered

Rome, but we remained bumpkins. As documents of the time indicate, we were treated as such by the élites of the Empire.

Charlemagne was not simply claiming historic legitimacy when he had himself crowned Roman Emperor by Pope Leo III in St. Peter's on Christmas Day of the year 800. He was giving in to his own colonial emotions by claiming the status of those who had been superior to his people. As with the classic *nouveau riche*, he had succeeded in his own terms but felt obliged to wrap himself in the trappings of the thing he could never be. Charlemagne was the great king of a large but backward tribe called the Franks (see: PROGRESS). He wasn't a Roman emperor. He was a Barbarian.

The long see-saw battle among the tribes of Europe over the crown of the Holy Roman Emperor continued this seemingly indigestible inferiority complex. In its wake, German and Russian kings declared themselves Caesar (Kaiser, Czar). In our own century the Roman overlord past has been repeatedly claimed by dictators and democrats.

In any case, for the last half-century this sort of squabbling has been over the illusion of appearances. After all, the reality of power had slipped away from the three European tribes and moved on to North America, yet another step removed from Rome. The inferiority complex followed in a cumulative manner.

No country has more imitated Roman architecture and mannerisms than the United States. An early identification with the honest but militaristic ideal of Cincinnatus quickly declined into a taste for "triumphs" and "bread and circuses." George Washington would have been horrified, but he was dead when Congress had him sculpted, larger than life, as Zeus dispensing liberty.[1] Why Zeus would dispense liberty isn't clear, except to provide mythological legitimacy.

As the American dream gradually falters, so the sense of national superiority asserts itself with a growing reliance on Roman-style trappings of power. The most obvious element is a weakened emperor who today surrounds himself with more than 1,000 personal advisers. This was what the Romans called a praetorian guard. It follows that as government officials leave for the airport from their Washington houses, which are fully equipped with alarms and window-bars to protect them against their fellow-citizens, it is to tell non-Americans, rich and poor around the world, that they ought to be doing things the American way. See: SUPERIORITY.

WHITE BREAD Post-modern urban individuals, who spend their days in offices, have taken to insisting that she or he is primarily a physical being equipped with the muscles of a work-horse and the clothes of a cowboy. The rejection of white bread in favour of loaves compacted with the sort of coarse, scarcely ground grains once consumed solely by the poor follows quite naturally.

White bread is the sophisticated product of a civilization taken to its logical conclusion: essential goods originally limited by their use in daily life have been continually refined until all utility has been removed. Utility is vulgar. In this particular case, nutrition and fibre were the principal enemies of progress. With the disappearance of utility what remains is form, the highest quality of high civilizations.

And whenever form presides, it replaces ordinary content with logic and artifice. The North American loaf may be tasteless but remains eternally fresh thanks to the efficient use of chemicals. The French baguette turns into solidified sawdust within two hours of being baked, which creates the social excitement of having to eat it the moment it comes out of the oven. The Italians have introduced an intriguing mixture of tastes—hand towels on the inside and cardboard in the crust. The Spanish manage to give the impression of having replaced natural fibre with baked sand. There are dozens of other variations. The Greek. The Dutch. Even the world of international hotels has developed its own white roll.

In each case, to refine flour beyond utility is to become refined. This phenomenon is by no means limited to bread or even to food. Our society is filled with success stories of high culture, from men's ties to women's shoes.

WHITE HOUSE STAFF Like all praetorian guards it separates the leader from the legally constituted parts of a government. In the process, it also separates the leader from the populace. Whether this protection is accomplished with physical or political weapons is irrelevant.

Those who serve in a praetorian guard have no legal status in the structure of government. They serve at the pleasure of the leader. This means that, whether armed like the Romans or in courtly dress or on leave from Harvard, they are courtiers.

One of President Clinton's first acts on taking office in 1993 was to reduce the White House staff from 1,394 to 1,044. It is always good to save a few million dollars. But what was the president doing with 1,394 personal advisers? The constitution provides him with an official set of counsellors—his Cabinet officers—who are approved and regulated by the legislative body. Each of these has responsibility over a large and competent bureaucracy whose job it is to advise and serve the president through their Cabinet Secretary.

The only purpose a president can have in surrounding himself with a fat doughnut of extra-constitutional courtiers is to protect himself from the institutions which were created by the constitution in order to give a responsible shape to democratic government. Of course, presidents have always had personal advisers. Woodrow Wilson had five. This is one of those cases when a gradual increase in size over a long period of time eventually constitutes a qualitative change. Those who serve in the White House may not feel this historic slide.

But from Richard Nixon on, every elected president has eventually been victimized by the White House staff. It could even be argued that their presidencies were seriously damaged and in some cases virtually destroyed by the courtiers surrounding them.

After all, praetorian guards do eventually destroy the leaders they serve. That's one of their characteristics. It is the natural result of leaving responsibility in the hands of people, whatever their intentions, who exercise public power outside the legal structures of the state. They exist only as reflections of the leader, yet they can act as if they were themselves real. They resemble the living dead in a horror story. See: COURTIERS.

WIND Caused by:

1. Mountain ranges pierced by passes through which air rushes, such as the *Chinook* (hot) through the Rockies and the *Mistral* (cold) down the Rhone.
   Common effects: depression, headaches, suicide.
2. Dried beans soaked and cooked in the same water. See: POLITENESS.
   Common effects: embarrassment, unpleasant smells.
3. Skyscrapers, which simulate the effect of a mountain range.
   Common effects: unpleasant, depressing streets.

WISDOM The purpose of doubt.

Wisdom, then, is life with uncertainty, the opposite of power or ideology. There is a simple story of two buildings which illustrates the difference.

In the centre of imperial Rome, just behind the Pantheon, you would once have found the Temple of Minerva, goddess of wisdom. By the Middle Ages it was an abandoned ruin. The various Christian orders which usually built their churches on the solid foundations of old pagan temples had been curiously discreet around Minerva, placing themselves to one side or the other.

But in 1280, the Dominicans decided to build their Roman headquarters on top of the old temple. They had run the Inquisition since its creation forty years earlier and had invented and developed its methods. Their job was to eliminate heresy by actively "inquiring into" it. They inquired in order to establish *a priori* truth. They had begun using torture in 1262.

The Dominicans baptized their new Gothic basilica Santa Maria Sopra Minerva. Saint Mary Over Minerva. Power over wisdom. Power over doubt. But theirs was a highly intellectual power. The Inquisition was the first truly modern organization and it developed a method of formal rational inquiry in order to establish documented legal truth.

It was also a profitable business. The basilica was enlarged in the fifteenth century by Cardinal Torquemada, uncle of the first Grand Inquisitor of Spain who had inquired into and burned approximately 2,000 individuals. A great deal of money went into decorating the chapels. In 1514 a large statue of the Redeemer was commissioned from Michelangelo and is still in its place.

On June 22, 1633, Galileo Galilei was brought to Santa Maria Sopra Minerva for the third day of his trial by the Inquisitor. The controversy surrounding his ideas had actually been going on for twenty-two years. At first, sensible church leaders had accepted his explanation of the Copernican theory, which demonstrated that the earth moved around the sun and not the opposite. They had been fascinated and intrigued by such new understanding. But the leading academics of the day—the Aristotelian or scholastic experts—had built their careers on other truths which they also could demonstrate, and with great INTELLIGENCE moreover. So they denounced him to the Inquisition.

On June 22nd, in the morning, in the great hall of the Convent of Santa Maria Sopra Minerva, Galileo was found guilty of holding a false doctrine. He went down on his knees and both abjured and condemned his own errors. He swore never to argue such doctrines again. It was thus definitively confirmed that the sun did rotate around the earth.

The lesson of this victory by a corporation of Aristotelian scholastics was not lost on succeeding generations of salaried experts. It had been shown, as Voltaire put it in his *Dictionary*, that people could be convinced to believe what they didn't believe.[2] In the last few decades alone, our own scholastics have been able to prove multitudes of unbelievable things

and so have carried society off in their desired direction.
(See: **ARMAMENTS** and **DEPRESSION**.)

Is this wisdom? It's better than wisdom. It's a sure thing.

WORLD CLASS   A phrase used by provincial cities and second-rate entertainment and sports events, as well as a wide
variety of insecure individuals, to assert that they are not
provincial or second-rate, thereby confirming that they are.

X

XENOPHOBIA (PASSIVE)   The English are fair, French bread is the best, Americans are individualists, Italian women are beautiful, Germans are real men because they are not circumcised, Canadians are nice, the Russians are courageous, the Welsh are poetic, Greece is the cradle of democracy, Argentinians are the essence of the male, Swedes are fair, the English are courageous, the Swiss are hardworking, Frenchmen are the best lovers, American culture is an expression of freedom, Australians are tough, the Chinese are smart, the Poles should have been superior to everybody, the Italians have style, language is the great love of the Irish, the English don't queue-jump, Canadians are courageous, God speaks directly to Iranians, *Que la France est belle*, Germans are efficient, Scots are smart, the Spanish are tough, the Brazilians are not racists, Norwegians are good-looking, Czechs are efficient, the English are at their best in a crisis, the Germans are courageous, the French are individualists, Canadians are hardy, the Swiss are efficient, the British are masters of understatement, Israelis are the best soldiers, Italians are romantic, Americans are courageous, the Scots are diligent and other reassuring, repetitive and boring fetishes.

XENOPHOBIA (ACTIVE) Passive xenophobia inverted so that the admirable qualities listed above become other people's unacceptable flaws. If this is expressed with sufficiently pure logic, it may become acceptable to control, exploit, even punish and if necessary kill those who belong to another blood line. See: BLOOD.

Y

YACHT One of the belongings from which a press **BARON** can fall and drown when the relationship between his **INFERIORITY COMPLEX** and his **BANKER** is no longer viable.

YES An affirmation which results in sexual, commercial or political consumption. Deliberate confusion of the three is central to advertising and public relations.

The underlying argument which accompanies this word is that we must not be afraid to say yes. "Say yes to life." The suggestion is that it takes courage to take a risk. In reality, yes is the traditional response of the passive party to the lover or the salesman or the person with power. If courage is to be treated as a serious factor then it must take the form either of a no or of a negotiation for better terms. Modern politics at their most cynical sell the courage to say yes. See: **REFERENDUM**.

YUGOSLAVIAN CIVIL WAR A common form of late-twentieth-century reality.

This typical postwar conflict involves irregular, mobile combat which mixes armies and civilians, professionals and amateurs, low-cost equipment and public terror. From 1960 on, the concurrent number of these wars has steadily risen to more than fifty. At the same time, Western armies have concentrated on developing a post-modern, hi-tech, abstract idea of professional warfare, which involves large-scale formalized clashes of titans and, above all, of titanic equipment. The result is that the largest and most sophisticated armies in the history of the world are by training, equipment and attitude incapable of fighting real modern wars.

Like the urbane French knights before Agincourt, they await a suitably superior enemy. Periodically, as with the Falklands or Iraq, they get a chance to strut their stuff with sandbox formality. Then they they go back to waiting for Armageddon.

Meanwhile, the fifty or so real wars go on. About one thousand soldiers die each day. Five thousand-odd civilians. Cities crumble. Children starve. Nations are destroyed. All of this as if real war and the armies of the West exist on the same planet but on separate planes, invisible to each other.

Periodically our titans manage to pierce this science-fictionlike separation and arrive on the scene with tanks and helicopters and parade about like magnificent knights in full armour on white stallions. Before and behind their progress the killing goes on.

The inflexible, managerial mind-set fixed in place in the staff colleges and general staffs in the two decades before 1914 remains firmly in place. From the trenches to the Maginot Line to Korea, Vietnam, even to Somalia, the determination to impose an abstract form on reality remains undented.

Z

ZAP The action of changing television channels by continually pressing the thumb onto a cordless remote control held like a gun. This may indicate the level of aggressive frustration in a disaffected population. Or perhaps it signals the death of linear narrative—the death of the story as we have known it for thousands of years. Perhaps this is the inevitable truth of a post-modern society which has wedded itself to electronic communications in the hope of being unified only to find itself fracturing. Or it could just be that there isn't much worth watching for more than ten seconds.

ZEALOT Someone who has the answer to a problem.

Originally a religious fanatic given to violence, the zealot is as likely today to be a **CORPORATIST** expert. They are, as Samuel Johnson defined them, "passionately ardent in any cause."[1] They are the bearers of truth.

ZENO Father of the paradox. Philosopher of the fifth century BC. A source of Socrates' technique and of humour as a weapon against power and pedantry. The other Zeno, also a philosopher and father of the Stoic movement, committed suicide.

ZINNIA   The ugliest flower in any garden.

The paradoxical idea that words have real but relative meaning leaves room for misrepresentation by those who wish to capture language for their own use. From ideologues to deconstructionists, they take the piece of the paradox that suits them and deform it by ignoring the rest.

Those who wish to resist this falsification of communication need only plant a zinnia and wait for it to bloom. With the meaning of the word "ugly" clearly established, the rest will fall easily into place. If that doesn't work, try marigolds.

NOTES

The Grail of Balance

1 Tom McArthur, *Worlds of Reference* (Cambridge: Cambridge University Press, 1986), 94.

2 Quoted in Michel de Montaigne, *Essais*, Volume II, 1588, Chapter 17, "De la praesumption": "Plus haut monte le singe, plus il montre son cul."

3 Samuel Johnson, *A Dictionary of the English Language* (1755; facsimile, London: Times Books Ltd., 1983). Quoted from the introduction. Johnson's original edition had no page numbers.

4 Denis Diderot, *L'Encyclopédie, un dictionnaire raisonné des sciences, des arts et des métiers*, edited by Alain Pons (Paris: Flammarion, 1986).

5 McArthur, *Worlds of Reference*, 105.

6 The edition in eight volumes quoted throughout is: Voltaire, *Dictionnaire Philosophique* (Paris: Librairie de Fortic, 1826).

7 Noah Webster, *An American Dictionary of the English Language* (New York: Johnson Reprint Corporation, 1970). This is a reprint of the original Webster's Dictionary, published in 1828.

8 Actually published posthumously in 1911.

9 Originally published as *The Cynic's Word Book* in 1906.

A

1 **A BIG MAC**—John F. Love, *McDonald's—Behind the Arches* (New York: Bantam Press, 1986), 15.

2 **AIR-CONDITIONING**—*The New York Times,* 21 October 1993, A10. Re: the tuberculosis incident, 7 June 1993, *IHT,* 1. Quote from Joseph Hopkins, a spokesman for United Airlines.

3 **ARMAMENTS**—Charles Mackay, *Extraordinary Popular Delusions and the Madness of Crowds* (New York: Harmony Books, 1980). Originally published in 1841.

B

1 **BABY SEAL**—George Orwell, *Animal Farm* (London: Penguin Books, 1987), 90. Originally published in 1945.

2 **BAD PEOPLE**—Voltaire, *Dictionnaire Philosophique,* "*Patrie,*" vol. 7, 252. *"Celui qui brûle de l'ambition d'être édile, tribun, préteur, consul, dictateur, crie qu'il aime sa patrie, et il n'aime que lui-même."*

3 **BAD PEOPLE**—*Le Monde,* 9 June 1993, 26. The third task was dealing with the inability of national governments to apply law in a world dominated by transnational economics. *"des intolérances ethniques"* and *"la quête extraordinaire et effrénée de l'argent sous toutes ses formes... Les classes dominantes de la politique et de l'économie...l'argent n'a pas d'odeur...sale, douteux et illicite."*

4 **BANKERS**—Samuel Johnson, *Pocket Dictionary of the English Language* (Chiswick: C. and C. Whittingham, 1826).

5 **BEES**—Voltaire, *Dictionnaire Philosophique,* "*Abeilles,*" vol. 1, 41.

6 **BURKE**—Conor Cruise O'Brien, *The Great Melody—A Thematic Biography and Commented Anthology of Edmund Burke* (Chicago: University of Chicago Press, 1992), 115.

7 **BURKE**—Ibid, 390.

8 **BUSINESS SCHOOLS**—Alain Chanlat, *"Lettre à Richard Déry:*

L'Occident, malade de ses dirigeants," June 1993, unpublished essay.

9 **BUSINESS SCHOOLS**—*The New York Times,* 14 November 1993, 26.

C

1 **CARLYLE**—Thomas Carlyle, *On Heroes, Hero-worship and the Heroic in History* (Philadelphia: Henry Altemus), 5. Originally published in 1841.

2 **CARLYLE**—Ibid, 114.

3 **CARLYLE**—Ibid, 322.

4 **CARLYLE**—Ibid, 269.

5 **CARLYLE**—Ibid, 265.

6 **COMEDY**—Salman Rushdie, speaking during an unannounced appearance at the Third Annual Benefit of the Canadian Centre of International PEN, Toronto, 7 December 1992.

7 **CONSULTANTS**—Xenophen, *Memorabilia,* I, vi, 11–13, Loeb Classical Library (Cambridge: Harvard University Press, 1992), 73.

8 **CONSUMPTION**—Eric Hoffer, quoted in James Hillman and Michael Ventura, *We've Had a Hundred Years of Psychotherapy and the World's Getting Worse* (San Francisco: Harper, 1992), 159.

9 **CORPORATISM**—Frederick Copleston, *A History of Philosophy* (New York: Image Book, Doubleday, 1985), Book 3, vol. vii, 214.

10 **CORPORATISM**—Information and quotations in this paragraph are drawn from James Hillman and Michael

Ventura, *We've Had a Hundred Years of Psychotherapy and the World's Getting Worse*, 137.

11 **CURE**—*The Globe and Mail*, 13 August 1993, 1.

D

1 **DECONSTRUCTIONISM**—This is an observation made by the author Eugene Benson.

2 **DEREGULATION**—*Le Monde*, 8 January 1994, 23.

3 **DIALECTS**—Vaclav Havel, "On Evasive Thinking," a speech to the Union of Czechoslovak Writers' conference, 9 June 1965. Translated by Paul Wilson.

4 **DICTIONARY**—Sources for the three definitions of truth are:
"consistent with," *The American Heritage Dictionary* (Boston: Houghton Mifflin Company, 1976);
"conformity to," Noah Webster, *An American Dictionary of the English Language.*
"in accordance with," *The Shorter Oxford English Dictionary* (London: Book Club Associates, 1983).

5 **DUAL USE**—Conversation with the author, 15 January 1994, Toronto.

6 **DUAL USE**—Three quotes from Jacques S. Gansler, "Transforming the U.S. Defense Industrial Base," in *Survival, The IISS Quarterly*, vol. 35, no. 4, Winter, 1993–4, 138, 141.

7 **DUAL USE**—In addition to Mr. Gansler's article see, in the same issue of *Survival*, Julian Cooper's "Transforming Russia's Defense Industrial Base," 147; *Le Figaro—Economique*, 26 January 1994, xi, *"Vers une 'liberalisation' des ventes d'armes"*; *Le Monde*, 28–29 November 1993, 9, *"La délégation générale pour l'armement veut être authorisée à exporter les matériels les plus modernes."*

E

1 **EDUCATION, PUBLIC**—*Newsweek*, 20 September 1993, 44. The study was carried out by the U.S. Department of Education.

2 **ELECTORS OF BRISTOL**—O'Brien, *The Great Melody*, 75.

3 **ETHICS**—John Rawls, *A Theory of Justice* (Cambridge, Mass.: Harvard University Press, 1971).

F

1 **FACTS**—Denis Diderot, *L'Encyclopédie*, vol. 2, 97. *"Fait" "...On peut distribuer les faits en trois classes, les actes de la divinité, les phénomènes de la nature, et les actions des hommes. Les premiers appartiennent à la théologie, les seconds à la philosophie, et les autres à l'histoire proprement dite. Tous sont également sujets à la critique."*

2 **FAITH**—From "The Apology" in Plato, *The Last Days of Socrates* (London: Penguin, 1954), 71.

3 **FRIENDSHIP**—William Blake, "The Marriage of Heaven and Hell," in *The Writings of William Blake*, ed. Geoffrey Keynes (London: The Nonesuch Press, n.d.), Plates 17-20, 157.

G

1 **GANG OF FIVE**—Voltaire, *Dictionnaire*, under *"Cartésianisme,"* vol. 3, 82.

H

1 **HELL**—Voltaire, *Dictionnaire*, vol. 4, 308. *"Enfer." "Dès que les hommes vécurent en société, ils durent s'apercevoir que plusieurs coupables échappaient à la sévérité des lois; ils punissaient les crimes publics; il fallut établir un frein pour les crimes secrets; la religion seule pouvait être ce frein."*

2 **HELL**—Diderot, *L'Encyclopédie*, vol. 2, 125, under *Fortune* (*Morale*).

3 **HUMANISM**—René-Daniel Dubois, 9 October 1991, Présentation du Mémoire conjoint de l'AQAD et du C.A.D., *"Nous ne voulons pas d'un monde dans lequel le sentiment d'être un humain est une maladie."*

I

1 **IMAGE**—*The Toronto Star,* 26 March 1994, A15.

2 **INAUGURATION GALA**—Kitty Kelley, *His Way—The Unauthorized Biography of Frank Sinatra* (New York: Bantam Books, 1986), 285.

3 **INFERIORITY COMPLEX**—Alfred Adler broke away from Sigmund Freud in 1911 and is known as the father of the inferiority complex. His key writings on the subject are:
1909: *Study of Organ Inferiority and Its Physical Compensation.*
1908: *Aggression Drive.*
1910: *Inferiority Feeling and Masculine Protest.*
1912: *The Neurotic Constitution.*
1918: *Social Interest.*

4 **INSTRUMENTAL REASON**—Max Weber, *The Theory of Social and Economic Organization,* trans. A.M. Henderson and Talcott Parsons (Illinois: The Free Press), 115.

5 **IRRADIATION**—Compiled by Barbara Dinham, *The Pesticide Hazard: A Global Health and Environmental Audit* (London: 2 ed Books for The Pesticide Trust, 1993).

6 **IRRADIATION**—Ibid.

J

1 **JOBS**—*The Guardian Weekly,* 28 February 1993, 4.

2 **JOBS**—*The Globe and Mail,* 23 February 1994, B7.

L

1 **LUDDITES**—Quoted by David Suzuki, *The Toronto Star*, 17 July 1993, D8.

2 **LUDDITES**—Oscar Douglas Skelton, *Life and Letters of Sir Wilfrid Laurier*, vol. 1 (Toronto: Oxford University Press, 1921), 321.

M

1 **MEMORY**—Johnson, *Dictionary*, 116. "Memory: the power of retaining or recollecting things past; that faculty by which we call to mind any past transaction."

2 **MEMORY**—*The Shorter Oxford English Dictionary*, vol. II (London: Book Club Associates, 1983), 1306. "Memory: 1. The faculty by which things are remembered.... 3. Recollection, remembrance.... An act or instance of remembrance; a recollection...."

3 **MUSSOLINI**—Denis Mack Smith, *Mussolini* (London: Paladin, 1983), 144.

4 **MUSSOLINI**—*Le Quotidien de Paris*, 7 June 1993, 15. A study of the football strategy has been done by the historian Paul Dietschy.

5 **MUSSOLINI**—*The Economist*, 2 April 1994, 5 and *The Economist*, 9 April 1994, 13.

N

1 **NEO-CONSERVATIVE**—Smith, *Mussolini*, 134.

2 **NIETZSCHE**—Ibid, 15.

3 **NIHILISM**—E.M. Cioran, quoted in an interview by Branka Bogavac Le Comte in *Les Lettres Français*, no. 33, June 1993, 18. *"Si vous essayez d'être libre, vous mourez de faim, et on ne vous tolère que si vous êtes successivement servie et despotique!"*

O

1 **ORAL LANGUAGE**—Harold A. Innis, *The Bias of Communication* (Toronto: University of Toronto Press, 1951).

2 **ORAL LANGUAGE**—Dante, quoted in Innis. Ibid, 22.

3 **ORGASM**—*The New Yorker*, 29 November 1993, 8.

4 **ORGASM**—Johnson, *Dictionary*.

P

1 **PLATO**—For a remarkable portrait of the atmosphere in Athens, see Donald Kagan, *Pericles of Athens and the Birth of Democracy* (London: Secker and Warburg, 1990).

2 **POWER, PUBLIC**—Diderot, *L'Encyclopédie*, vol. 2, 275. *"Pouvoir"* (*Droit nat. et politiq.*). *"Le but de tout gouvernement, est le bien de la société gouvernée. Pour prévenir l'anarchie, pour faire exécuter les lois, pour protéger les peuples, pour soutenir les faibles contre les entreprises des plus forts, il a fallu que chaque société établît des souverains qui fussent revêtus d'un* pouvoir *suffisant pour remplir tous ces objets."*

3 **PROGRESS**—Prof. Andrew Watson (Toronto), 26 June 1993. See also *The Islamic City*, ed. A.H. Hourani and S.M. Stern (Oxford: Bruno Cassirer, 1970), Chapter on Housing and Sanitation, 174–194.

4 **PUBLIC RELATIONS**—Smith, *Mussolini*, 144.

R

1 **ROTTEN BOROUGH**—*The New York Times*, 25 January 1993, A13.

S

1 **SAT**—*The New York Times*, 28 February 1994, A12, "New SAT sets students cramming."

2 SCHOLASTICISM—Diderot, *L'Encyclopédie*, vol. 2, 15, "Ecole (*philosophie de 1'*)," "...*scholastique, qui a substitué les mots aux choses, et les questions frivoles ou ridicules, aux grands objets de la véritable philosophie; qui explique par des termes barbares des choses inintelligibles ... Cette philosophie est née de l'esprit et de l'ignorance ...on raisonna sur les abstractions, au lieu de raisonner sur les êtres réels: on créa pour ce nouveau genre d'étude une langue nouvelle, et on se crut savant, parce qu'on avait appris cette langue. On ne peut trop regretter que la plupart des auteurs scholastiques aient faits un usage si misérable de la sagacité et de la subtilité extrême qu'on remarque dans leurs écrits.*"

3 SCHOLASTICISM—Frederick Copleston, *A History of Philosophy*, Vol. II: *Medieval Philosophy* (New York: Image Book, Doubleday, 1993), 312.

4 SCHOLASTICISM—Innis, *The Bias of Communication*, 80.

5 SCHOPENHAUER—Leni Riefenstahl, *The Sieve of Time: The Memoirs of Leni Riefenstahl* (London: Quartet Books, 1992), 178.

6 SCHOPENHAUER—Copleston, *A History of Philosophy*, Book 3, vol. VII, 263, 277.

7 SEX—John Ralston Saul, *Voltaire's Bastards: The Dictatorship of Reason* (New York: The Free Press, 1992), 488.

T

1 TALENT—*Milano Citta*, Spring 1993.

2 TASTE—*The Spectator*, 20 February 1993, 39.

3 TECHNOCRAT—John Ruskin, *The Stones of Venice*, 1851, Everyman's Library, ed. Ernest Rhys (London: J.M. Dent & Co., n.d.).

4 **TECHNOLOGY**—Johnson, *Dictionary.*

5 **TECHNOLOGY**—Charles de Gaulle quoted in *Charles de Gaulle, jour après jour,* Olivier Germain-Thomas et Philippe Barthelet (Paris: Nathan Press, 1990) 53, "...*les sociétés préservent la liberté, la sécurité et la dignité de l'homme. On ne voit pas d'autre moyen d'assurer en definitive le triomphe de l'esprit sur la matière.*"

6 **THINK TANK**—Edited by Alan J. Day, *Think Tanks: an International Directory* (Harlow, Essex: Longman, 1993).

7 *TRIUMPH OF THE WILL*—Robert Dassanowsky-Harris, "Leni Riefenstahl's Inner Migration, Self-Reflection and Romantic Transcendence," from *Nazism in Tiefland,* 1994, unpublished paper.

8 *TRIUMPH OF THE WILL*—Analysis by Elizabeth Kolbert of "The Living Room Candidate: A History of Presidential Campaigns on Television, 1952–1992," *The New York Times,* 17 July 1992, 81; an exhibition at the American Museum of the Moving Image, New York.

9 *TRIUMPH OF THE WILL*—Anton Kaes, *From Hitler to Heimat* (Cambridge, Mass.: Harvard University Press, 1989), 5.

10 **TRUTH**—Engraved over the fireplace in the living room of the house Frank Lloyd Wright built for himself in Oak Park, Illinois.

V

1 **VISION**—Euripides, *The Bacchae and Other Plays,* translated by Philip Vellacott (London: Penguin Classics, 1954).

2 **VISION**—Shiva Naipaul, *North of South* (London: Penguin Books, 1980), 119.

3 **VOLTAIRE**—Voltaire, *Dictionnaire*, vol. 6, 350, "*Lettres, Gens de Lettres, ou Lettrés.*" "*Les gens de lettres qui ont rendu le plus de services ... ont presque tous été persécutés.*"

W

1 **WESTERN CIVILIZATION**—Twelve-ton statue of George Washington by Horatio Greenough, 1840. Placed in the Capitol. Inspired by Phidias's Zeus.

2 **WISDOM**—Voltaire, *Dictionnaire*, vol. 8, 128, "*Sens Commun.*"

Z

1 **ZEALOT**—Johnson, *Dictionary*.

ACKNOWLEDGMENTS

Many of the people who made *Voltaire's Bastards* possible—
even if I don't name them again—have offered advice and
information, answered desperate phone calls at strange
hours and been good enough to disagree in long discussions.

Adam Bellow and Cynthia Good have again given great
help as editors and applied their imaginations and persis-
tence. Indeed, the enthusiasm of everyone at Penguin Books
and The Free Press has been very important to me.

Laura Roebuck and Donya Peroff have been a constant
support. Advice, information, criticism and dozens of other
forms of help have come from Alain Chanlat, Anoukh Foerg,
Pier Daniele Napolitani, Hans Wuttke and Jagoda Buic, Scott
Sellers, de Montigny Marchand, Noël and Dominique
Goutard, Christine Klose, Elisabetta Sgarbi, Rolf Puls, Gilbert
Reid, Margaret Atwood, Niels de Groot, Jean-François
Garneau, Mary Adachi, Charles Rubinsztein, Matthieu
Debost, Francesca Vallenti and my good friend, Father Joe
Maier.

WORD LIST